Who Should Care for the Elderly?
An East-West Value Divide

Who Should Care for the Elderly?
An East-West Value Divide

Edited by
WILLIAM T. LIU & HAL KENDIG

SINGAPORE UNIVERSITY PRESS
NATIONAL UNIVERSITY OF SINGAPORE

World Scientific
Singapore • New Jersey • London • Hong Kong

© 2000 Singapore University Press
     Yusof Ishak House, National University of Singapore
     31 Lower Kent Ridge Road, Singapore 119078

and

     World Scientific Publishing Co. Pte. Ltd.
     PO Box 128, Farrer Road, Singapore 912805
     USA office : Suite 1B, 1060 Main Street, River Edge, NJ 07661
     UK office : 57 Shelton Street, Covent Garden, London WC2H 9HE

ISBN 9971-69-232-5 (Case)

Typeset by: International Typesetters Pte. Ltd.
Printed by: Chung Printing

CONTENTS

About the Co-editors   ix

List of Contributors   xi

Preface   xiii

Critical Issues of Caregiving: East-West Dialogue   1
William T. Liu and Hal Kendig

Part One: The Western Perspectives

1. Societal and Family Change in the Burden of Care   27
   Rhonda J.V. Montgomery, Edgar F. Borgatta
   and Marie L. Borgatta

2. Family Change and Family Bonding: Conceptual   55
   and Policy Issues
   Marvin B. Sussman

3. The Social Context of the Nature of Care   68
   Allen Glicksman

4. Sharing Long-term Care Between the Family   78
   and the State — A European Perspective
   Alan Walker

v

5. Family Change and Family Bonding in Australia   107
   Hal Kendig

6. Care and Social Support — The Example of   126
   Ageing Migrants
   Ken Blakemore

7. The Value of Old Age in Modern Society: 143
   Social Responses to 'Elder Abuse'
   Richard Hugman

Part Two: The Eastern Perspectives

8. The Social Psychological Perspective of Elderly Care   165
   Ying-Yi Hong and William T. Liu

9. Values and Caregiving Burden: The Significance   183
   of Filial Piety in Elder Care
   William T. Liu

10. Filial Piety, Co-residence, and Intergenerational   200
    Solidarity in Japan
    Wataru Koyano

11. The Cultural Politics of the Asian Family Care   224
    Model: Missing Language and Facts
    Yow-Hwey Hu and Yah-Jong Chou

12. Caring for the Elderly in Singapore   249
    Kalyani Mehta

13. Living Arrangements and Elderly Care: The Case   269
    of Hong Kong
    Rance P.L. Lee, Jik-Joen Lee, Elena S.H. Yu,
    Shong-Gong Sun and William T. Liu

14. Children and Children-in-law as Primary   297
    Caregivers: Issues and Perspectives
    Odalia M.H. Wong

15. Caregiving Survey in Guangzhou: A Preliminary   322
    Report
    Elena S. H. Yu, Lai Shihlong, Wen Zehuai and
    William T. Liu

16. Middle-aged Women's Supporting Behavior to   339
    Elderly Parents: The Comparison of Parents-in-law
    and Own Parents
    Byung-Eun Cho

ABOUT THE CO-EDITORS

William T. Liu is a Visiting Senior Fellow at the East Asian Institute of the National University of Singapore, and Professor Emeritus of Sociology and Public Health at the University of Illinois (USA). He received his Ph.D. in Sociology (Florida State), his Post doctoral training in Social Psychology (University of Chicago), and his NIMH Post Doctoral Training in Psychiatric Epidemiology (Yale University). He had previously taught at the University of Notre Dame where he also headed the Department of Sociology and later, the Associate Dean of Arts and Sciences in charge of Social Science; and at Johns Hopkins University, the University of California at San Diego, and the University of Illinois where he had joint appointment in Sociology of the Arts and Sciences Faculty, School of Public Health, and the College of Medicine in Psychiatry, as well as the Director of Pacific/Asian Mental Health Research Center, a national R and D Center funded through a long term grant from the National Institute of Mental Health. He later became the Dean of Social Science Faculty at Hong Kong Baptist University and later as the Acting Head of Social Science Division at the Hong Kong University of Science and Technology until his retirement.

William Liu's major research in the past decade had been in the epidemiology of Alzheimer's Disease, where field work was conducted consecutively in Shanghai, Hong Kong and Guangzhou with the collaboration of local institutions. He has authored and edited 12 books. His more than 100 papers and chapters in books can be found in social science journals, journals in social gerontology, neurology, social psychology, and psychiatry. His forthcoming books are: *The Class of '47,* which is a study of China's first Socialist generation of intellectual-technocrats; and *The Social Origin of Alzheimer's Disease,* which is a study of the social isolation of the brain.

Hal L. Kendig holds an appointment as Dean of the Faulty of Health Sciences at the University of Sydney. From 1989 to 1998 he directed the Lincoln

Gerontology Centre, a Key Centre of the Australian Research Council, and was a Professor of the School of Public Health at La Trobe University. At the Research School of Sciences in the Australian National University from 1975 to 1988, he served as Senior Fellow and Coordinator of the Ageing and Family Project. His Ph.D. studies were completed at the Arndrus Gerontology Center at the University of Southern California.

He has contributed regularly to research on international aspects of ageing. He is Chair of the Social Research and Planning Section, Asia-Oceania, International Association of Gerontology and he serves on the United Nations Expert Group for a Global Research Agenda on Aging for the 21st Century. He has held visiting fellowships at Nihon Universities and the Tokyo Metropolitan Institute of Gerontology, and he has contributed to research efforts by the United Nations Economic and Social Commission of Asia and the Pacific and the World Health Organization, and a co-editor of *Family Support to the Elderly: the International Experience* (Oxford University Press, 1992; Chinese edition, 1998).

Professor Kendig edited or authored 12 books including *The Sociology of Ageing* (International Association of Ageing, 1996) and *Towards Health Ageing* (Collins Dove, 1994). Over recent years he has published in *Ageing and Society, The Gerontologist, Disability and Rehabilitation, Medical Journal of Australia, Australasian Journal on Ageing,* and *The Australian and New Zealand Journal of Public Health.* Findings are reported on spouse-caregiving, widowhood, driving, spirituality, social support in Australia and Japan, childlessness, retirement, health and social class, falls, impacts of disability, and community care. His current research focuses mainly on longitudinal studies of health and well being of older people including health promotion, social support and community services.

LIST OF CONTRIBUTORS

Ken Blakemore, Professor of Gerontology and Social Policy, University of Wales Swansea.

Edgar Borgatta, Professor of Sociology and Editor of Encyclopedia of Sociology, The University of Washington.

Marie Borgatta, Professor of Sociology and Managing Editor of Encyclopedia of Sociology, The University of Washington.

Byung-Eun Cho, Professor of Sociology, Korea National University of Education.

Yah-Jong Chou, Associate Prof., Department of Psychology, National Chung Cheng University.

Allen Glicksman, Project Director, Philadelphia Geriatric Centre.

Hong Ying-yi, Assistant Professor, Division of Social Sciences, Hong Kong University of Science and Technology.

Yow Hwey-Hu, Associate Professor, Institute of Health and Welfare Policy, National Yang Ming University.

Richard Hugman, Professor of Sociology, Edith Cowan University.

Hal L. Kendig, Dean, Faculty of Health Sciences, University of Sydney.

Wataru Koyano, Professor of Gerontology, Seigakuin University.

Shihlong Lai, Director and Professor Department of Clinical Epidemiology, The Guangzhou University of Chinese Traditional Medicine.

Jik-Joen Lee, Associate Professor of Social Work, The Chinese University of Hong Kong.

Rance Lee, Professor of Sociology and Head, Chung Chi College, The Chinese University of Hong Kong.

William T. Liu, Professor Emeritus, University of Illinois, Chicago; and Visiting Senior Fellow, National University of Singapore.

Kalyani Mehta, Assistant Professor of Social Work, The National University of Singapore.

Rhonda Montgomery, Professor of Sociology and Director, The Gerontology Center, University of Kansas.

Marvin Sussman, Professor of Human Development and Family Studies, The University of Delaware.

Alan Walker, Professor of Social Policy, University of Sheffield.

Zehuai Wen, Senior Lecturer – Applied Clinical Ep., Guangzhou University of Chinese Traditional Medicine.

Odalia Wong, Associate Professor of Sociology, Hong Kong Baptist University.

Elena S. H. Yu, Professor of Epidemiology, The Graduate School of Public Health, San Diego State University.

PREFACE

This book has arisen from the belief that cultural understandings can be advanced by contrasting the work of scholars who share academic concerns but who work from different cultural vantages. In our estimation, knowledge in the caregiving field has reached the point where such comparisons can shed useful insights into not only differences between cultures but also between the perspectives of the scholars who study them.

We believe that the chapters in this book provide a rich information base for these purposes. They have been prepared from papers presented at an invited conference on East-West Values in Elder Care organised by William Liu and convened in Hong Kong in 1996. We wish to thank Hong Kong University of Science and Technology for the initial grant that enabled the gathering of participants for this meeting. Gratitudes also are extended to Hong Kong Baptist University through its facilities of David Lam Centre for East-West Studies, for providing both venues and staff help during the conference. The East Asian Institute at the National University of Singapore provided the auspice for William Liu during editing and publication.

Participants to the Conference were invited on the basis of their capacity to contribute to the increasing dialogue between East and West in considering the value and culture-laden issue of caregiving. To help focus of the work, invitations from the West were restricted to participants from the English-speaking countries of Australia, the United Kingdom, and the United States of America. Invitations to contributors from East Asia were limited to countries which are relatively more advanced economically and share a common cultural base of Confucian beliefs in filial piety. They include Japan, China, Korea, Taiwan, and Singapore. In our estimation, this emphasis helps to clarify better the differences attributable to culture from those attributable to the economic gap between the developed and developing worlds.

Participants were invited largely on the basis of colleagial networks and, in very broad terms, fall into two groups. Some are well-established scholars from the West who have summarised and reassessed their areas of knowledge for purposes of cross-cultural comparisons of caregiving. We are particularly pleased to have contributions from emergent scholars in the East, working in their own cultural traditions with conceptual and analytical skills informed by the West. Participants were invited to develop their own conceptual approaches and to incorporate empirical findings which illuminate aspects of caregiving which are important from their own cultural and scholarly points of view.

As with most publications based on conference proceedings, this volume also has had a long gestation. Contributors were invited to re-work their papers in the light of conference discussions and additional time was taken for the publisher's review, two external reviewers, and our own efforts to emphasise a common thread to bring papers together to form a more coherent manuscript. In the end we believed it necessary to exclude some papers read at the Conference on the basis of their inconsistency with the volume as a whole rather than the quality of these papers. We wish to apologise to the authors for our joint decisions.

Co-editing was the original idea in order to represent more fully an effort in the East-West dialogue on elder care. William Liu, the primary organiser for the conference and the book, is an American academic with a Chinese background; he also has worked extensively in research in East and Southeast Asia. Hal Kendig had helped with the organisation of the conference and returned to the project later to assist with editing. He is an American originally, has lived and worked in Australia since 1975, and he has done comparative research in Japan and elsewhere in Asia-Oceania.

We owe a particularly great thanks to Professor Alan Walker who has read all these papers and made cogent and important comments on them. Unfortunately, because of his extraordinary schedule first as a policy advisor with the European Union, and later in his advisory capacity to the Labour Party's election and eventual victory, he had not been able to devote the time to continue his editing.

Many individuals have contributed significantly to this effort, particularly the assistance and supervision of Wendy Chan, Assistant Director of the Lam Centre. Our thanks to Professor Ch'i His-sheng, then the Dean of the School of Humanities and Social Science, and Andrew Walder during his tenure as the Head of Social Science Division, both at the Hong Kong University of Science and Technology for their support. We wish to thank the publishers, Singapore University Press and World Scientific and their editors, for reviewing and eventual publication of this volume. Last but not least, we wish to thank all participants who spent the time to write papers that contributed to the Conference.

In closing we wish to remind readers that these proceedings have the modest aim of presenting interpretations of caregiving studies in the West and new caregiving studies from the East. The papers were completed in 1996. We believe that they can contribute to conceptual and policy advances but we have not embarked on such an ambitious agenda in this publication.

WILLIAM T. LIU
East Asian Institute
National University of Singapore

HAL KENDIG
Faculty of Health Sciences
University of Sydney

Critical Issues of Caregiving: East-West Dialogue

William T. Liu and Hal Kendig

This introduction provides a brief backdrop to issues of East-West contrasts in caregiving for older people. It begins by considering the context of rapid population ageing and emergent views on ageing and caregiving from economic, welfare, and feminist perspectives. We then consider the concept of caregiving and ways in which they may be construed differently accordingly to cultural prescripts and expectations for government. We also wish to provide the reader with an overview of the chapters and their authors. The chapter concludes by commenting on recent policy development and possible research strategies for the future.

The International Context

The demographic revolution of the first half of the 20th century was notable for the reduction of infant and maternal mortality rates, and the gradual decline of the ten infectious diseases in the world. The second half of the century has been noted for population ageing. In 1990, the population aged 60 years and older was estimated at about one-half of a billion worldwide. By 2050, this figure will triple to more than 1.45 billion. Most of the growth of the old population will take place in developing economies in Asia, South and Central America, and in Africa. China alone will contribute to one-fourth of the increase.[1]

Population ageing generally has been more advanced in the West than the East but such generalities are dissolving rapidly. Japan, for example, already has a slightly older population than Australia. The most notable divide is the extraordinarily fast pace of population ageing in the East. Indeed, the demographic change that took two centuries in the West is now being achieved in the East over a remarkable two generations (Myers, 1992). This rapid population change — combined with industrialisation, urbanisation, and westernisation — has raised questions concerning the world's capacities to maintain family support for older people throughout the world (Hashimoto and Kendig, 1992).

The reality of greying populations is accompanied by related trends. First, there is the widening gap in life expectancy between men and women, and the narrowing gap between developing and developed countries. Second, at least in the developing economies, more old people are living alone or otherwise without their adult children. Third, average household size has been decreasing and there are increases of single person household and household with no dependent children. In East Asia, for example, the proportion of Japan's households containing at least one older person rose from 3.11 million in 1985 to 5.54 million a decade later in 1994. The 2.43 million increase is about 78% jump in ten years. A faster pace will be achieved in China under the current one-child policy. Similar trends are reported in Hong Kong, Taiwan, and Singapore; the same is true for other societies in the ASEAN region.

The 1982 International Plan of Action on Ageing (United Nations, 1989) provided comprehensive recommendations for improving world responsiveness to the ageing of the population. Six of the sixty-two recommendations concerned "the family as a fundamental unit of society". They argued that women had reduced their traditional role as "caretakers", as a result of entering the paid labour force in greater numbers. The report recommended that men and social services would need to support the family in caring for older people.

In the lead up to the International Year of Older Persons in 1999, the UN General Assembly [97-23409 (E)] again outlined a range of issues in working towards "A Society for All Ages". This Operational Framework for the Year shows the emergence of active ageing and caregiving strategies as pre-eminent in the situation of older persons (paragraphs 42 and 94). It recommends research, policies, and programmes for "an appropriate caregiving mix for frail older persons, encompassing family, community, and institutional care systems that distribute tasks equitably among state, community, family, and the primary caregiver" (paragraph 94a).

Feminist perspectives on family care have been articulated clearly in the United Nations "Expert Group Meeting on Caregiving for Older Persons: Gender Dimension" convened in late 1997. The meeting shows the centrality given to caregiving by its two organisers: the United Nations Division for Social Policy and Development and the Division for the Advancement of Women. The papers (e.g., Brody, 1981; Brody, Johnson and Fulcomer, 1983; Lang and Brody, 1984) highlight the problems of caregiving particularly for women who, relative to men, are more likely to care for older parents and also to be left with inadequate care in their own old age. Western academics have made similar comments for women in developing as well as developed countries.

The World Bank has reported various views of economic orthodoxy on population ageing in *Averting the Old Age Crisis*. The 1994 document argues that, in the West, the costs of health care and income support will soon reach limits that cannot be borne by younger taxpayers. Particularly in developing countries, there is concern that the costs of supporting older people will take away income, which is badly needed, for economic advancement. The report argues that income security for older people in the future will depend on inculcating habits of savings over the working years.

These illustrations show that ageing and caregiving have emerged much more prominently as concerns in the developed countries of the West than in other parts of the World. The different interpretations depend as much on the commentators' value and ideological perspectives as they do on the intrinsic issues of population ageing. With the notable exception of Japan and a few other countries, caregiving has not emerged as major issues on the political agendas of governments in the East.

What is Caregiving?

The word caregiving involves a broad spectrum of meanings that go beyond the limits of single disciplines. Reviewing writings on the subject, Chappel (1990) used a general concept of "social care" to denote a wide range of assistance provided to the elderly that ranges from social and health services, formal care and care provided by kins and friends. In actual practice, finer delineations of "social care" may be difficult to separate, since they often overlap. However, health and social care may be viewed as distinct and separate assistance, depending on whether physicians play a central role in rendering and coordinating such services. But even then if community social care develops with a medical dominance, it could be viewed as a component of the health care system, particularly if the cost of such care comes from existing national health insurance dollars. The word can simultaneously involve restoration of health and quality of life, nursing care, and high technology assisted physical therapy, as well as assisting the elder with basic activities of daily living (ADL). The division of formal and informal care does not provide an entry to delineate the concept of caregiving either. In the literature on informal caregiving activities, Dunlop (1980) stated that caregiving day-to-day housework and personal attention, rather than nursing care, although, as reported by the Frankfather, Smith and Caro that administering medicine is one of the tasks that is most frequently undertaken by caregivers. Generally speaking and for research purposes, distinctions should be made between services that are essential for subsistence and survival (one which could be approved by long-term care insurance), and effective involvement and social support in the family and community organisations (that may not be recognized by health insurance for payment). In a capsule, four major and *not mutually exclusive* categories are mentioned relative to caregiving. These are: medical care, personal care, help with instrumental activities of daily living (IADL), and other non-specific care tasks such as staying with and watching the elderly because of the necessity of supervision for personal safety. Staying in the same room to make sure that these tasks are properly carried out (by someone else) may also be regarded as caregiving. Helping with nursing care also included assistance with physical, occupational, or speech therapy. Caregiving through formal organisations included help with transportation, arranging services and benefits on behalf of the care recipient, generally carried out by social services personnel have also been used in the caregiving context. In some cases the term is used to refer more to relationships in which instrumental and expressive support are fused inseparably.

Health service professionals and academic researchers used different yardsticks to measure the scale of needed care. This made it exceedingly difficult to assess necessary and appropriate care, especially in cross-cultural comparisons. The problem of defining the need and nature of caregiving is twofold in the context of cross-cultural comparisons. First, the concept of "need" is in itself a function of social values as well as the political culture of voters in a democratic system in what can be regarded as entitlement. Second, there are also wide variations in the ways people consider transitional stages in life (see Keith, 1992) and this life-span view may affect caregiving in some ways.

In East Asia, for example, caregiving is a continuous and reciprocal process for support that emphasizes mutual dependency among certain familial members throughout the life span. The cut-off point as to when the young is old enough to provide care to parents while still in some

ways being cared for by parents is not always clear (see also Fry and
Keith, 1982). This last point leads to the concept of *decrepit* at old
age and the necessity of assistance. In societies that emphasise personal
independence, ageing without decrepitating makes caregiving
irrelevant and unnecessary (see also Glascock and Feinman, 1981 and
1986; as discussed in Keith, 1992:16). Decrepitating then is perceived
as the pre-requisite for needing assistance. On the other hand, in
cultures that value *inter-dependence*, decrepitating may not be required
before caregiving is received or expected. A merely negotiated
recognition of "getting old" is sufficient for the young to render —
and for the old to receive — assistance. Aside from a medical
definition, the concept of elder caregiving may have been frequently
used to mean different things in various research settings.

Contributors to this volume provide a wide variety of perspectives,
disciplines, and methods in understanding caregiving in the context
of their chosen theme. In this overview we wish to present them to
the reader in the context of the intended East-West contrasts as the
objective of this book project. This is obviously a difficult task. The
reader will soon notice that ageing research, like social science research
in general, is largely based on the Western experience, and is built on
concepts and methodologies originated in Euro-American societies.
Asian ageing policies, particularly those in Japan and China, where
adult children are held responsible for parental care, have frequently
been criticised as being impractical and not keeping with the trend of
global ageing. We are not discouraged by the difficult task because,
first, we soon discovered that there exist more consensus of opinions
than there are differences when it comes to global elderly care for the
future when the majority of the societies in the world are fully aged.
Fully aged society can no longer provide the needed elder caregiving
by either the family or the state alone. Welfare entitlement as the basis
of elder care policy has proven to be both costly and not meeting the
emotional needs of the elder. On the other hand, family care alone is
neither sufficient nor workable in the future when fertility rates
continue to decline with rising life expectancy.

After having reflected on the best way to present a contrast between the East and the West, editors of this volume decided simply to group them by the locus of the author's research reference. We are sure that perhaps there are better ways to handle this problem. This is perhaps a simpler way.

Western Approaches to Caregiving

The opening chapter by Montgomery, Borgatta and Borgatta provides an elegant articulation of a key position from the perspective of the West. Their position reminds us of the argument of the late William F. Ogburn, who, in 1922 wrote his first sociological treatise on the impact of technologies on changing social institutions. In their analysis of caregiving, Montgomery and the Borgattas have focused on the technologies of modern medicine. They reflect a strong Western belief that medicine can greatly increase the quality of life, with the goal that people could maintain this quality and then die quickly when their biological clock runs out of "batteries". This chapter, however, has less to say about family and community contributions to needs that are more inclined to be the core of a policy debate.

Marvin Sussman has long been a leading sociologist in applying exchange theory to understanding inter-generational relationships in the United States. In the modern society of his vision, he suggests that a way to maintain positive family values is to have them written into a relational contract as a reciprocal lifetime help package. It may not be realistic to assume that parent and child relations are defined solely by filial love nor that all such relationships really are imbedded in selfless devotion. While social contracts between the generations may seem cold, and therefore would meet resistance from those who adhere to more traditional values. In reality, however, the legality of contractual obligations can offer increased security for older people and increased justice, if not rationale, for adult children who assume the role of caregivers.

Allen Glicksman's paper reminds us that even in one society, there are heterodox values with respect to the care of the elder. Glicksman's anthropological perspective and qualitative analysis show major differences between Calvinists, Catholic and Jewish values and how they are expressed in the American context with respect to elder care. This cultural diversity raises major questions in how governments can work appropriately and sensitively in sharing aged care responsibilities with ethnic communities, which can have very different expectations for families and governments.

From the vantage of a British political economist, Alan Walker provides an insightful analysis of elder care in the European Union. He argues that social values have changed from the modern era to a post-modernity. The socio-demographic transition, and the political and economic changes in the West have necessitated the change in the management and delivery of care. Drawing on his own extensive writings in the field, Walker's chapter provides one of the best-articulated statements for policies that advocate shared burden of elder care between the state and the family.

Hal Kendig's paper applies concepts of inter-generational reciprocity to understand family support to older people in Australia over the post war era. His evidence shows that Australia has maintained considerable stability of core family values. The rising resources of older people have facilitated their independence and their contributions to younger relatives. Government support for aged care arguably has strengthened family ties by augmenting family care in the community and providing residential alternatives when the family was not available. New policies to support caregivers hold promise to reduce gender inequalities in caregiving and reflect the rising political recognition of caregivers.

International migration of a segment of the larger kin is perhaps the most significant reason for what had been regarded as the process of nuclearisation of the family in the 20th century. More of such will be reflected in censuses throughout the world in the coming millennium. Ken Blakemore's paper addressed itself to the problem of migration among elders in English-speaking countries, raised questions on how migrations at old age has adapted to welfare benefits as well as determined by them. Government benefits and old age entitlement so far have not been a factor in migration.

Hugman's paper touched on a previously not asked and perhaps not askable question on elder abuse. He does so by looking at the functional role of the elders in a society. Whereas in the capitalist society, productive age is viewed as being young and functionally useful to the society, old age is not. Since we view *old age* differently from one society to another, the concept of *old age abuse* also varies from one culture to another. The ambiguity of social values ascribed to old age can be the root cause of social values that underlie policy formulation with respect to the care of the elder. It is notable that papers in this volume on care giving may also have been viewed in various ways by different authors. For example, Montgomery, Borgatta and Borgatta (Chapter 1, this volume) are concerned primarily with instrumental assistance in the activities of daily living. Other authors, reporting caregiving in East Asia, included affective support as a part of caregiving. In our estimation, this variability of definitions reveals different disciplinary viewpoints and cultural values that shed light on the diversity and complexity of caregiving as a concept used in old age research.

Western value of individualism presupposes that caregiving is essentially a service rendered by a caregiver regardless of the nature of social ties. As a service, it should be compensated either monetarily or considered as non-payable obligation. The former is based on voluntary exchange between the caregiver and the recipient of care; and the latter is defined in either kinship or friendship terms, or both. It is the latter that creates a tension to strive for a relative balance between an obligatory norm and the norm of reciprocal and relatively equal exchange. The subjective feeling of the former gives a theoretical basis for the query of burden in caregiving as a major research area in ageing.

Furthermore, it follows that research in the West has long recognised the central role of women in family support for older people. The term caregiver, when it came into wider use in the 1980s, signalled a greater valuing of the personal costs paid by *individual* daughters or other female members of the family. Along with the rise of the worldwide social force of women's movement, it is perhaps not a surprise that this research has focused overwhelmingly on the stresses and other burdens of caregiving, particularly for middle-aged daughters. By the 1990s, caregiving research had emerged as the single largest area for gerontology publication. In the original publication of the *Handbook of Aging and the Social Sciences*, three position papers dealt with the topic of caregiving (see chapters by Chappell, 1990; Keith, 1990). The seminal paper on the "Women in the Middle" by Brody (1981), which appeared in the *Gerontologist,* has triggered off a whole generation of writings on the role of women in caregiving.

However, even in the West there can be ambiguity and non-recognition of caregiving when the cultural prescripts are very strong. For example, an elderly wife may not recognise herself as a caregiver when she looks after her frail husband with the same support provided earlier during times of good health for both of them (Wells and Kendig, 1997).

Prevailing views about family care as essentially "care by women" care need to be examined and interpreted in the context of the social value foundations in that society. As Finch and Grove (1980) have argued, the term community care has equally obscured the fact that women are caring for women without acknowledgement or reward. The astonishing growth of research on the burden of caregiving suggests the subjective experience of personal costs by the caregiver. Frustration, annoyance, and stronger stresses can be interpreted as a consequence of people performing unwilling kinship duties.

In the Western literature there has been for some time a view of caregiving in the context of *exchange theory*. In a capsule, this theory builds from a Western axiom of individualism: individuals and the relationships between them form social structures. From this viewpoint the sense of burden and frustration varies with the amount of excess of benefits over costs in the caregiving relationships. For example, if the caregiver expects to be awarded handsomely, usually through money, the perceived burden would be neutralised by the obvious benefit. In this volume, Sussman has articulated the idea that reciprocal benefits between the elder and her caregiver can be legally specified and guaranteed through contracts.

There remain notable weaknesses in employing *exchange theory* in assessing caregiving relationships, or the burden imposed by a rigid kinship of patriarchy, as it is the case in East Asia. Under both conceptions, there is no room for genuine affection in the caregiving relationship, that is, a sense of diffused mutual devotion to one another. In the same vein, caregiving is not entirely a form of functional assistance and affective neutral, although professional nursing and health intervention can to some extent have a very delimited personal element. It is within the realm of affection and diffused obligations in caregiving that we need to be particularly flexible in the use of research instrument for data collection. The bottom line is "knowing what it is being measured".

Most of the early ageing societies in the West had adopted, at one time or another, social values that favoured welfare policy for the state to take care of the old and the frail. The social value of the welfare state stemmed from a broader base of "individualism", and more narrowly on the belief that, as mentioned in the paper by Montgomery, Borgatta and Borgatta that one's relationship with parents was one of duty, rather than sentiment.

At the time of mass ageing toward the end of the century, most of the countries in Europe and North America had already developed the policy of social security and welfare legislation based on the social value of individualism. It is essentially the society that must provide the needed *security* and *sustainability* for its citizens. Before the *Elizabethan Poor Law* in England, the charity organisations and religious bodies help the poor, the employed, old and infirmed. The *Poor Law* was a legal pioneering effort for the state to assume that responsibility. As the state has became more engaged in helping the individual, there has emerged a strong "entitlement mentality".

The Western sense of public responsibility emerged foremost in the area of income support and health care and more recently in the area of aged care. The extent to which aged care is viewed as a private or a public responsibility still varies considerably from one country to another. For example, aged care is viewed more as a public responsibility in Europe and relatively more as a private responsibility in North America. There arguably is increasing convergence, as signified in United Nations publications, in the view that aged care is appropriately viewed as *both* a family *and* government responsibility.

Many Western governments are now caught between conflicting trends. On one hand, populations are ageing and electorates continue to expect high levels of support; the reverse of such policies imposes the risk of being voted out of office. On the other hand, either high levels of economic growth or a willingness to pay higher taxes does not match the costs of meeting high expectations. This dilemma of the welfare democracy is considered further in Alan Walker's paper in this volume.

Eastern Approaches to Caregiving

In traditional Eastern cultures, the individualistic assumptions underlying the Western caregiver literature do not always hold very well. It may be true that an individual, nearly always a woman, does perform primary tasks in providing support for older people in the family. However, it is also recognised from Confucian precepts that the son assumes the responsibilities in providing care for old parents as a structural requisite of the system of patriarchy. This support is conceptualised more as a (inevitable) responsibility, within the unquestionable family systems, rather than as either an imposition or as a "choice" on or by any individuals. Anthropologists have long argued that cultural values provide a strong behavioural predisposition with respect to elder care (Kiefer, 1974; Palmore and Maeda, 1985; Keith, 1992; Fry and Keith, 1982). Sociologists similarly argued that patterns of social organisations, based on systems of social roles, norms, and shared meanings that provide regularity and predictability to social interaction (see George, 1990; Ikels, 1983; Glascock and Feinman, 1981 and 1986) also shape the way people take care of their elders. Since family structure varies greatly from one society to another, it is no surprise that the predominate caregiving responsibility may be assigned to different genders (see Hsu, 1963), in spite of the overlapping nature of domestic role assumed by women in general in the majority of the world's societies.

East Asian societies, that include China, Hong Kong, Taiwan, Japan, and Korea, the *Classics of Filial Piety*, or *Xiao Jing (*on the teachings of Confucius) was the primer on children's selfless devotions and respects to one's parents. There are two major obligatory norms to depict the essence of *xiao*, or filial piety. On the passive side, children must show unqualified obedience to parents even if parents were known to be wrong. On the active side, children at any age throughout their life must always show their efforts to please parents. Though changing times have greatly altered the interpretation of filial piety, taking care of aged parents has remained an unquestioned and unquestionable virtue. Since East Asian governments' ageing policy is based on the moral persuasion of Confucian ethics, the ageing policy is for adult children to take care of the needs of their own ageing parents. Both Japan and China had such a policy written into their current and respective constitutions.

As a corollary of the social value of filial piety, East Asian values base social welfare on the family as the fundamental unit of social organisation. In Southeast Asia where Confucianism has had little or no influence except in Chinese overseas communities, traditional values of familism prevails throughout, as it prevailed in most traditional societies. Needy individuals are seen as families with older people as contrasted with those without older people. Caring for the elderly members is thought to be unquestionably a collective (familial) responsibility, and (at least in the ideation) is not the responsibility of a single or specific kin role. In any case, the assumption of having one primary caregiver — most likely a middle-aged daughter — as it was reported in the literature, did not receive empirical support here, as reported in an on-going Guangzhou study by Yu in this volume; and in studies reported in Shanghai and Hong Kong as well. It seems that this concept of caregiving, more as a collective responsibility, rather than a single person's duty, requires a paradigm shift in the research thinking developed in a Western context.

In addition to the cultural perspective, there is also the structural significance of a society dominated by patriarchal lineage in East Asia. The role of the daughter-in-law is a central issue when social scientists deal with the institution of patriarchy. Obviously this is the critical role that intersects gender and generation status in the kinship structure. Consequently, elder care by the daughter-in-law as compared to the daughter flushes out the structural significance of the kinship structure relative to perceived filial piety. The obligatory norm of filial piety is unevenly loaded on the son that characterises the essence of a patriarchy system. A daughter-in-law, by virtue of her position as the wife of the son, normally assumes domestic responsibilities of caring for both her husband's children (who are *also* her own children), and her husband's ageing parents (who are *not* her natal parents). As a mother to her husband's children, the affection is both natural and instinctual. On the other hand, as the wife of a son, her affinity to the mother-in-law is only significant with respect to the role structure of the system, and not necessarily with respect to affective relationships.

Two papers in this volume that are based on the data of caregiving collected in Shanghai (Liu) and Guangzhou (Yu) seem to have clearly demonstrated this point. The authors argued separately that the burden of care is explained largely by the specific kin role that is prescribed by the Confucian precepts of proper obligations associated with specific dyads within the family. Liu's paper on caregiving in China specifically examines the crucial distinction between subjective and objective senses of burden (as measured by using Montgomery, Borgatta and Borgatta method). His re-analysis of the caregiving data collected for the Shanghai Epidemiological Survey[2] shows that daughters-in-law exhibited inordinate amount of subjective burden even though the objective burden remained relatively low. This suggests that the problem is less of the caregiving as it is the role of the daughter-in-law in the system of patriarchy.

Of course social values are expected to change, mostly as adaptation to the changing social structure and modes of economic production. The industrial revolution has changed both the family structure and intergenerational relations in the Western world. There are, however, some unsettled questions as to whether this is also true in the process of modernisation in East and Southeast Asian economies. Both Japan and Taiwan have shown a mixed bag of both modernisation and family based elder care policy.

Singapore's successful programme of the Central Provident Fund, which was designed to put the emphasis of an ageing policy on the individual through a compulsory personal savings scheme (see Mehta's paper, this volume), is nonetheless fully loaded with the value of filial piety, which enables the "middle generation" to take care of both the parental generation when money is needed for caregiving, and their children's needs for education. Mehta's paper also provides us with other detailed information about government policies and measures that anticipate a faster growth of an ageing population. These incentives include tax credits and special housing related privileges in order to maximise the opportunity for an adult child to live close to an ageing parent(s), a policy that is being considered for adoption by other East Asian governments, which at the moment do not have a well articulated ageing policy, such as Hong Kong and China.

Hu also reported that Taiwan's government also encourages adult children to live close to, if not residing with, their ageing parents through legislative incentives. In China, where the government controls the right to migrate and to relocate, moving for the purpose of taking care of aged parents have always received priority as a national policy.

It seems that the social value of individualism that provided the legal provisions of welfare state policy on ageing in the West, is clearly contrasted with the social value of familism and filial piety in the East as the family policy on ageing. While at the turn of the millennium, the West faces an economic crisis in continuing its welfare policy. The East also faces a crisis that the family is no longer able to continue to take care of its elder, because of both the limited human and financial resources of a smaller family, even if there is no convincing evidence that there is an erosion of family values.

There are, of course, strong voices within the Asian academic circles that disagreed with the so-called Asian model. The debate is not new. There is, of course, absolutely nothing wrong with a known value assumption when considering social policy. No workable social policy can be void of social values. After all, the success or failure of an enduring policy depends largely on whether there is a minimum degree of consensus in a society to sustain such a policy.

To search for a theoretical paradigm that defies cultural peculiarities, Hong and Liu's paper raises questions about the way culture may influence our way of defining dyadic relationships within the context of primary social relations. Elder care, as seen by Hong and Liu, is a special type of social relations that should be studied as a micro-process of helping relationships that evolve around disability as a result of aging. Their paper suggests that caregiving relationships involving members of the primary family has a natural history of the family and its various dyads peculiar to that family. To generalise caregiving burden across the board in terms of an exchange theory is perhaps over simplistic.

Similarly, Koyano's paper clearly reflected a new generation of Japanese sociologists whose analysis touches directly on the actual flows of support between the generations and has critically examined the support, which flows between households. The ageing crisis in Japan has perhaps reached a point that required considerable rethinking on the part of the government and academicians. Japan is the most fully-aged society in Asia. In spite of the urgent nature of a most rapid ageing structure of its demography, the Japanese government defies all the predictions by research scholars of the signs of erosion of filial piety. Confronting household statistics that compared the in-residence of elders in the home of adult children from decade to decade, the Government of Japan made no specific plans to take over the elder care chores from the family. The issue understandably seems to be a much more urgent matter to many Western observers. Perhaps that is why an East-West dialogue is needed. Would the Japanese government hold a traditional position at the expense of the quality of life of younger families with old relatives? What about those families that continue to hold the practice of the three-generation household? To them, would that give the nuclear unit better or worse quality of life? Would the elder generation be of help or a burden in the middle generation's care for his own young? Would a supportive role be sufficient for the government in Japan and other East Asian societies to play instead of moving into the driver's seat to assume all the responsibilities? Is it financial consideration or is it the impact on the functions of the family that is the real issue? The reader has much to ponder.

The Hu and Chou chapter is a good example of looking at a social policy from the viewpoint of human values. The priority issue is that of gender, and gender pushes to the front of the discussion on the unequal distribution of responsibilities (and therefore sufferings) as a result of having to care for someone within the family. Hu and Chou failed, however, to marshal evidence to show that elder care in Taiwan has fallen largely on the shoulder of the daughter-in-law. But the assumption that older women had a higher than expected rates of suicide was the basis of their argument. We know, however, traditional inequality between men and women that was reflected in the educational and employment opportunities as well as the complex nature of gender roles are all in some ways responsible for higher suicide rates among women. It should also be noted that a higher rate of clinical depression among women are reported in most Western societies as well. In the United States, the most recent large-scale psychiatric epidemiological surveys conducted in six sites of both urban and rural samples showed that the ratio of major depressions was 2:1 for female and male subjects respectively. Though suicide causes are complex, and not all depressive patients are suicidal, the Hu and Chu paper deserves attention for those who argued for the Asian model in elder care.

Odalia Wong, by using intensive interviews with both daughters and daughters-in-law in Hong Kong, reported that the structural characteristics of women's role in elder care differ considerably between daughters and the wives of sons. Obviously, the daughter-in-law took precedence of her relations with her husband over her relations with his parents, a once removed norm of filial responsibility compared with the daughter. The daughter-in-law therefore is expectedly to be less attached and therefore feels more burden if undertaking the caregiving role.

Wong and Cho independently addressed to the question of the role of daughters-in-law respectively in Hong Kong and Korea. Though their methods of data collection are different, the conclusion drawn from the two studies are amazingly similar. Cho's study, based on path-analysis of causal relationships and subsequent burden felt, deserves special attention.

In this sense, Cho's paper about caregiving by daughters-in-law in Korea has also shed considerable light on some points raised by Hu and Chou in their paper about female suicide in Taiwan. The reader will notice that Hu and Chou had not demonstrated that the relationship between differential suicide rates for women and the presumed burden of caregiving. They simply did not have caregiving data at this moment. Their inferences were made by showing a greater participation of women who provide care for the elder relatives and suicide statistics from different sets of statistics. However, Cho has shown that in Korea factors such as one's value of familism, age, and educational status of the women do intervene with regard to supportive behaviour. Cho's sample of 259 middle-aged women may be small, the conclusion, however, is convincing.

On the same point, Liu argued that because of the organizational characteristics of the patriarchy, the obligation of Confucian ethics of filial piety is structurally asymmetrical, and unevenly distributed among all adult children within the family according to birth order and gender of the child. The first-born son has both the priority of caregiving responsibilities and the expectation of being filial amongst all members of the younger generation. As a result, the son should have a lower sense of caregiving burden compared with other positions in the family because of the predisposition to perform caregiving duties when needed by parents. The alternative hypothesis states the opposite: that greater responsibilities to care for the parents would result in both higher subjective and objective burden. The daughter-in-law, if being culturally assigned as the primary caregiver, should have a much higher subjective caregiving burden, because the kin-relationship is an indirect one, through marriage, and is derived from her husband's sense of filial piety. There is the added complication of the marital relationships between herself and her husband, as well as her husband's relationships with his parents. Liu's analysis on the son's filial duties and burden scores suggested credence for the original hypothesis. His data also suggested that the daughter-in-law has the built-in propensity to feel burdened subjectively, though objective measures of burden may be the same as other members in the family. There are undoubtedly many other factors that may contribute to the burden scores, which had not been identified at this time. Any quick conclusion, however, about the role of the daughter-in-law and caregiving burden to her mother-in-law here is perhaps premature at this point without further rigorous testing of these hypotheses.

Finally, the paper by Rance Lee and his colleagues, on the elder caregiving in Hong Kong through a sample survey[3] deserves attention for two reasons. First, Hong Kong may provide Western observers with information as to how Asian social values can shape government policies even under British rule. Second, statistics reported in this paper has cleared the myth that Hong Kong, being a former British colony, and a densely populated urban society, has adopted the nuclear family of the West only in the household type. In Hong Kong, despite the appearance of prevailing nuclear-household families, the over-whelming majority of the elderly do live with their younger relatives, or at least close by. The caring of elder parents by their offspring is the same in Hong Kong as it is in Japan, Taiwan, or Korea. The uniformity of practice, at least for the foreseeable future, shows the proof of an East Asian model. One cannot resist the temptation to raise the obvious question: "how long can the individual family continue to take care of an increasingly large number of elderly in the future?" While Western welfare states are turning to the family for help in providing the kind of elder care that the formal bureaucracy could not, families of East and Southeast Asia anticipate the time when the family must turn to the state for assistance in caring for the elder. When all societies are fully aged in the next two decades, plans to have a state-family partnership in elder care may converge between the East and the West.

Dialogue between the East and the West

Cross-cultural understandings of ageing and caregiving have a sound foundation in research from Western perspectives to encompass Eastern cultures. Anthropological inquiry is of course a Western construct but it has been applied to focus equally on caregiving and its meanings in the context of underlying ways of life in local communities both East and West (Fry's Hong Kong work-give citation). Survey research has taken quite a different path in attempting to adapt Western instruments (through rigorous processes of translation and back translation). However, with the fixed and close-ended questions of surveys, it is not clear how much the original Western frame of reference overpowers the attempt to represent and contrast across cultures equally.[4]

In our view, there is much to be gained from studies conducted by researchers from within their own cultures who also have a strong appreciation of other cultural perspectives as well. While all these are new ways to dissect the various components of research on caregiving in societies with different social values, more studies with rigorous research design are needed, especially in the East where only a few studies are in print, to further elucidate a complex social process of caregiving.

One very significant payoff of the project was the polemics of values in research. Those who subscribed to one view argued that demographic realities and family care burden for the small nuclear family left no room for doubt about the role of the government in elder care. Those who argued for the continual responsibilities of the family argued that government should have the duty to uphold the cohesion of the family and its role in providing care for the collective, both young and old. The argument is reminiscent of William F.

Ogburn's thesis of social change (not without intellectual influence from Karl Marx) which posited that technological change calls for changes of social values on one hand; and Max Weber who argued that social values often determine the way social change takes place. Weber cogently pointed out that Protestant Reformation shaped the way Industrial Revolution took place in Europe rather than the other way around. If the role of the government is to shape the way social policy is formulated, institutionalisation of practices may be difficult to alter once the process has began. Leaders in Asia, may determine to follow an Asian value model, and, in doing so, largely ignore the current academic views on elder care.

We have no reason to argue for or against any views in this book because, rightly or wrongly, a lot of people support them. But nor do we believe that there is any universal belief system, since by and large, we as social scientists, also believe that social relationships are learned behaviour. As learned behaviour, cultural values do intervene.

Notes

1 World Bank, 1994, "Averting the Old Age Crisis: Policies to Protect the Old and to Promote Growth", A World Bank Policy Research Report, Oxford University Press, p. 3.

2 The Shanghai Epidemiological Survey results were published elsewhere. See Liu, W.T. *et al.*, "The Shanghai Epidemiological Survey", pp. 65–70 in W.T. Liu (ed.), *A Decade Review of Mental Health Research, Training and Services,* Chicago: The University of Illinois at Chicago, 1987; Zhang, M.Y., *et al.*, "The Prevalence of Dementia and Alzheimer's Disease in Shanghai, China", *Annals of Neurology* 27:428–37, 1990; and Yu, E. *et al.*, "Cognitive Impairment among Elderly Adults in Shanghai, China", *Journal of Gerontology: Social Sciences* 44:S97–106, 1989.

3 The survey is a collaboration with the Department of Census and Statistics of the Hong Kong Government as Part II of the Annual Household Survey that took place in 1991.

4 Numerous authors have written on the problems of asking the same
   questions cross-culturally. The major contention lies in the controversy
   between identical wording (translated and back-translated) versus
   phenomenal equivalent wording (finding culturally appropriate
   expressions). These theoretical questions were first raised in a special
   1964 issue of the *American Anthropologist*, and specifically discussed
   by minority researchers in the seventies and the eighties. See Liu, W.T.
   (ed.), *Methodological Problems in Minority Research*, Chicago: P/
   AAMHRC Monograph Series, 1982; Yu, E.; M.Y. Zhang; W.T. Liu and
   Z.Y. Xia, "Translation of Instruments: Procedures, Issues, and Dilemmas",
   pp. 75–83 in W.T. Liu (ed.), *A Decade Review of Mental Health Research,
   Training and Services*, Chicago: The University of Illinois at Chicago,
   1987, and K.S. Markides, J. Liang and J.S. Jackson, "Race, Ethnicity,
   and Aging: Conceptual and Methodological Issues", pp. 112–25 in R.H.
   Binstock and L.K. George, *Handbook of Aging and the Social Sciences*,
   3rd edition, New York: Academic Press, 1990.

References

Brody, E.M. (1981), "Women in the Middle and Family Help to Older
   People", *Gerontologist*, 21: 470–80.
Brody, E.M.; P.T. Johnson and M.C. Fulcomer (1984), "What Should Adult
   Children Do for Elderly Parents? Opinions and Preferences of Three
   Generations of Women", *Journal of Gerontology*, 39: 736–46.
Chappel, N. (1990), "Aging and Social Care", in Binstock, R.H. and L.K.
   George (eds.), *Handbook of Aging and the Social Sciences* (3rd edition).
   New York: The Academic Press.
Finch, Janet and Dulcie Grove (1980), "Community Care and the Family: A
   Case for Equal Opportunity", *Journal of Social Policy,* 9, Part 4: 487–
   511.
Fry, C. and J. Keith (1982), "The Life Course as a Cultural Unit", in M.W.
   Riley (ed.), *Aging from Birth to Death: Sociotemporal Perspectives*.
   Boulder, CO: Westview Press.
Glascock, A. and S. Feinman (1981), "Social Asset or Social Burden: An
   Analysis of the Treatment for the Aged in Non-Industrial Societies", in
   C. Fry (ed.), *Dimensions: Aging, Culture and Health*, New York: Praeger.

Glascock, A. and S. Feinman (1986), "Towards a Comparative Framework: Propositions Concerning the Treatment of the Aged in Non-Industrial Societies", in C. Fry and J. Keith (eds.), *New Methods for Old Age Research*. South Hadley, MA: Bergin and Garvey.

Keith, J. (1990), "Aging in Social and Cultural Context: Anthropological Perspective", in Binstock, R.H. and L.K. George, *Handbook of Aging and the Social Sciences* (3rd edition). New York: The Academic Press.

Keith, J. (1992), "Care-taking in Cultural Context: Anthropological Queries", in Kendig, H.L.; A. Hashimoto and L.C. Coppard (eds.), *Family Support for the Elderly*. WHO. Oxford: Oxford University Press.

Kiefer, C. (1974), *Changing Cultures, Changing Lives*. San Francisco: Jossey-Bass.

Lang, A. and E.M. Brody (1983), "Characteristics of Middle-Aged Daughters and Help to Their Elderly Mothers", *Journal of Marriage and the Family*, 45: 193–202.

Myers, G.C. (1992), "Demographic Aging and Family Support for Older Persons", in Kendig, H.L.; A. Hashimoto and L.C. Coppard (eds.), *Family Support for the Elderly*. WHO. Oxford: Oxford University Press.

Palmore, E.B. and D. Maeda (1985), *Elders Revisited: A Revised Crosscultural Analysis of Aging in Japan*. Durham, NC: Duke University Press.

United Nations, Economic and Social Council (1989), *Second Review and Appraisal of the Implementation of the International Plan of Action on Aging: Report of the Secretary-General*. The United Nations (E/1989/13), New York.

United Nations General Assembly [97-23409 (E)].

PART ONE
The Western Perspectives

Chapter 1

Societal and Family Change in the Burden of Care

Rhonda J.V. Montgomery
University of Kansas
Edgar F. Borgatta and Marie L. Borgatta
University of Washington

Introduction

Caregiving burden is a concept that needs to be considered with regard to the parties involved, the situation that exists, and the values that are relevant. These three foci will be considered before presenting information on how caregiving burden has been measured and reviewing research related to this concept.

Who Needs Care

Children

At one time or another, everyone is potentially a person needing care. The most prevalent group of dependents is infants and children. In most parts of the world families, which are usually based on biological relationship, are the most common social structure ordered by socially defined rules that provide for this care. The variety of family structures range from extended families in tribal situations to nuclear and single parent families in industrialized nations, with the birth mother most commonly given the responsibility for infant nurturing and care. Since family and kinship types may vary greatly both within and across cultures, the care seen as appropriate and who to provide it also varies greatly. In extended families responsibility for care of infants and children may be shared by many adults and older children. Surrogate arrangements are not uncommon, especially among the rich and the powerful. Wet nurses, nannies, and other surrogates have been and are used to care for infants and children.

In general, as children grow, care takes on other meanings, including education and indoctrination into the family and the culture/ society. In some Western nations, there has been a tradition for the upper social strata to send children to boarding schools, where parental responsibility is effectively transferred to the school masters.

Disabled

Special caregiving may be required as persons grow from children to mature adults, when, for whatever reason, they are or become in-capable of caring for themselves. This is especially the case with those incapacitated from birth or by later injury or illness. How much attention the incapacitated get may also vary greatly across cultures. In industrialized nations there has been a tendency in medical and related areas to use extraordinary (or what have been called "heroic") procedures to maintain life for newborns and others who in earlier times might not have survived initially or who would have died in a short time. There are at least two foci with regard to extraordinary care for infants and children. The first is the attempt to support survival techniques during the fetal period in order to accomplish a live birth and viability. Aside from prenatal care, this is most commonly seen in the "heroic" attempts to keep early premature infants alive, which may involve enormous mobilization and expenditure of resources. The second is the determination to keep infants and children with major disabilities or infirmities alive, even when it is known that the quality of life for them will be sorely limited or meaningless. Some of the recent vast investment in life support systems has involved great controversy because it has often required massive costs with little social justification when alternate options for the use of funds is considered.

In some broader discussions of life-support measures, the controversy has been described as one with two poles: The first is usually thought of as a neutral or "natural" orientation to life, i.e., permitting ordinary termination of life as it would have occurred before the recent advent of the extraordinary technologies for keeping people alive. In earlier times, people commonly died when they were not able to carry out normal body functions without the assistance of currently available medical resources, ranging from intravenous supply of nutrients to implantation of mechanical devices. Such deaths without intervention are sometimes identified as "natural". Thus, people died because such things as dialysis, intravenous feeding, mechanical heart valves, organ transplants, etc., were not available. There are many life-prolonging procedures now available, and these may involve quite different things. Obviously, the use of antibiotics, immunizations, and other general medical, hygienic, and sanitary procedures that have become available are not at issue in the consideration of extraordinary interventions.

However, the position taken by those who resist total avoidance of "natural" death is that while technology is often available to keep tissues alive, keeping tissues alive is not justifiable unless people can consciously experience ordinary pleasures associated with a good "quality of life". A second implication of this position is that in some cases, especially with less than "normal" healthy infants, a negative eugenic policy may be supported. This is also manifest at two levels. The first is the reproduction and extension of severely defective or deficient humans. The second involves the differential use of resources to maintain the defective and deficient rather than to support those

30   *Rhonda J.V. Montgomery, Edgar F. Borgatta, Marie L. Borgatta*

who are more fortunate biological products. (For example, the expenditure to keep one early premature infant alive may have the equivalent cost of providing minimum life support for several hundred people in a developing nation.) When this position is stated in order to be provocative, it is phrased as stating that "humane" policy involving extraordinary interventions simply counters any notion of the survival of the fittest in society. (There is, of course, some irony in this position since in most modern societies the most successful and powerful strata, no matter how defined, rarely is the most productive of children for the next generation.)

Extraordinary interventions rarely are economically affordable by families even in most prosperous industrialized nations. Caregiving in most industrialized nations where this kind of investment occurs commonly involves the biological families for at least some of the pre-adult years of their children, but since most often the expense reaches extraordinary sums impossible for most families to afford, the cost becomes publicly supported.

Countering the position of those who resist extraordinary investments in the survival of infants and children who are infirm and incapacitated are those who feel that all life must be supported and saved no matter what cost or investments have to be made. The arguments offered commonly have a morality and/or religious base, in contrast to the opposite position which often is based on humanistic, relativistic, and pragmatic values.

The Elderly

The comments thus far have focused on infants and children to indicate that the issues of caregiving are not merely problems in dealing with the old and the dying, but range through the life cycle and involve both practical issues of cost as well as philosophical positions on the value of life. It is within this context that we now address the growth in need for elder care.

Caregiving in families has been the situation in most of the world over known history. However, family types and needs have been changing quite quickly in many societies. Transitions such as those associated with the industrial revolution have changed family types substantially, and modernization and post modernization periods have led to further changes. Along with these changes have also come changes in medicine, hygiene, and sanitation, which have improved the health and living conditions of people. The development of and access to improved medical, hygienic, and sanitation resources has resulted in an impressive increase in life expectancy. Roughly, in the industrialized nations the life expectancy of both men and women was 50 years at the beginning of the 20th century. Currently it is about 80 years for women and six or seven years less for men. Concomitantly, during the 20th century there has been a corresponding drop in fertility which has shifted population distributions from an age pyramid to an age column with a small pyramid sitting at the top, beginning roughly at 50 years of age. The shift has changed the situation from one in which a small proportion of persons survive into old age to one in which most persons survive into old age, but, further, often old and feeble enough to be dependent on care by others. Death from exposure to infectious diseases during the life course has been replaced by a situation in which most of the older population die from heart and circulatory diseases or failures, from progressive diseases like cancer, or from the general deterioration of health with a withering away of physical and/or mental capacities to a state of dependency that requires progressively more and more care.

What has become the circumstance, at least clearly so in the modern industrialized nations, is that more old persons survive to a point of needing care. This fact has received attention from social scientists and social planners in a number of ways.

Issues Surround the Care Needs of the Elderly

Family Changes and Filial Responsibility

One focus of scholars and policy-makers has been the changes in the family. Part of the change in the population pyramid is due not only to older age survival, but also to the lowering of fertility performance. Thus, the number of children in the industrialized nations has dropped in general to an average of two or less, with many families having one or no children. The pattern is towards achieving a stable population size. Even in a number of less developed nations fertility patterns have been reduced markedly in response to international concerns with over-population reflected through UNESCO and other sources. This shift in family structure has important implications for the care for the elderly.

Filial Responsibility

In the literature that touches on caregiving for the old, but also often incorporated in legal systems of the societies, there traditionally have been expectations that children will care for their aging parents. This expectation has been bolstered by the myth of *filial responsibility* in Western nations, that is, that children in prior centuries somehow voluntarily cared for their aging parents. In consideration of other cultural areas the concept is often identified as "filial piety". A serious look at Western history has suggested that there is little corresponding reality to the myth for two reasons. First, as noted, old persons were formerly relatively uncommon, with life expectancy being on the average 50 years even as late as the beginning of the 20th century, and substantially lower before then. Actually few persons survived to what is currently thought of as old age. Second, family wealth, if there was any, was in the hands of the elderly, and that was the basis for family control and receipt of care from children and the younger generation.

The literature on this topic largely pivots on Schorr's monograph (Schorr, 1980), which established that the relationship with parents was one of duty, rather than sentiment and satisfaction on the part of the children. The likely situation if persons survived into older age was that they were not really dependents of children, since land and other possessions were held by them, and the parents would be the key to income and support for others until they died. The children were, in these circumstances, the more likely "dependents" in the broader meaning of the word. As Schorr points out, the industrial revolution altered the sources of income for individuals and families so that the economic ties to the extended family were reduced and often did not exist at all. There is some debate on what the reasons for development of laws holding children responsible for the welfare of their parents has been in England, the United States, and other industrialized nations. The justification is often phrased in moral terms, the explicit statement of which involves the notion that as a matter of love and respect for parents the children should accept the responsibility. However, a more cynical but realistic view is that the state and other government units see the care of dependent persons as a public expense and burden to avoid (Bulcroft *et al.,* 1989). Where laws exist holding children responsible for the welfare of their parents, they are commonly sporadically distributed in jurisdictions, not uniform, and enforced capriciously, which according to most legal scholars means they are not good laws. (At least, this has been the case in the United States.) With regard to older persons who become dependent, some order exists in the expectations of responsibility by family members, with spouses first in order, then children. The topic of filial responsibility has been reviewed extensively (Montgomery, 1992).

Fairness of Filial Piety

The notion of individual responsibility for family members and relatives, whether parents, children, spouses, or more distant relatives, raises questions of fairness that are in part seen as the reason for the difficulty in enforcing responsibility laws. In particular, having a relative who becomes a dependent is not under the control of the individual. To illustrate the question of fairness in the abstract, take the extreme *example* of a married person who may have as dependents two parents, two parents of the spouse, and correspondingly eight grandparents. Compare such a person with one who has no parental elders at all. Theoretically, why should one person be held responsible for the welfare of twelve persons and the other have no such burden? Is the word burden correct here? Some will say that the person with all the parental survivors has good fortune. The example is extreme, of course, but it is formulated to illustrate the principle. (Those who like to be provocative in raising this type of example often also point to the fact that the children do not choose the families in which they are born.)

Let us take as another *example* the situation that appears to be modal for industrialized nations at this time with regard to family structure. Suppose we have a couple who marry young and are the only children of relatively young parents. The young couple establishes their own household. Then, with life expectations being what they are, suppose fifty years pass. Since in many places there commonly is the expectation that in marriages females will be somewhat younger than males (probably the most common form of hypergamy), and as we have noted males have life expectancies about 7 years shorter than females, the female is most likely to have the responsibility for taking care of a dependent husband rather than the other way around. (In the United States the odds are about eight or nine to one that the wife will survive her husband.) Rarely does the husband have to take care of a dependent wife. This family structural situation that is so common in societies raises some interesting questions about how families are formed and what possible changes may occur in what appears to be the modal pattern in societies.

But, independently of the situation of husband and wife in the example above, let us note for another *example* that when the young couple has been married for about 40 years, and, if they have parents who are survivors, they would presumably be the persons responsible for the care of these very old dependent persons. The old parents who survive, of course, are statistically most often females. What is expected, thus, is that now in their early 60s the couple who has lived in a separate and independent household for forty years, has probably had and raised children who are themselves now in independent households, who at this point should take responsibility for the very old survivors. In considering this family structure situation from the point of view of policy formation, the question has been phrased as follows: Is it reasonable to expect 65-year-old persons who have had their own independent household and family and likely also have been in the labor force most of their lives to assume responsibility for the care of 90-year-old mothers whom they have not lived with for forty or so years? Is this a timely reward for persons reaching retirement age? More will be said about this below as we discuss the basis for measurement of caregiving burden.

Possible Decrease in Care Needs

A second area of interest affecting the consideration of the need for care, or the possible decrease of such need, is the notion that there is a genetic basis for how long any individual will live (Fries and Crapo, 1981; Borgatta, 1987). Presumably, with the advent of modern medicine, hygiene, and sanitation, people will no longer die from communicable diseases or disorders and failures of the human organism that can be medically controlled. The theory suggests people will die simply because they have reached the end of their genetic clock. A part of this notion is that when the genetic clock strikes the death toll, people will die promptly with only short periods of dependency related to incapacity or incompetence. When this theory was first circulated it received considerable attention, but subsequently the notion has faded from the scene, as it has become apparent that in the absence of disease, the dying process commonly is one of slow deterioration into incapacities that require assistance and care, with possibly even half such cases that become dependent involving mental deterioration of one type or other. Little actual research directly bears on this, but the idea of life effectively being shut off rather than of parts slowly wearing out or deteriorating simply has not developed any strong research support.

Gender Inequalities

Spouses

A third notion that has needed attention is the inequalities between the sexes in both care responsibility and dependency. As noted earlier, the differential death rate that favors women means that they more often are left to take care of their expiring male partners. The fact that in marriages men are usually older than women accentuates the circumstance in industrialized societies, so that women not only live on average 7 years longer than men, but wives commonly live 9 or 10 years longer than their husbands. Thus, women are most often caregivers for their spouses. This is a situation in which the notion of caregiving burden becomes problematic beyond what has been indicated earlier in considering a concept of fairness.

There are, also, additional issues of fairness in a system that has this sex role unbalance. There has been some practical basis historically in the industrialized societies for the sex role differences, since in earlier times women were infrequently in the labor force. When private retirement pensions were available in those days they were usually attached only to the male worker. So keeping a husband alive had some economic value. However, this has changed both in the reflection of laws and policies to protect survivors, especially wives and children, but also in the shift to the increasing participation of females in the labor force and thus to personal access to retirement benefits of their own.

There is no direct evidence to suggest that the differential death rates are genetically based, so equal attention should, in theory, be given to examining how the life expectancy of males might be increased to equal that of females, avoiding of course the recourse to blaming the victims or to suggest that women should in some way be deprived or corrupted so they die earlier.

Adult Children

When the older person needing care has no viable spouse, often the caregiving task may be allocated to a child. In this circumstance a number of points must be made: (a) If there is no child, this cannot be the source of caregiving, (b) In industrialized societies, older persons are quite old when they become dependent. Thus, as implied earlier in an example, the children are likely to be older themselves, (c) Additionally, if there is only one child in the family, or only one child is available when very old persons need the caregiving, it is not the same concept as an extended geographically local family with many members available to provide assistance. From experience in research and observation in the United States, it appears that when children are caregivers, female children actually do the caregiving, and, if male children do so, they are most often involved only indirectly, either by having their own spouses assist or by providing funds to purchase care.

Population Control and Care Needs

World Trends

What is clear so far is that a need for caregiving of old dependent persons is becoming a common circumstance in industrialized nations and as less developed nations move in the same direction with regard to life expectancy, family structure, and the economy, the problems noted will also more frequently be theirs. Population expansion increasingly becomes a major issue in the world, with general acceptance of the validity of at least a modified Malthusian view. In particular, the balance of population and standard of living is obviously not uniform throughout the regions of the world. While there has been a massive growth of population in the last few centuries, the rates of industrial development and resource use have not been uniform. The industrialized nations have already gone through the demographic transition and tend to have relatively low fertility rates at this point. Thus, they have not had an extraordinary problematic situation thus far with regard to over-utilizing available resources (which include those drawn from other nations). However, with problems of pollution, of waste disposal, of maintenance of water supplies, of availability of power resources, etc., limits required to maintain a reasonable environment become obvious. In the most industrialized nations the vast majority of persons have access to modern technology, including automobiles and a variety of mechanized recreational vehicles including boats, to television, radio, telephone, personal computers, washing machines and laundry driers, dishwashers, vacuum cleaners, etc. This democratization of wealth is, of course, only one reflection of the differences in the industrialized nations compared to the less developed ones.

It is a fortunate part of history that the decline of fertility has slowed the increase of population in the industrialized nations. If the population of the industrialized nations were twice the size it is now, would there be enough available energy and natural resources to maintain the level of consumption that now exists? Would there be enough of everything to go around? This is a tough question to ponder, but it also has to be considered with regard to the less developed nations, which presumably are under pressure to move up the scale of industrialization and modernization, and, most importantly, of consumption. They already have in existence much larger populations than do the industrialized nations do.

Population control will be a critical issue in the whole world, but as has been pointed out many times, the industrialized nations have been deluded in some of their stereotypic presentations of this subject. To put it crassly, one child born in an industrialized nation may consume several hundred times more of the world resources than a child born in primitive circumstances in a less developed nation, but population control as a critical issue is often denied with regard to the industrialized nations.

Different nations have taken different approaches to the question of population control, and it has become a prevailing topic of importance in many, if not most, nations. The involvement of the United Nations in studies of population statistics and analysis of trends has resulted in the production of major documents of international importance. Education for population control has been socialized in many nations, but in others it is effectively a taboo subject, because of religious and other beliefs, which may be nationally indoctrinated, or may be controlled less formally at local levels. However, it is hard to restrict all communication, so changes can occur quickly even in places where the belief systems are highly controlled and restrictive. Often a conflict occurs between traditional beliefs and changes that occur. For example, the Pope in the Catholic Church still categorically rejects contraception and safe pregnancy termination, yet in some nations where the Catholic religion is dominant, such as Italy, the fertility levels are among the lowest. Individuals face conflicting values if they wish to obtain some of the benefits of the technology and material opportunities available in the industrialized nations, and these include a balance between being locked into supporting and rearing children and access to an increased standard of living.

However, fertility control is also associated to a large extent with access to medical and health resources for women and children, so there is the potential for conflict with and modification of traditional values simply on these grounds. This access, certainly, is also supported in the commitment of most nations to documents and treaty agreements which explicitly cover civil rights and civil liberties (United Nations, 1948, 1966, 1989; Cohen and Naimark, 1991).

In any event, when fertility control becomes effective, the collective changes in family structure will alter the familiar population pyramid to a column, and if the fertility performance decreases below replacement, the bottom of the column actually becomes smaller than the top.

Fertility Control in China

In China, where a national policy restricting family size has been imposed quickly and with considerable success, the old family pyramids based on extended families increasing each generation will no longer persist, and the family structure change is well recognized. The policy in China is a unique social experiment in response to definition of population control as a critical problem. Some have been critical of the policy in China, and even Hillary Rodham Clinton, who is usually characterized as a liberal, has implicitly taken a negative position, stating: "It is a violation of human rights when women are denied the right to plan their own families, and that includes being forced to have abortions or being sterilized against their will." (*Seattle Times*, September 11, 1995). However, critics do not point out how an effective policy can be imposed if some persons do not voluntarily control their own fertility. As a matter of fairness, the "right to plan their families" may need to involve limited choices of plans. According to a newspaper report, President Jiang Zemin covered issues of the complexity and difficulties in maintaining the policy in China, and the impact of current experience on population growth. A projection of 1.2 billion persons in the year 2000 required revision to almost 1.3 billion persons (*Seattle Times*, March 21, 1995).

Family planning policy is no different from other matters governing individual control that come under societal control. With regard to fertility control, practically, modern medicine has made remarkable strides in the development of effective contraceptive techniques, which are the basis for anticipating undesired pregnancies. These include not only the common mechanical means such as the condom, IUDS, diaphragms, but also spermicides, pills, injections, and implants, not to mention voluntary sterilization of both males and females. The procedures for surgical termination of undesired pregnancies are well developed, but pregnancy termination is becoming even more effective and less intrusive with the availability of medical drug therapies. In any event, the feasibility of changing family structure in China and in other areas will profit from the advances in medical and hygienic care. Managing the social and political problems that may arise in the process because of traditions and beliefs, however, will generate considerable challenge.

Thus, with the arrival of effective and reasoned fertility control, attention to issues of caregiving for incapacitated elderly will become more acutely required. The role likely to be played by families should be anticipated realistically. Caregiving burden has been considered primarily with regard to family caregiving and needs to be understood in terms of current family situations, but from a point of view of planning for the future, the changes in family structures must be underscored in terms of societal burden and the practical problems and issues of fairness.

Study of Caregiving Burden in the United States

In the United States the focus on caregiving burden has received attention in two major ways. First, attention have been given to the definition and measurement of caregiving burden. Second, investigators have focused on the correlates and consequences of caregiving with regard to burden for family members? How does the assignment of caregiving occur? Who or what family members accept the responsibility for caregiving? How is burden a part of the caregiving process, and how does it relate to the needs of both the elder and the caregiver?

Measuring Caregiver Burden

Over the past decade a large body of literature has emerged that is focused on the burden of care for the elderly. As is often typical of new areas of study, however, there is great variation within this literature in the conceptual definitions of burden and in the measurement of burden. Yet, a careful review of this burgeoning literature by the authors revealed some consistent patterns in the definitions of burden. Generally, burden has been conceptualized in three broad ways. First, burden has been defined as the extent of work load and measured in terms of the number and types of care tasks performed (e.g., assistance with household chores, banking tasks or personal care tasks) and/or the number of hours spent performing these tasks (e.g. Carey *et al.*, 1991). Second, burden has been defined as the caregiver's judgement concerning the distress or difficulty associated with performing the care tasks (Miller *et al.*, 1991; Poulshock & Deimling, 1989). Third, burden has been defined as the "perceived" impact of this workload on the caregiver's life (e.g. Miller *et al.*, 1991; Montgomery *et al.*, 1985). It is this third conceptualization of burden that is most prevalent in the literature and that has received the most attention.

This conceptualization of burden as the perceived impact of care tasks has been further refined by distinguishing between emotional impacts and impacts on resources such as time, physical health, physical space and/or finances. Emotional impact has been variously called subjective burden, stress, or strain and has been linked to depression. In addition, several investigators have focused on the impact of care tasks on the dyadic relationship between the caregiver and the care receiver, and referred to this unique form of burden as elder-family conflict, relative stress, provocateur, relationship burden or subjective demand burden (e.g. Kosberg *et al.*, 1990; Poulshock and Deimling, 1989; McFall and Miller, 1992; Montgomery *et al.*, 1993).

Although the earliest investigations of burden employed global or multi-dimensional measures of burden which incorporated both the emotional impacts and the impacts on caregiver resources, most recent studies have distinguished between these types of burden (see Montgomery, 1989). Measures of impact on resources have most often included items pertaining to restrictions on social and work activities, financial costs, and/or health costs.

Our own study of caregiving burden was initiated more than a decade ago (Montgomery *et al.*, 1985; Montgomery and Borgatta, 1986), and, of course, is only a small part of the many studies and research on caregiving by family members. It should be emphasized that these are results restricted to the culture of the United States. Our approach to measurement, while broadly based initially, has led to a set of concepts which are simple and easily understood. Three relatively independent main variables (drawn from exploratory factor analytic studies) appear to cover most of the variance of the concept. First, there is *objective burden*, which is measured in our studies by six items that involve the following content: Amount of time one has for one's self; amount of personal privacy one retains; time available for recreational activities; restrictions on vacations and trips; amount of time available to do one's own work and daily chores; and amount of time for friends and relatives. The internal consistency of this measure (Cronbach Alpha) for recent examinations have ranged between .87 and .90. Second, there is *subjective demand burden*, which is measured by four items that involve the following content: Attempts by the dependent relative in manipulating the caregiver; unreasonable requests of the caregiver; feeling by the caregiver of being taken advantage of by the dependent relative; and demands made by the dependent relative that are over and above what is needed. The internal consistency of this measure has ranged from .68 to .82. Third, there is *subjective stress burden*, which is measured by four items that involve the following content: Stress in the relationship with the dependent relative; tension in the caregiver's life; nervousness and depression related to the relationship with the dependent relative; and anxiety about things. The internal consistency of this measure has ranged between .81 and .87. Thus, it can be concluded that caregiving burden measures are reasonably well defined. Our measures have more recently been further refined. A review of measures of caregiving burden is found in a recent article which also implicitly underscores the recurrence of at least concepts of objective and subjective burden (Vitaliano *et al.*, 1991).

Establishing the three relatively independent variables associated with the concept of burden provides one finding that has been reported in other forms. In particular, the fact that the variables are relatively independent means that many persons who have dependent relatives with objectively defined burdens do not subjectively feel they are burdened. The opposite, of course, is also a finding, namely that many persons who have dependent relatives who do not have many objectively defined burdens may still subjectively feel they are burdened (also see: Zarit *et al.*, 1980; Noelker and Poulshock, 1982).

Who is Burdened

Research on caregiving burden has been stimulated in part by a particular reality orientation among policy-makers. That is, if caregiving burden is too high, the caregiver may not be able to continue to provide the support and service required. Then, if substitute family relatives cannot be found, the dependent relative must be cared for by a public agency. Indeed, in our observations and that of others, a relationship is readily found between caregiving burden and admission of dependent family relatives to nursing homes or other institutional care (Kosloski *et al.*, 1990; McFall and Miller, 1992).

For the past decade, the majority of research on caregiver burden has focused on questions that are consistent with this orientation of policy makers and reflect the underlying premise that family members are, and should be, the primary source of help for the impaired elder. The most frequent research questions concern the identification of correlates of caregiver burden with the underlying purpose of using this information to develop and target interventions to keep the family as the primary source of care for the elderly. Two patterns have emerged from this research.

First, the consistency among findings regarding gender and generation differences in the type and extent of tasks performed (see Dwyer and Coward, 1992). In particular, spouses provide more personal and more extensive care, which is easily understandable in terms of the long history of intimacy usual for marital couples. Spouses also provide assistance over a longer period of time than do adult children. Among children, daughters tend to provide more personal care and greater amounts of care than do sons. Daughters also tend to share the care load with siblings or spouses less often than do sons.

Second, in contrast to the observed consistency in care patterns, a recent review of findings of research on caregiver burden (Montgomery, 1996), revealed the inconclusiveness of studies regarding correlates of caregiver burden. Characteristics of the caregivers may have some relationship to the existence of felt burden, but the findings on this matter tend to be sporadic and not necessarily consistent. For example, no consistency is found in the differences of felt burden between men and women who are caretakers of their spouses. However, some studies note that the role changes in becoming caretakers can be documented for male spouses. Similarly, the closeness of the relationship of the caregiver to the dependent person has not provided consistent evidence on differences in subjective burden. With regard to differences between spouses and children as caretakers, possibly the majority of studies indicate that spouses report more objective burden, but there is inconsistency even on this. Other factors that have been investigated as correlates of burden include caregiver employment status, duration of caregiving tasks, sibling networks, living arrangements and social support. Findings from studies focused on each of these factors remain inconsistent.

At least in the United States, one negative finding (i.e., absence of a finding) must be reported. In particular, in the abundance of studies that have been carried out and reviewed by Montgomery, little or no consistent evidence has been found that the characteristics of the dependent relative are associated with the burden felt by the caretaker (Montgomery, 1989). This is in contrast to some of the common clinical lore which suggests that the greater the impairments, especially in the mental area, the greater the burden on the part of the family caregivers.

The implication in this very brief report of the research on caregiving is that while there may have been many studies focused on caregiver burden, it is not clear that an agenda of questions about the caregiving process has actually been formulated in any systematic way. Moreover, the inconsistency in findings reflects a certain naive understanding of the caregiving role and process. Much of the work to date has been formulated without sufficient attention to the established structural and historical family relationships from which the dyadic caregiver-care receiver relationship emerges. To successfully understand caregiver burden it is necessary to acknowledge that there is no single, generic caregiver role. Rather, caregiving is a role that emerges from beliefs, and circumstances of the role occupant. Consequently, burden must be understood within this context of variations in normative and personal expectations. Additionally, future research on burden must recognize caregiving as a dynamic process that unfolds over time with corresponding changes in implications for burden.

The Need for Realistic Perspectives on Caregiving

Changing Family Contexts

What else needs to be given attention? One thing is that as people realize that the historical descriptions of what families might have been or might be are commonly romanticized and idealized, there is also a realization that care for the elderly is something that at a practical level becomes a community responsibility. In a sense, in the past it was a community responsibility when the extended family, the clan, the tribe, or other close social organization was the community. Suggestion that the public agencies are now the community is not a mean spirited comment, but reflects the fact that the practical situation for care is not found in the family relations that are being generated in the modern world. And, although this has not been noted earlier, older dependent persons, for example, in general do not want to be burdens on their few close biological and marital relations, or on their close friends.

Still, it is necessary to emphasize that changes in families have occurred and will continue to occur. In the structural analysis of the family that has been presented emphasis has been on the transition from the extended family to the nuclear family. However, this is an over-simplification of changes that have occurred in the United States and other industrialized nations, particularly in the idealized notion of stable families. Divorce is common and in some nations half of all marriages end in divorce. For children in divorced families there are complex relationships, and these relationships cannot be assumed to involve the kind of sentiments that are presumed for the idealized stable complete family. Further, differences between parents and children, the classic notion of generational differences, appear to be great in some cultural situations and quickly changing cultures. Many post World War II children do not have the traditional values of their parents, and dating, cohabitation, and other patterns, including increases in single-parent families, are additional changes. There is an anecdote of the Japanese father, who asked if he understood his son, states he does not, for his son seems to be from another planet, so different is he from the traditional expectations. The anecdote is particularly acute because Japan is one of the nations in which strength of family ties and veneration of the elders has been traditionally strong. But even when there is no divorce, it does not mean the married couple as it ages is a representative of mutual respect and supportive sentiment. The literature on family relations, at least in the United States, notes that couples stay together for many other reasons, including the economy of a single household and the fact that alternatives for the divorced are often less than attractive or practical. These and other reality factors associated with family relations that exist or may be anticipated complicate the idealized notion that family members should be caretakers for each other.

Quality of Life and Assisted Death

Some additional questions will also need to be raised with some degree of seriousness. To cite one, policies that exist and develop often may be well intentioned, but may result in becoming restrictive or punitive. For example, there is a notion that quality of life ought to be included as a consideration in the expectations we have about life and death. We know tissue can be kept "alive" by extraordinary procedures, and death in this sense gets some extraordinary meaning. In the United States, for example, a recent report of critically ill patients indicated that "only 49 percent of the patients who requested do-not-resuscitate orders actually got them, and 70 percent were never asked their preference" (*Newsweek*, December 4, 1995). For many, surviving only as "live tissue" is not an attractive or desired prospect, and so some would prefer to "check out" by a humane procedure before becoming burdens to themselves and to others as well. How is this to be managed? With regard to choices, there is a propensity in many societies to move, out of pity, kindness, moral philosophy, or religious dogma to what become negative eugenic policies with massive economic and other consequences. How should this be controlled? What mechanisms should be used to control this and in whose hands should the controls be placed?

There is a need for reconsidering concepts of suicide and assisted death. While it is extraordinarily delicate as a subject, even questions of managing the dying process for those who become incapable will require attention. What should be done when persons are reduced to "live tissue" before expressing their preferences or when preferences that have been expressed are ignored?This topic is touched on by Moody in a recent article discussing the prolongation of morbidity.

"Groups advocating for the disabled have had misgivings about reference to quality of life as a standard for allocating scarce health care resources.... How then to acknowledge the quality of life standard as a basis for allocation while at the same time maintaining individual rights?

Political efficiency might suggest that an allocation policy guided by quality of life can be achieved by indirect if not covert means. An example of such a policy shift would be a judicial determination that the "best interest" of a "reasonable person" whose intent is not otherwise known is presumed to be termination of treatment under conditions where quality of life dips below some threshold. There might be a rebuttable presumption not to treat — e.g., to withhold Medicare reimbursement — from Alzheimer's patients certified as mentally incompetent or who are suffering from some other identifiable ailment. Many will respond that there is a dangerous slippery slope here once we accept the idea that quality of life is a valid factor for allocating scarce health-care resources in the last stage of life. But the point here is that the "slope" is actually an implicit claim about the meaning of life in old age, where "meaning" is understood as quality of life, defined in different, often controversial ways." (Moody, 1995, pp. 168–69)

What needs to be added to Moody's comments is that there may be more practical ways of handling the matter. For example, a policy could be proposed that anyone who wishes to be kept alive when totally incompetent (essentially, what is usually termed a "vegetable") should record this desire formally in an established procedure. At the present time in most of the industrial societies the procedure, as noted, is the opposite. Often the client is not consulted, or, even when persons have made "living wills" requesting termination under particular conditions, their wishes are not carried out.

Conclusion

The emphasis in this paper is that the issues that deal with caring for the disabled, the incompetent, the sick, and the incapacitated dependent aged are complex, and the practical problems that societies face will become greater rather than lesser. Attention to the changing structures of society and of the family in particular cannot be reserved as topics for the future, for in these matters the future is now. In many circumstances the family is not the sufficient structure it has been in the past, and thus the social community becomes the fallback locus of support and security. Attention needs to be given to how a baseline safety net can be provided. Giving importance to values based on beliefs rather than to the rational analysis of practical problems for humanity is not a reasonable way to anticipate the needs of the future.

Appendix A

Caregiver Burden Measure

Now, I'd like to know whether assisting or having other contact with your [relative] has affected the following aspects of your life.

Please tell me whether the amount of each of these aspects in your life has changed due to your caregiving activities.

Alternative introduction for nursing home populations:

Since your [relative] was placed in the nursing home, how has assisting or having contact with him/her affected the following aspects of your life?

Do you have a lot less, a little less, the same, a little more, or a lot more

	A lot less	A little less	The same	A little more	A lot more
... time to yourself?					
... stress in your relationship with your relative					
... personal privacy?					
... attempts by your relative to manipulate you?					
... time to spend in recreational activities?					
... unreasonable requests made of you by your relative?					
... tension in your life?					
... vacation activities and trips?					
... nervousness and depression concerning your relationship with your relative?					
... feelings that you are being taken advantage of by your relative?					
... time to do your own work and daily chores?					
... demands made by your relative that are over and above what s/he needs?					
... anxiety about things?					
... time for friends and other relatives?					

Scoring and Reliability of Scales

Objective Burden Items:

	A lot less	A little less	The same	A little more	A lot more
... time to yourself?	5	4	3	2	1
... personal privacy?	,,	,,	,,	,,	,,
... time to spend in recreational activities?	,,	,,	,,	,,	,,
... vacation activities and trips?	,,	,,	,,	,,	,,
... time to do your own work and daily chores?	,,	,,	,,	,,	,,
... time for friends and other relatives?	,,	,,	,,	,,	,,

Range (5–30): Range of Cronbach's Alpha in previous studies (.88–.91).

Subjective Demand Burden Items:

	A lot less	A little less	The same	A little more	A lot more
... attempts by your relative to manipulate you?	1	2	3	4	5
... unreasonable requests made of you by your relative?	,,	,,	,,	,,	,,
... feelings that you are being taken advantage of by your relative?	,,	,,	,,	,,	,,
... demands made by your relative that are over and above what s/he needs?	,,	,,	,,	,,	,,

Range (4–20): Range of Cronbach's Alpha in previous studies (.79–.88).

Subjective Demand Burden Items:

	A lot less	A little less	The same	A little more	A lot more
... stress in your relationship with your relative	1	2	3	4	5
... tension in your life?	"	"	"	"	"
... nervousness and depression concerning your relationship with your relative?	"	"	"	"	"
... anxiety about things?	"	"	"	"	"

Range (4–20): Range of Cronbach's Alpha in previous studies (.81–.88).

References

Borgatta, Edgar F. (1987) "Active Life Expectancy", in *The Encyclopedia of Aging*, edited by E.F. Borgatta and M.L. Borgatta. New York: Springer.

Bulcroft, Kris; June Van Leynseele and Edgar F. Borgatta (1989) "Filial Responsibility Laws", *Research on Aging*, 11: 374–393.

Carey, Phyllis J.; Marilyn T. Oberst; Marilyn A. McCubbin and Susan H. Hughes (1991) "Appraisal and Caregiving Burden in Family Members Caring for Patients Receiving Chemotherapy", *Oncology Nursing Forum*, 18:1341–1348.

Cohen, Cynthia P. and Hedwin Naimark (1991) "United Nations Convention on the Rights of the Child: Individual Rights Concepts and Their Significance for Social Scientists", *American Psychologist*, 46: 60–65.

Dwyer, J. W. and R. T. Coward, eds. (1992) *Gender, Families and Elder Care*. Newbury Park, CA: Sage.

Greene, J. G.; R. Smith; M. Gardiner and G. C. Timbury (1982) "Measuring Behavioral Disturbance of Elderly Demented Patients in the Community and Its Effects on Relatives: A Factor Analytic Study", *Age and Aging*, 11:121–126.

Kosberg, Jordan I.; Richard E. Cairl and Donald M. Keller (1990) "Components of Burden: Interventive Implications", *The Gerontologist*, 30: 236–242.

Kosloski, Karl D.; Rhonda J.V. Montgomery and Edgar F. Borgatta (1990) "Predicting Nursing Home Utilization: Is This the Best We Can Do?", pp. 186–200 in *The Legacy of Longevity*, edited by S. Stahl. Newbury Park, CA: Sage.

Krulik, Tamar and Miriam J. Hirschfeld (1984) "The Continuation of Home Care to Severely Impaired Children and Aged in Israel: Family Attitudes", *Home Health Care Services Quarterly*, 5: 283–313.

McFall, Stephanie and Baila H. Miller (1992) "Caregiver Burden and Nursing Home Admission of Frail Elderly Persons", *Journal of Gerontology: Social Science*, 47: 573–579.

Miller, Baila (1990) "Gender Differences in Spouse Caregiver Strain: Socialization and Roles Explanations", *Journal of Marriage and the Family*, 52:311–321.

Miller, Baila; Stephanie McFall and Andrew Montgomery (1991) "The Impact of Elder Health, Caregiver Involvement, and Global Stress on Two Dimensions of Caregiver Burden", *Journal of Gerontology*, 46: S9–S19.

Montgomery, Rhonda J. V. (1996) "Burden" (mimeograph classified abstracts).

Montgomery, Rhonda J. V. (1989) "Investigating Caregiver Burden", in *Aging, Stress and Health*, edited by Kyriakos S. Markides. New York: John Wiley.

Montgomery, Rhonda J. V. (1992) "Filial Responsibility", pp. 721–725, in *Encyclopedia of Sociology*, edited by Edgar F. Borgatta and Marie L. Borgatta. New York: Macmillan and Co.

Montgomery, R. J. V. (1992) "Gender Differences in Patterns of Child-parent Caregiving Relationships", pp. 65–83 in *Gender, Families, and Elder Care*, edited by J. W. Dwyer and R. T. Coward. Newbury Park: Sage.

Montgomery, Rhonda J. V. and Edgar F. Borgatta (1986) "Creation of Burden Scales", Paper presented at Gerontological Society of America, 1986.

Montgomery, Rhonda J. V.; Judith G. Gonyea and Nancy R. Hooyman (1985) "Caregiving and the Experience of Subjective and Objective Burden", *Family Relations*. 34:19–26.

Montgomery, R. J. V.; K. Kosloski and M. Datwyler (1993) "Factors Defining Caregivers", Final Report to the National Institute on Aging. Contract No. R01-AGO5702.

Montgomery, Rhonda J. V.; Donald E. Stull and Edgar F. Borgatta (1985) "Measurement and the Analysis of Burden", *Research on Aging*, 7:137–152.

Moody, Harry R. (1995) "Ageing, Meaning and the Allocation of Resources", *Ageing and Society*, 15: 157–184.

Noelker, L. S. and S. W. Poulshock (1982) "The Effects of Families Caring for Impaired Elderly in Residence", Cleveland, Ohio: The Benjamin Rose Institute.

Poulshock, S. W. and G. T. Deimling (1984) "Families Caring for Elders in Residence: Issues in the Measurement of Burden", *Journal of Gerontology*, 39: 230–239.

Schorr, Alvin L. (1980) *Thy Father and Thy Mother ... A Second Look at Filial Responsibility and Family Policy*. Social Security Administration, Number 13–11953. Washington, D.C.: Government Printing Office.

United Nations (1946) *Universal Declaration of Human Rights*.

United Nations (1966). *International Covenant on Civil and Political Rights*.

United Nations (1989) *Adoption of a Convention on the Rights of the Child*. U.N. Document No. A/44/736. New York: United Nations.

Vitaliano, Peter P.; Heather M. Young and Joan Russo (1991) "Burden: A Review of Measures Used Among Caregivers of Individuals with Dementia", *The Gerontologist*, 31: 67–75.

Zarit, S. H.; K. E. Reever and J. Bach-Peterson (1980) "Relatives of the Impaired Elderly: An Invisible Crisis", *The Gerontologist*, 20: 649–655.

Chapter 2

Family Change and Family Bonding: Conceptual and Policy Issues

Marvin B. Sussman
The University of Delaware

Introduction

In this paper I will briefly describe historic patterns of extended family care of its older members; generational connections and the willingness of family members to care for its elderly; the reconstitution of intergenerational relationships involving non-kin in creating a temporal family form; and the prospects of relating care to inheritance transfers, a component of the new story for the care of the elderly in the 21st century. Whenever possible I will draw upon my research and scholarship approaching the half century mark.

The Early Period

Care for the elderly members of preliterate societies has seldom been a problem. Recent studies of Neanderthal man, precursors of Cromagnon, our ancestors indicate that few survived to what we would call old age (Gore, 1996). Tests of bone fragments indicate that few Neanderthals lived beyond thirty years of age and death was usually a violent one. Those who grew too feeble to contribute to the hunt were allocated women's activities. A few whose lineage was not an issue became shamans.

In a fast leap of time we see societies bound to the land, engaged primarily in agricultural production with concomitant support services, organizations, and institutions. Owned or rented land becomes the stabilizer of created social structures. Inheritance, in its manifest forms induces the continuity of intergenerational relationships over historic time. Customs and laws emerge to regulate such transfers. While these vary in form and complexity one characteristic is the dominance of the older generation in any transfer system. Possession of the land and attendant or related enterprises means power and control. Heads of family and kin based households now can negotiate with younger generational members for their survival and well being over generational time.

Historians such as Gaunt (1983), Kochanowiz (1983), Plakans (1989), and Sorensen (1989) describe the patterns of impartible inheritance and "stepping down" phenomena of 18th and 19th century Eastern European families which provide some security and care of elderly family members. Established by statute impartible inheritance is a situation in which property and other resources are indivisible and are given to one person, the devisee. This is unlike partible inheritance where there are many takers under intestate conditions or where testamentary freedom is exercised under a will formulated by the testator. The generational transfer of resources helps maintain the families' position in the society and stability to social caste and class arrangements.

Where land was the primary family asset in 19th century European a "stepping down" process was engaged (Gaunt 1983; Plakans 1989). Stepping down was a transfer of resources and equities from parents to the oldest son, usually occurring when the oldest son married. In effect a retirement contract, an intervivos transfer is entered with the hope of maintaining the property in the family over generations; and the promise of care in old age.

Changes in a society's demographics, such as fertility and mortality, changes in the means of producing goods and services, and development of society-wide systems of generational transfers resulted in lessened need for impartible inheritance. Partible inheritance became identified with the modern period of Western civilization.

Family Members as Caregivers

The potential role of inheritance in the care of elderly persons will be proposed in the final section of this paper. At this juncture I want to examine briefly the role of the family network in providing a home environment for its elderly members. This issue is important for policy and practice since national governments today are reducing their major programs and are espousing a "back to the family" exodus of older adults.

The study I am reporting is 20 years old. It is up to date not in lineal but subjective time. The issues covered in this Cleveland, Ohio, USA study are still being debated. Only a few findings are presented from one component of this study of 356 family members (Sussman, 1977).

The principal research objectives were to investigate the feasibility, circumstances, and conditions under which the family network — in lieu of institutionalization — could be utilized as an alternative or complementary long-term care system and provider of a home environment for its aged members. Family network in this study refers to those persons who are "perceived" to be family and include those who are distantly related by blood or marriage such as second cousins, uncle or aunt-in-law. It does not imply only members of the immediate family, e.g., children and parents of the nuclear family of procreation.

Other objectives were:

Would economic and service incentives make a difference by increasing receptivity and willingness to provide an enhancing environment for the aged family member? Would elderly family members be willing to live with their kin if the potentials of economic and service burdens for family members were removed?

A few findings:

(1) The data suggest that most families (81 percent) will accept older people in the household in some circumstances. There is, however, a hard core of approximately 19 percent (of the total 356 cases) who have indicated that they would not take in older persons under any conditions.

(2) Over half of the respondents who expressed the view that they would not take in an elderly member under any circumstances indicated that family or relatives were responsible. Of particular interest is that almost 40 percent said that the government was responsible. Although these individuals are a fairly small proportion of the total sample (19 percent), they do indicate a willingness to place the responsibility for care of the elderly in the domain of the government.

(3) Service incentives are preferred over economic ones by a larger proportion of individuals who cared for or had an older person living with them some time previously. This suggests that service programs would be more positively received by individuals and families who currently have an older person living with them or who have had such experiences in the past.

(4) Age is the most important demographic variable affecting incentive programs. The older the respondent, the less likely the individual will perceive such programs to have positive influences and most likely, such individuals will be resistant to incentive programs designed to encourage home care for the elderly.

(5) Elderly persons have incentive priorities similar to those of potential home providers but for different reasons. Forty-two percent thought that the monthly check was the best incentive in our proposed program because it was the most flexible, it helped older people stay independent, and it would help with

both the older person's and the family's expenses. Twenty-six percent of the respondents liked the medical care incentive best because they perceived it as the most useful one for older people because of the high risk of getting sick and needing costly medical attention.

(6) The majority (76 percent) of the group of elderly interviewees said that they preferred to live in their own home. It seems that only when older individuals cannot fend for themselves is there an expressed willingness by the elderly person to live with a family.

(7) In a multiple classification analysis of variables related to the willingness of families to take in an elderly relative, age, prior experience in caring for older people and attitudes towards older people were significantly related to willingness. Programs using currently proposed economic and service incentives are most likely to be least successful among older individuals and families. Prior experience and positive attitudes towards the elderly may be attitudes indicating an earlier willingness to interact with older people which is reflected in the willingness score and not with causal significance. If, however, these variables are of direct causal significance, then the success or failure of such incentive programs will be based more on attitudinal and experiential factors than financial hardships or inconvenience.

(8) The majority of respondents do not believe that institutionalization is a desirable alternative for older individuals who do not want to live alone. Slightly over 58 percent indicated that older persons should not have to go to a home for the aged. In addition, over 75 percent of those who responded negatively to having homes for the aged indicated that the family or relatives should care for the older person, although it should be noted that about 20 percent placed conditions on care in the home. It is interesting to note that very few of the respondents felt that communities or apartments for the elderly are desirable alternatives.

(9) Familial responsibility is also recognized among a relatively
     large percentage of individuals who felt that older people
     should go (including those who said "it depends") to a home
     for the aged. Approximately 37 percent indicated that this
     alternative was desirable if the family or relatives could not
     care for them. Most of the other respondents who were in
     favor of homes for the aged suggested that such homes could
     provide better care or that older persons would be happier
     there.

During the ensuing years I have not noted any elimination in
willingness to care for an elderly relative if economic and social
supports are available to the caregiving kin family member(s). Most
respondents opt for cooperation with governmental and community
based organizations in developing and supporting creative living
environments for elderly relations. Respondents as potential caregivers
want to be named, recognized and rewarded if they opt for the helping
role. A monthly cash payment is to be used at the discretion of the
receiver who is not obligated to spend it for the care and maintenance
of the elderly family member, although this is likely to occur. Services
such as health care should be available not only to the older person
but to the members of the caregiving household. Such incentives do
not invite a mind set to care. Rather their availability enhance the
possibilities of quality family interactions.

These possibilities for family caregiving beg an equitous policy of
shared family and agency action. Such partnerships will reduce the
power and control of existing hierarchically and bureaucratized human
service systems; and involve more extensively the kin family network
in caregiving.

Non-Kin Connections

Contact and connection between older adults and youth is a viable
process to enhance the lifeways of the participants. Older adults not
living in households of relatives may find joy and satisfaction in the

short-term from activities with non-kin youth. Long-term consequences are possible such as creating a new family form from the resultant bonding.

Preliminary work on the older adult-youth connection led to an AARP, USA funded project on the viability of intergenerational program modules in different settings. These were nursing homes, senior centers and community environments. In this study ten groups of children consisting of boy and cub scouts and 4H members agreed to participate in the study (n=100). Elderly adults (n=86) residing in nursing homes and the community also participated in the activities. Recreational, craft, and social activities occurred in the nursing home and senior center settings while service projects took place in the community setting. These were systematically introduced lasting one to three hours over a two-month period. The post-test scores were higher than the pre-test ones although not statistically significant. The potential range within which change could be measured was truncated because of the initial high scores.

The success of this program was measured in several ways. Elders who participated in the six to eight activity sequence and their controls were tested before and after the completion of the program regarding changes in life satisfaction, self esteem and morale. Youth were given instruments to measure changes in self concept and attitudes toward aging and the aged. Changes in self concept, morale, and attitudes which did occur from the time before and after the program were not statistically significant.

However, while the results of the quantitative measures did not indicate a change in self esteem, self concept, and morale, it is imperative to point out that the children's and elder's pretest scores were very high. A change would have indicated a detrimental program effect.

In addition, interesting behavioral changes of the children were observed by the youth and elder group leaders. One significant observation was that the youth and elders paired spontaneously. No one was "assigned" to another person. Many of the youngsters developed a "special friend" relationship with an older adult and continued their visits and exchanges after the project was completed.

In addition, reports from program leaders emphasized that the children, youth, and elders related to one another in a positive manner that was beyond explanation. These findings are consistent with other research results on intergenerational relations which debunk the myth of intergenerational conflict. On a personal (micro) level, critics comment that these types of findings may be romantic, subjective findings influenced by biases of the researchers.

We found that older adults and youth were not equally enthralled to begin the intergenerational program. Elders in the community setting were particularly cautious. They wanted a trial period to "test" the nature of the relationship that was unfolding. While the youth were eager to start the program, many elders were hesitant. Older adults probably value their time and energy differently from their younger counterparts. The commitment required to become engaged in a deep friendship cannot be entered into lightly. As a result of our work in intergenerational relationships we have recognized the need for continued support of programs of this type. The strategy of linking older adults with youngsters regardless of their respective mental or physical conditions has the potential of producing short-term outcomes as well as long-term consequences. In the short-term as previously stated, intergenerational linkages can substitute or complement existing intergenerational family connections. The basic assumption is that as a consequence of this bonding children will improve their coping skills, increase their self-esteem, develop an understanding of the aging process, obtain new friends, and learn of the past — its lifeways, skills, and knowledge. In turn, older adults will flourish in their roles as teachers and guides, and obtain in some measure the warmth, love, and care basic to human life and survival.

The connection of older adults and youngsters not related by blood or marriage is predicted to increase in incidence in the coming decades. In all likelihood, this will occur regardless of public policy. The non-kin nexi have the potential to become "like flesh and blood generational families", long in duration where individuals have a deep commitment to each other. Other formations may be for shorter periods of time, providing the participants with memorable experiences, resources, associations, knowledge, skills, caring, affection and intimacy within a less than lifetime frame. The development of multiple "special" friendships between older adults, children and youth may be the insurance for loneliness in old age, and its devastating morbific consequences.

In conclusion, the following areas for further study in non-kin intergenerational relationships are recommended. First, communication patterns between elders and children within group settings and on a one-to-one basis be examined. Second, the long lasting effects of "special friend" relationships and the basis for their continuity be explored. Third, it is imperative that the impact of non-kin connectedness on the family system be considered. Finally, it is most imperative that a new set of quantitative evaluation tools be developed. There measures must be sensitive to small or microscopic changes in attitudes, beliefs, and feelings, as well as incorporating time sequencing and setting constraints which are indicative of this type of field study.

Inheritance and Caregiving

In a paper co-authored with Roma Hanks we document the historical precedence for personal contracting as well as existing and potential linkages, existing and potential, between inheritance and caregiving.

We propose an agreement among family members for the transfer of property at death or during the life of the benefactor in exchange for caregiving services. This inheritance contract can be written into the will or as a separate document. As with other personal contracts, the inheritance contract will be negotiated by the principals, and will be communicated to interested parties, particularly the heirs and beneficiaries of the benefactor. More than one beneficiary may be named in an inheritance contract if agreements are made among multiple caregivers.

The inheritance contract offers several advantages for the family system and the larger social interests. These advantages are listed here and discussed in greater depth in the remainder of this paper. The inheritance contract is expected to:

(1) increase family communication, particularly around the needs of members for care and the real costs and expectations for care, and generally begin to open communication in all other areas;

(2) enlarge the pool of caregivers by giving recognition to caregiving and inheritance arrangements beyond the nuclear family; and

(3) help families and society avoid costly litigation processes over filial fiscal responsibility, unexpected inheritance outcomes, and victimization of elders who are the recipients of care.

Policy Implications

Response to trends toward family care. Trends toward deinstitutionalization and home care, entrepreneurism in the provision of caregiving services, and rising costs of dependent care point to a need to equip families with means to effectively respond to the care needs of dependent members. Medicare and Medicaid are inadequate to meet the rising costs of care for many older individuals. The Tax Equity and Fiscal Responsibility Act of 1982, which required that patients be categorized under Diagnostic Related Groups (DRGS) and hospital stays covered by Medicare be predetermined, in effect mandated the return of long-term health care to the family. Elders, already seeing the values of their resources routinely reduced by expenditures for services not covered by public programs, began to face concerns related to family caregiving, namely the need to purchase substitute care when family members were prohibited from providing care by fulltime work commitments or geographic separation from the care recipient. Managed care emerged as a growing industry which offers surrogate care for families that can afford to pay.

The inheritance contract recognizes the costs of caregiving. Financial reward neither supersedes affectional bonds nor eliminates stress in poor relationships. However, financial reward during the life of the care recipient or anticipation of reimbursement in a will may: (1) remove barriers for potential kin and wider kin caregivers who have deep emotional feelings for dependent elders but lack financial means to act on those feelings to provide the needed care and (2) provide an alternative way of paying for surrogate care.

Although at first blush, any idea which suggests paying family members to "do their duty" seem crass and suggestive that family relationships are more economic than emotional. By suggesting inheritance contracting one is not denying the critical affective nature of relationships in family and wider family networks. Rather, a viable alternative to publicly or privately funded surrogate care is to offer a mechanism under which families recognize and plan for the financial costs of caregiving. In those cases where the financial means of a family are limited or where financial resources are great and caregivers do not need reimbursement, transfers under the inheritance contract may be of more sentimental than monetary value and may be largely a recognition of the great affectional bonds between caregiver and care recipient.

Change in the balance of large scale/family transfers for care. Policy-makers recognize the need to strike a balance in the allocation of resources among the generations (Riley & Riley, 1990; Callahan, 1986). Intergenerational competition must be replaced with intergenerational cooperation. In the United States the call has come for a comprehensive national health care policy that recognizes the changing needs of caregivers and care recipients across the life span (Hooyman, 1990; Gilliland & Havir, 1990). While families wait for society to recognize its obligation to support caregivers as well as dependents, they continue to customize caregiving arrangements to meet specific caregiving needs and to make intergenerational transfers that support those arrangements.

If social policy is to continue to place a substantial proportion of the burden of care on the family or wider family, there must be policy level supports to allow families to develop creative solutions to their caregiving needs. The inheritance contract could work together with a complementary policy to subsidize family caregivers who are willing to give up outside employment to provide fulltime care for dependent

relatives to substantially increase the availability of family caregivers
and reduce the personnel demands on public care programs. The
diversity of arrangements resulting from the enactment of these
policies would flow from the affectional bonds that draw humans
together into families and wider family networks.

In the 21st century there will be a complementarity of public and
private systems in meeting needs for dependent care. The challenges
of an aging society will be met by judiciously expanding society-wide
transfers, developing effective benefits in the private employment
sector, and at the same time rewarding caregivers who go beyond the
limits of filial piety and responsibility.

Conclusions

(1) Patterns of elderly care involving families emerged during the
     period of settlement of the land. Negotiations regarding
     maintenance of the elderly family members were part of the
     generational transfer.

(2) Research undertaken in the 1970s indicates a strong
     willingness of family and kin network members to care for
     an elderly relative under certain circumstances. Policies and
     practices of organizations and families with an emphasis on
     superordinate goals which, forces dialogue and cooperation
     necessary for a successful outcome, is germane in this period
     of institutional downsizing and bashing.

(3) Developing activity programs linking together children, youth,
     and older adults has more than intrinsic value for the
     participants. In this period of history and the coming century
     more and more of the "Baby Boomers" now in their 50s will
     be "in search of a relative". Cultivating generational relation-
     ships of non-kin may, for some, be the most appropriate
     activity to enhance friendships and caregiving in old age.

(4) The use of an "inheritance contract" to increase the probability
     that there will be available a caregiver in one's old age is an
     idea which needs empirical testing and evaluation. Whether

it can be readily integrated into current inheritance and descent systems is problematic. I would like to think that it can in order to avoid a traditionectomy of current policies and laws governing inheritance, a difficult and arduous task.

References

Callahan, D. (1986) "Health Care in An Aging Society: A Moral Dilemma", in M. A. Pfifer & L. Bronte (eds.) *Our Aging Society: Paradox and Promise,* pp. 319–340. New York: W. W. Norton.

Gaunt, David (1983) " The Property and Kin Relationships of Retired Farmers in Northern and Central Europe", in Richard Wall, Jean Robin and Peter Laslett (eds.) *Family Forms in Historic Europe.* Cambridge: Cambridge University Press.

Gilliland, N & Havir, L. (1990) "Public Opinion and Long-Term Care Policy", in M. D. E. Beigel & A. B. Lum (eds.) *Aging and Care Giving: Theory, Research and Policy,* pp. 242–253. Newbury Park, CA: Sage.

Gore, R. (1996) "The Dawn of Humans, Neanderthals", *National Geographic,* 189: 6–35.

Hooyman, N. R. (1990) "Women as Caregivers of the Elderly", in M. D. E. Beigel & A. Blum (eds.) *Aging and Caregiving: Theory, Research and Policy,* pp. 221–241. Newbury Park, CA: Sage.

Kochanowicz, Jasalav (1983) "The Peasant Family is an Economic Unit in the Polish Feudal Economy of the Eighteenth Century", in Richard Wall, Jean Robin and Peter Laslett (eds.) *Family Forms in Historic Europe.* Cambridge: Cambridge University Press.

Plakans, Andrejs (1989) "Stepping Down in Former Times: A Comparative Assessment of Retirement in Traditional Europe", in David I. Kertzer and K. Warner Schaie (eds.), *Age Structuring in Comparative Perspective.* Hillsdale, N.J.: L. Eribaum.

Riley, M. W. & Riley, J. (1991) "The Lives of Relatives and Changing Social Roles", Paper presented at XIIth World Congress of Sociology, July 9–13, Madrid, Spain .

Sorensen, Aage B. (1989) "Old Age, Retirement, and Inheritance", in David I. Kertzer and K. Warner Schaie (eds.) *Age Structuring in Comparative Perspective.* Hillsdale, N.J.: L. Eribaum.

Chapter 3

The Social Context of the Nature of Care

Allen Glicksman
Polisher Research Institute, The Philadelphia Geriatric Center

Introduction

Our goal in this paper is to define what we mean when we speak of a "social context" and why the "social context" is important in understanding the dynamics of caring for older persons. In the social sciences, and especially in sociology "social" is a term that includes those domains that define the determinants of human action and are themselves the products of human action. The social is usually further broken down into "cultural" and "structural" aspects of the social world. "Cultural" usually refers to collectively held values, beliefs, ideas and the rituals and institutions explicitly designed to perpetuate and preserve those values, beliefs and ideas. On the other hand "structural" refers to the demographic, political, economic and general societal environment.

We will use this second definition of "social", that is cultural and structural, to better illuminate the experience of caring for older persons and, in fact, family members in general. This paper is divided into three parts. The first part will review the cultural and structural context matter in caring for the elderly. While this may seem obvious to some, one could argue that the core of the experience of physical aging is impervious to variation due to social factors. After all, the fact of physical aging is universal. Nevertheless, we will argue that even while acknowledging the universal aspects of these biological processes social domains are determinative in the experience of caring for elders.

The second part of the paper will use American society for examples of the general observations made in section one. This will be done both in order to illustrate the points already made and to lay the groundwork for the third section of the paper. American society provides a particularly useful vantage point to discuss these issues because of the explicit way in which the cultural and the structural have been interwoven from the beginning and because the rich variety of racial, religious and ethnic groups within American society allow us to examine a wide range of responses to the challenges of caring for the elderly within a single national framework. The third section will take materials from my ongoing and completed research projects to demonstrate how these issues play out in daily life. In particular, we will take examples from four research projects to understand the role of the social in the experience of caring for elders within the family and to understand what happens when cultures collide in the context of caring for the elderly.

1. Why Does Social Context Matter?

While the importance of social context for caring for the elderly could be argued from many perspectives, the most important may be that social context defines the parameters within which choices are made regarding care. That is, the cultural and structural domains within which the social actor operates define the limits within which the social actor can choose options for the care of elders, or for any other decision for that matter. Take nursing homes for example. Some societies which might wish to, simply lack the resources to offer nursing home placement for impaired elders. Others choose not to allocate as much resources as might be needed to building nursing homes. A family from a minority group within a society that does offer at least some nursing home placement may not consider placing their elder in a home because their cultural traditions consider such choices immoral, or because of prejudice and fear that they will not get access to the service. These differences concerning the use of services such as nursing homes can also lead to a clash of expectations and values between the family from one culture and professional providers of services from another culture. A provider may consider a family uncaring because they seem to want to place their elders in a nursing home, if home placement seems to the provider as abandoning the elder. The provider might deem a family uncaring because they refuse to place an elder in a home, even though the provider feels that the elder would be safer and better cared for in an institutional setting. In either case, the clash of expectations between the provider and the family may reflect different sets of values.

2. The American Experience

The United States usually traces its cultural origin to the immigrants who came from England in the 17th century and settled in New England. These Puritans as many were called (in both senses of the term) came with a vision for a new society which, among other things, gave religious sanction to the values of capitalism. As Max Weber has demonstrated, although capitalist values, such as the accumulation of profit and a focus on the individual, had existed for a very long time before the 16th century, Protestantism in general and Calvinism in particular, by giving religious sanction to these ideas, allowed them to become organizing principle for an entire society, rather than the beliefs of marginal sectors of a society. This means that the structural (capitalism) and the cultural (Calvinist belief system) were intertwined from the beginning. Since biblical injunctions about the obligation to the poor and the elderly (two groups closely linked in Government service programs) remained part of the belief system of American society, in one way or another services were provided. However, these services were often and continue to be, sub-standard and reflect a continuing belief in some parts of American society, especially among current presidential candidates, that poverty is somehow the fault of the poor. These issues have become more acute in the post-World War Two era when elders are able to live much longer in a more frail state. The more conservative elements in American society argue that it is the family that must bear the cost of caring for these elders because if the government assumes the burden, the family will abandon their traditional responsibilities. The liberal viewpoint is that the government has an obligation growing from society's duty to care for the elderly, and that families will not abandon their elders if the government helps with the cost of their care. While research has shown that the liberal position that families will not abandon their elders is generally correct, the fact that this debate continues to rage reflects the reality that although American society has a general "point of view" from its Calvinist/Capitalist roots, more than one interpretation of the American tradition co-exist.

Changes in the interpretation of the American tradition is also affected by the influx of immigrants throughout its history. While there is a process of assimilation, where immigrants from other cultures begin to take on some of the characteristics and values of America's Calvinist heritage, there are also continuities from the immigrants' culture of origin. During the decade of the 1980s this process was in full swing because during that decade the U.S. absorbed the largest absolute number of immigrants in the nation's history except for the decade of 1900–1910. This decade also saw a much greater proportion of immigrants from non-European cultures than in previous decades.

Conflicts sometimes arose between the new immigrants and their adopted land because of different values and assumptions concerning appropriate elder care and if the decision-making authority rests in the autonomous individual (a western concept) or in a larger network such as the family (the attitude of many non-Western migrants). Aside from the norms of what constitutes appropriate care and family behavior in regard to elders, there were also differences in the manner that various groups dealt with the dominant affective style in American society.

The traditional affective style considered appropriate in American society arises from the Calvinist tradition concerning appropriate responses to challenges in life and to pain and suffering in particular. In this tradition the way one "takes" pain is a measure of one's moral character. To "take pain well" or to have a "stiff upper lip" is a sign of having done the right thing by accepting the fate God has ordained for you. This value has become secularized in American society so that even without a belief in the original Calvinist principles it is taken as the "right thing to do". Although this particular tradition does not exist within Catholic teaching, Catholicism does teach that one can use pain and suffering in a productive way by donating one's pain. One can release souls from purgatory and accomplish other religious goals by using pain. Although the Catholic tradition is different from the Protestant one, in both cases complaining about pain is morally wrong — the pain provides an opportunity for a moral act and it is this opportunity that must be taken. A little later we will see what happens to a religious minority that does not place the same emphasis on the redemptive value of pain.

Attitudinal differences can be products of structural domains as well as differences in value systems. Such structural differences may include length of time in the United States, income levels, history of services to the elders in the home country, desire to remain in the United States or return to the home country (for political refugees) and family structure on arrival (some with full families, some partial families, etc.).

3. Case Studies

We want to tie these issues together by using four examples of what the implications are for the "social" context of the nature of care. In particular, we will present examples from four different studies to better understand how the social context of caring operates in specific instances. The first two examples demonstrate how cultural and religious traditions can be called upon either to deal directly with family issues or to avoid talking about family relations. The second two cases take two examples of the relation of culture and structure to demonstrate how these domains can either help maintain continuities across national boundaries or create confusion and problems for older persons moving from one society to another.

The materials for these descriptions come from four completed and ongoing research projects. Although the projects have somewhat different goals, one is designed to examine access to services for older refugees, another to understand how members of different ethnic groups talk about their own lives, the third (completed) was an investigation of the service use of long-term immigrants and the fourth set of data comes from field work conducted in Ukraine (the former Soviet Union), they do share the common aspect of attempting to understand how differences in life experience and world view affect the lives of people as they age.

I will begin with a discussion of data from two studies designed to examine how older Jews (among others) respond to questions concerning their personal well-being. The first study was a secondary analysis of data from two national and one local surveys. Each of these surveys contained one or more scales designed to measure subjective well-being. The second ongoing study is designed to take this topic one step farther by asking some of the well-being questions in an open-ended manner to better understand how the subjects arrived at their answers.

Jews represent an interesting group for the study of well-being in Western societies. As a minority community with a distinctive tradition they can be used in contrast with the majority Christian population (as in Durkheim's *Suicide*) to draw more general conclusions about the nature of social issues. At the same time they are well integrated within most Western societies and so serve to remind us that structural integration dos not always mean cultural integration as well.

In contrast to Calvinist and Catholic traditions as described above, Jewish tradition does not place great value on the experience of suffering — it places value on the alleviation of suffering. For example Jewish tradition forbids pious Jews from living in cities without doctors. One of the effects of this is that there is no moral stigma associated with complaining about aches and pains. In fact, one might argue that it is morally worthy to make such complaints, because unless others are aware of the need for help how can they fulfil their duty to alleviate the distress?

Perhaps for this reason, Jewish patients are known (or notorious) for being complainers. And when Jews answer standard questions concerning their own well-being, they often give what are considered to be negative answers. But their negative answers do not only reflect their willingness to report health problems in sometimes excruciating detail, as I am discovering in this research. They also reflect the fact that because Jews can be so expressive about their health they sometimes use health issues to talk about other, more difficult subjects. The most important of those subjects is family. American-Jewish parents have told their children that they (the parents) expect two things: success and family responsibility. That is, the children are expected to succeed in economic and social terms, something that often requires geographic mobility, and at the same time care for their parents, something that requires physical proximity to their parents. This creates a double bind that is often not discussed directly in Jewish families. Rather, the elders and sometimes their children use the topic of health to work around family issues. For example, we had a subject in one of our studies at the Philadelphia Geriatric Center (not my study) who said that she worried so much she lost sleep at night. When asked what she worried about, she reported that her grandson was in his third year at the Harvard Medical School and she thought he worked too hard. This comment also reflects another reason for negative answers to health questions among Jews: an old tradition that the Evil Eye would be attracted by good news and inflict some harm. Even among Jews who have no belief in an Evil Eye, the tradition persists of presenting good news in a negative way. To cite only one more example, again not from my study but from the work of the late Barbara Myerhoff, concerning an older Jewish woman in California who told Myerhoff that she had "teased" her daughter who lives far away in Chicago. How did she tease her daughter? By telling her daughter that she had put her breakfast in the trash and the trash in the refrigerator. The woman knew perfectly well that her daughter would come immediately to see if her mother was all right, and her mother could say that she never asked her daughter to visit. The mother had used a clear hint of mental degeneration as a way of getting a much wanted visit without saying directly to her daughter that she was lonely. In these examples Jewish cultural traditions had been used to work around the issue of family, rather than dealing directly with it.

Among African-American Baptists, discussing religion allows elders to talk directly about issues in their lives. This is much broader than the traditional view that religion plays a role in ameliorating the effects of negative events in the lives of older African-Americans. This material comes from the same study in which we are asking Jewish elders to talk about their feelings of well-being. This can be illustrated by the use of the term "feeling blessed", which among our subjects is used in the context of feeling blessed because things (income, health, family situation) could be worse than they are. This does not mean that the respondents are happy or content with their lives. The expression of "feeling blessed" may be used as a way of warding off worse fates. It also allows the subject to tell us and family members directly what is wrong and what is right while maintaining the traditional Calvinist notion that we must be thankful for what we have. Two Presbyterian women in our sample spoke of God as giving them the tools to fight for a better life and felt they would be judged on whether they had used those tools to the best of their ability. Here, rather than attempting to ward off a worse fate, religion plays the role of activating the respondents to struggle with their environment. Religion is a catalyst that allows these women to try to deal as best as they can with their situation. Religion does not play one role, positive or negative, in the lives of our respondents. Religious involvement is also used to bring the generations together.

We now turn to the other two examples. Our data, based on data collected in the United States in the summer of 1992 and in Ukraine in the summer of 1993 suggests that there are continuities as well as significant differences between women born in Western Ukraine who immigrated to the United States fifty years ago and women of the same age who remained in the small villages of Western Ukraine. We will concentrate here on the continuities between the two groups to demonstrate how cultural continuities can continue to affect the lives of older persons as they age. For example, embroidery played a significant role in the lives of older Ukrainian women both in the United States and Ukraine. It represents a moral, religious, and national activity as well as something decorative. Women in both places thought that their inability to embroider was the first sign of their decline. Because embroidery is a skill that requires a high level of function and dexterity, losing this skill is something that would never be identified by most standard scales designed to measure functional health. But in the minds of these women, both in the United States and in Ukraine, in losing their skill to embroider they are crossing a threshold that requires rethinking their own lives as well as what they want from their children. The differences in social, political, and economic structures between the US and Ukraine are less important than this internal "scale" carried by these women from childhood which also helps define their family relations independent of other considerations. In this way culture can transcend structure in defining the lives of older persons and their relations with family members.

Our second example is taken from a study of recent immigrants from the former Soviet Union, in this case Ukrainians and Jews from Ukraine. The American Jewish and American Ukrainian communities prepared for the immigrants from the former Soviet Union based on the assumptions that there would be cultural continuities between the members of the same ethnic group, and that the overall nature of services for older persons would be the same across all industrial societies, capitalist and communist.

This misunderstanding about the nature of persons coming from the former Soviet Union was compounded by a lack of understanding of how different the structures of caring for the elderly were in the two societies. It was thought that an explanation of services available provided in the native language of the immigrants (here Russian) would be enough to help these new immigrants establish new lives here. What was not understood was that behind the language there was an American cultural and social structure that the Soviet immigrants still needed to learn. Even after key terms, such as Supplementary Security Income, federal funding of sectarian religious bodies for non-sectarian purposes, the impact of refugee status on benefits, and other programs and activities were translated, they were still not well understood by the immigrants. Further, the notion of ethno-religious "communities", such as the "American Ukrainian community" and the "American Jewish community" were equally strange. These misunderstandings played a critical part in creating the difficulties between the Soviet immigrants and the agencies responsible for their adjustment to American life. These misunderstandings and misconceptions have led to a level of tension between the new immigrants and the long-term ethnic communities. The negative feelings toward the new immigrants can extend into the professional staff of agencies that deal with immigrants from the former Soviet Union. This tension can exacerbate the stressors on the Soviet immigrants, who are expected to turn to these very agencies for help in family matters.

In other words, the structure of the formal caring system as well as the structure of the ethnic communities themselves in American society have created barriers between the care recipients and the care receivers, barriers that were not supposed to happen because of supposed cultural continuities within each group.

In conclusion we can state that caring for the elderly and family relations in general use the social context both as backdrop and as tools to deal with issues that arise. We can further conclude that such context can be a source of support or can further strain already difficult situations. In either case, ignoring the social context of care leaves us with no real understanding of the struggles and challenges that face all families attempting to care for their elders.

Chapter 4

Sharing Long-term Care Between the Family and the State — A European Perspective

Alan Walker
University of Sheffield

Introduction

Despite the major differences in the provision of long-term care to older people between eastern and western societies the fact is that the family is the main source of such care in both parts of the world. Moreover modernisation brings with it changes in family structure, caring capacity and values. Therefore some of the questions currently being addressed by social care providers in Europe may become increasingly relevant in Hong Kong and other eastern societies in the early part of the 21st century. This is definitely not to suggest that European solutions are appropriate to meet Hong Kong's needs but, rather, that many similar issues will emerge here as in the west as the state tackles the equation of rising demand for care in old age and the declining capacity of the family to provide such care. In this context my chapter has three main aims.

First it outlines the reasons for the changes taking place in the social care systems of the European Union and particularly the recent pressure for more participation by older people and their informal helpers in decisions about the management and delivery of care. Social care systems in Europe are beginning to recognise this right of older people and their family caregivers to participate but the majority of health and social services have not progressed very far in implementing that right. Indeed these agencies are still important elements in the social construction of dependency in old age.

Secondly the paper focuses on some of the shifts in long-term care policy in Europe which are designed to promote a more mixed economy in the care of older people and other groups. Some critical questions are raised about the implications of these changes, particularly for the care burden being borne by the family.

Thirdly, it is argued that the most effective way in which a pluralistic system of care can enhance the ability of the family to meet the needs of the next generation of older people is for the formal providers to work in partnership with families. This entails a model of shared care in which older service users and their family caregivers are closely involved in decisions concerning the need for and supply of care services and are consulted regularly about their needs.

In conclusion it is suggested that empowerment is one of the most important challenges confronting all advanced health and social care systems.

Pressures for Change in Social Care Provision

The reason that change is on the social care agenda in all EU and, indeed, all western societies is relatively straightforward: they are all facing similar pressures. There are two general pressures:

Socio-demographic Pressures

The European Union is ageing rapidly. At present there are 48 million people aged 65 and over in the EU, 20 million of them are aged 75 or over. By the year 2000 they will represent more than one-fifth of the population and by 2020 they will comprise more than one-quarter. All EU countries face similar demographic patterns: lower fertility rates coupled with higher life expectancy — though they have different starting points. There is considerable convergence between member states in the proportion of their populations aged 65 and over.

The facts of the demographic revolution are well known so I will not labour the point, but it is important to guard against the tendency to regard population ageing automatically as a problem — what has been called in Britain a 'demography of despair' (Henwood and Wicks, 1984; Phillipson and Walker, 1986). Ageing populations are a sign of success in overcoming many of the causes of premature death that cut short people's lives in the last century. Moreover, even among the very elderly it is still only a minority that require care (one-third of those aged 80 and over in Germany and the UK).

But population ageing does present a challenge to service provision, partly because of the association between disability (including dementia) and advanced old age and partly because this change is coupled with other socio-demographic changes.

Most importantly there is the fertility trend towards smaller family size. This means that by far the main source of care for older people in need — their own families — are having more and more to face the prospect of caring for older relatives for longer and with fewer potential family members to help. Moreover since women are the main source of care within the family, smaller families mean that more and more women are being forced to shoulder both the labour and the responsibility for caring, on their own (Qureshi and Walker, 1989). This development is of profound importance for both families and the providers of social care services.

It means that family members are entering new inter-generational caring relationships — new in terms of both their intensity and duration —with both sides having to bear the strains these relationships can generate (Walker, 1996). The inevitable result is that these caring relationships will break down with increasing frequency, due to carer fatigue. Alternatively, given this prognosis, fewer and fewer women will be prepared to enter such long-term caring relationships. Either way, the result is increased demand for service provision (often residential). There are very few examples of western care systems having fully adjusted yet to the implications of the demographic revolution that we are experiencing currently.

The trend towards increased female participation in the labour market (often in roles, such as home care, that mirror their domestic one) puts additional burdens on the female dominated informal care sector. Although there is no widespread evidence at present that women are giving up family care for the labour market the case of Denmark gives some indication of the potential conflict between full time paid employment and unpaid domestic labour. In 1960 one-quarter of women aged 25–34 were employed. By 1986 this had risen to 89 per cent (Dooghe, 1991). At the same time Denmark is the one EU country to report relatively low 'family' participation in care (Walker, Guillemard and Alber, 1991). The example of Denmark gives some flavour of the distaste of Scandinavian women for the full-time housewife role (Waerness, 1990) and, therefore, the enlargement of the Community is likely to emphasise the social distance between north and south. This can be illustrated with reference to the recent Eurobarometer surveys of public opinion in the EU: 14 per cent of older people in Denmark said they see a relative everyday, compared with 60 per cent in Spain and Portugal, 65 per cent in Greece and 71 per cent in Italy (Walker, 1993, p.11).

The growth in divorce and family break-ups is also important because there is evidence that divorced children give less help to older relatives than those in stable marriages. As well as providing less direct personal care they are less likely to have social contact with their older relatives (Cicirelli, 1983). Of course there are obvious material reasons why divorced children may display lower levels of filial obligation than non-divorced ones, including limited financial resources.

There is one further point of importance in this socio-demographic matrix. In all European Union countries an increasing proportion of older people are living alone. This is partly a function of demographic change and geographical mobility, but it also appears to reflect a desire for separate dwelling places on the part of both older and younger people. The variation in the EU is from a low of 17.5 per cent of people aged 65 and over living alone in Ireland to a high of 49.3 per cent in Denmark. Again it is necessary to be cautious about this trend. There has been a great deal of speculation about the break-up of the family which is simply not borne out by the evidence. What the research shows is that, although they may live in separate households, older people and their adult children are still in close contact — they prefer 'intimacy at a distance' (Wenger, 1984; Qureshi and Walker, 1989; Walker, Guillemard and Alber, 1991). So caution is necessary, but the widespread trend towards living alone has important service implications: older people living alone are likely to be poorer than couples and in some countries, such as the UK, home care has traditionally been targeted at (or rationed to) those living alone.

The combination of these social demographic factors have created considerable pressures for change both as a reaction to the increasing demands for social care they create and, in some cases, in order to adapt to the changing nature of the family. Although reliable evidence is hard to come by the Eurobarometer survey did reveal a worrying perception, on the part of older people themselves, that the family is now less willing to care for older relatives than it used to be. In the EU as a whole some two out of three older people agreed that families are less willing to care and the strongest opinions were held in France, Luxembourg, Italy, Portugal and Spain (Walker, 1993, p. 29). Of course the factors I have already outlined indicate that families may be less *able* to provide care than they used to be rather than less willing. Nonetheless this perception on the part of older people must be taken seriously by policy makers, not least because it points to the importance of the changes taking place in family structure and location, particularly in the southern states of the EU.

Political and Economic Pressures

In all EU countries economic concern about the cost implications of population ageing — in terms of pensions, health and social services

— is coupled with political worries about the tax implications of increased welfare spending. In some countries this has led to a high level of pessimism about the so-called 'burden' of societal ageing (Walker, 1990). In general, economic concerns about the cost implications of population ageing are universal but, for the most part the policy responses to these concerns are relatively mild. However the more extreme forms of pessimism are associated primarily with those governments that, for ideological reasons, have adopted an anti-welfare state posture.

The service implications of these political and economic pressures are, as far as the mild form found in most EU countries is concerned, a cost effectiveness imperative that, for example, establishes the principle that older people should stay in their own homes for as long as possible and promotes a search for cheaper forms of care. While, in the extreme pessimistic form of these pressures, there is a desire to place even greater responsibilities on family members and to encourage the growth of the private and voluntary sectors in substitution for the public sector. Scandinavian countries are not immune to these pressures but, so far at least, they have taken the relatively mild forms of action with regard to social care (Waerness, 1990; Kraan *et al.*, 1991).

Within the EU the specific service implications of these political and economic pressures include: strict financial limits on care (Belgium, France, Green, Ireland, Italy, the Netherlands and the UK); a shift or a planned shift from residential to community care (for all countries but most radical in the Netherlands because the proportion of older people in residential care has been, on average, twice as much as other countries); deinstitutionalisation (Ireland, Germany, the Netherlands and the UK); increased expectation of financial contributions (Belgium, Germany, Italy and the UK); decentralisation (Germany, Ireland, Italy, the Netherlands and the UK); encouragement of family and informal service networks (Germany, Ireland, the Netherlands); failure to improve training and levels of pay for social care staff, which reinforces staff shortages (most countries); local experimentation with cheaper forms of care (most countries); and encouragement of the private sector (Italy, Luxembourg, the Netherlands, Portugal and the UK).

Although they are not the only factors underlying the emerging new agenda in social care for older people, political and economic pressures are key inspirations behind innovation and experimentation. In other words, if necessity is the mother of invention, then the primary necessity in many EU countries is shortage of public funds. Moreover such shortages usually result from political decisions about the proportion of national resources that should be devoted to the care of older people that have not taken full cognisance of the fact that their societies are ageing ones, a fact which should necessitate an increase in the resources devoted to social care.

Pressures for Increased Participation

These two intertwined factors — socio-demographic and political/ economic — set the general context for change in the management and delivery of social care and, for the present time at least, they provide the main driving force behind change. In addition, however, there are three specific factors that have acted to channel some of these pressures for change towards policies designed to increase the participation of service users in decisions about their social care.

The New Consumerism

In the first place there is a discernible shift in cultural and political discourse in all western societies away from the certainties of monolithic, universal, positivist and logical absolute truths and the belief in linear progress and rational planning, towards a more fragmented, heterogeneous indeterminate and pluralistic orientation. This shift — commonly labelled as the transition from modernity to postmodernity (Harvey, 1989) — is sometimes imbued with, frankly, ridiculously apocalyptic claims concerning, for example, the 'end of ideology' or the 'end of history'. However there is no doubt that the reassertion of individualism and, with it, the elevation of pluralism to a key policy goal in many countries, has profound implications for all welfare states and forms of welfare, including of course social care provision for older people.

This is especially the case when elements of postmodern thought are selected and amplified by the standard bearers of the pro-market ideology of neoliberalism, as may be witnessed in the former state socialist societies of central and eastern Europe. Within the EU the UK represents the extreme case in which, under the Conservative governments of the 1980s and early 1990s, strong central government direction was given to the creation of a 'mixed economy' in care for older people and other groups. Moreover this policy has been promoted by rhetoric concerning increased choice for social care 'consumers'. In reality this has meant the promotion of the private sector of care with public subsidies and the residualisation of the state as a direct provider (Walker, 1989). But the last stage of the Conservative policy emphasised flexibility, plurality and choice.

For example the 1989 White Paper, *Caring for People*, on which social care policy is based currently, defined four key components of community care. They are: services that respond flexibly and sensitively to the needs of individuals and their carers; services that intervene no more than is necessary to foster independence; services that allow a range of options for consumers; and services that concentrate on those with the greatest needs (DH, 1989, p. 5). In the White Paper 'choice' is defined as giving people a greater individual say in how they live their lives and the services they need to help them (DH, 1989, p. 4). This is to be achieved in two main ways: a comprehensive process of assessment and care (or case) management, which 'where possible should induce [the] active participation of the individual and his or her carer', and a more diverse range of non-statutory providers among whose benefits is held to be a 'wider range of choice of services for the consumer' (DH, 1989, pp. 10, 22). Unfortunately, however, these laudable aims exist largely in rhetoric rather than practice. The two main reasons for this are, on the one hand, that the policy derives from an ideology which is averse to making the increases in public expenditure necessary to realise the stated goals of participation and choice; and, on the other, that the model of participation on which the policy is based is a very shallow form of consumerism (Walker, 1992).

Grassroots Pressures

In the Northern EU states, with long established social care systems, a certain disillusionment with the nature and form of these services has set in recently, particularly with regard to monolithic public services. These care systems have been subjected to criticism from three distinct quarters: service users, the feminist movement and the providers of informal care.

More and more users of the social services are complaining about their bureaucratic organisation, complexity and lack of responsiveness to felt needs. In fact there is a long series of research studies pointing to the divergence between the perceptions of need held by users and professional providers in the social services (Mayer and Timms, 1970; Sainsbury, 1980; Fisher, 1989). Some groups of users — such as people with disabilities — have formed self-advocacy or liberation movements to press their case for greater influence over their own lives and the services they use. (In the UK it is these groups that have posed the most effective challenge to the rhetoric of choice by asking for resources to run their own services.)

At the present time groups of older people are not at the forefront of pressure for change in the social care services, but the recent emergence of grey political parties and the strengthening of EU wide organisations of older people suggests that this may change in the near future (Walker and Naegele, 1999). For example a Grey Party was formed in Germany, in 1989, to champion senior citizens' interests. A pensioners' party was formed in Belgium in 1990 and, in the same year, a party of older people (Party of National Solidarity) was created in Portugal. The radical C Team in Denmark and the mushrooming of pensioner action groups in the UK point to what is a growing self-confidence on the part of older people. This is already leading to reasonable demands for a 'voice', or participation, in the care decisions that are vital to their lives (either as carers or as cared for).

One indication of this growing desire on the part of older people for the right to full public participation was highlighted in the Eurobarometer survey when we asked older people what *they* would prefer to be called. Their rejection of the term most commonly used by professionals and politicians — 'elderly' — with its connotations of separate group status, was emphatic in all countries except Denmark and the Netherlands. The positive choice of 'older people' and 'senior citizens' suggests that they favour labels that portray them as participants in society: they want to be seen as people who just happen to be older than some others, or they want to be seen as civic actors with both rights and duties. Either way these favoured alternatives emphasise integration and participation rather than separation (Walker, 1993, p. 6).

A similar impulse may be detected in the increasing currency of terminology such as the 'third age' and 'productive ageing'. The distinction between the third and fourth ages helps to focus on the potential for continuing participation and activity among the former, through for example volunteering, education and quasi-formal roles, such as mentors, in the labour market. However, if crudely defined by age alone, it runs the risk of wrongly implying that the fourth age is dominated by dependency. Also it is important not to overlook the fact that in Europe informal care is concentrated in the third age. Thus, in the UK, some 46 per cent of all carers were aged 50–74 (in 1985) and one-fifth of those in this age group were carers. This suggests that they are already making a substantial contribution. The concept of productive ageing focuses on the link between activity or productivity and health and, if it is not too prescriptive, offers a useful model on which to develop a more participative future for older people.

Then there is the distinct feminist critique of the gendered nature of care which has developed, since the late 1970s, into a devastating indictment of both informal and formal care. Feminists have been primarily responsible for demonstrating that community care is, in fact, mainly care by female kin and also that care consists of two dimensions: labour and love (Land, 1978; Finch and Groves, 1980; Walker, 1981). This has led to a demand for alternative approaches that do not exploit women (Dalley, 1983; Finch, 1984; Waerness, 1986) and which recognise the right of women *not* to participate in care by offering them a genuine choice. This critique has been extended to many recent innovations in social care because they have relied on the unpaid or lowly-paid services of women.

Out of this feminist critique has come a specific case mounted by those people responsible for providing informal care. Informal (unpaid) carers are part of the 'taken-for-granted' context within which social care is provided (Twigg, Atkin and Perring, 1990). For example the provision of home care is based to some extent on assumptions about the availability of informal carers and their domestic duties towards the person in need of care. Thus the scope of home care is determined frequently by the activities performed, or assumed to be performed, by a caring relative. During the 1980s, in Britain and the Netherlands, carers began to form self-help and pressure groups to support themselves and represent their views. Together with researchers they have shown, for example in the UK, that community care in particular policies have paid very little attention to the needs and rights of carers and the state has done very little to support the activities of the 6 million carers (Oliver, 1983; Wright, 1986). So carers themselves are calling for a recognition of their right to be consulted on an equal basis with service users. This has been recognised to a limited extent in some EU countries. For example, in the UK, a carers' charter will was introduced in April 1996. The EU as a whole is likely to see the emergence of more politically active informal carers as more women enter the labour market and more men take on caring roles. Carers' pursuit of their own and their relatives' interests will inevitably lead to increasing demands for active participation in decisions concerning the provision of social care.

It is important to realise that these three forms of grassroots pressures are directed towards a fundamentally different form of participation to that favoured by consumerism: empowerment (Croft and Beresford, 1990; Walker, 1992). In contrast to the consumer-orientated model, which employs a simple market analogy based on exit, the user-centred or empowerment approach aims to involve users in the development, management and operation of services as well as in the assessment of need. The intention is to provide users and potential users with a range of realisable opportunities to define their own needs and the sort of services they require to meet them. Both carers and cared for are regarded as potential service users. Ideally services would be organised to respect users' rights to self-determination, normalisation and dignity. They would be distributed as a matter of right rather than discretion, with independent inspection and appeals procedures, and would be subject to democratic oversight and accountability.

Although I have distinguished the two models of consumerism and empowerment as if they represent the two extremes of a continuum, in practice they are confused. In fact the two polar forms of service organisation are the models of bureaucracy and empowerment (as shown in the diagram below). In operational terms the bureaucratic model may be said to enhance dependency in both physical and political terms (Walker, 1982b) while the empowerment model emphasises the interdependent status of older people as requiring assistance but with the right to autonomous decision making. The position of the consumerist model is subject to debate: its rhetoric is close to the empowerment pole but its organisational implementation is close to the bureaucratic one. This confusion may be seriously inhibiting progress towards empowering users because the limited goal of consumer consultation is sometimes mistaken for empowerment or regarded as a viable form of participation.

Bureaucratic Model	*Empowerment Model*
service/provider orientated	user orientated
inflexible	responsive
provider-led	needs-led
power concentrated	power sharing
defensive	open to review
conservative	open to change
input orientated	outcome orientated

The gulf separating the two approaches — consumerism and empowerment — and the difference between having a right to participate and being merely a consumer in the market can be illustrated with reference to a supermarket. Consumerism ensures that shoppers have a reasonably wide choice and some safeguards as to safety and quality. It is an entirely different matter, however, to expect that shoppers might be involved in the management and day-to-day running of the store. In other words, in the market analogy, the user remains relatively powerless. Is this an appropriate model for the development of social care for older people? The provision and receipt of social care entails complex inter-personal relations, vulnerability, frailty, invasion of privacy, life and death — it goes beyond mere production and consumption.

Professional Pressures

Finally there are changes in professional orientation and practice that are beginning to articulate new, more participative approaches to social care on the part of service providers. Partly in response to grassroots pressures and partly as a corollary to the critiques of professional dominance in medicine and social work, some social care professionals are beginning to question traditional models of training which emphasise professional autonomy and are seeking ways of working that are less oppressive and more open to user involvement (Ward and Mullender, 1991). (An important contribution to this self-questioning in the fields of both home care and residential care was made by Norman, 1980.)

This transition is at an early stage but already there are examples of service providers attempting to develop user-centred methods that emphasise, at the very least, the right of service users to be consulted. Some practitioners and social services departments are attempting to create partnerships in social work practice and social care in which older people are seen as active co-producers (Fisher and Marsh, 1993; Warren and Walker, 1992). There are also more radical examples of attempts to empower service users, including older people, to make their own decisions about care.

In order to tap the extent to which these changes in professional orientation have been picked up by the general public we addressed this issue in the Eurobarometer study by asking: "Who is the best person to decide on services for older people?" Older people themselves gained the highest vote in the EU as a whole, but only just. Professionals (meaning doctors) and a relative or close friend were just behind older people. In all countries except Italy the combined percentages for older people and their relatives or friends came to more than half of the total (Walker, 1993, p. 30).

These three sets of pressures are contributing to a disillusionment with social care services and, in combination with the demographic, political and economic factors, have created a significant impulse towards change in the organisation and delivery of services. They have begun to set a new agenda for the care of older people and other groups (Evers, 1991). Some changes are already underway, for example,

- standard, off-the-peg, services are being replaced by more flexible, 'tailormade' and coordinated care services;
- the role of the informal sector is becoming more explicit and attempts are being made to better integrate the formal and informal, rather than seeing them as substitutes for each other;
- in some cases the service user as a passive recipient is being replaced by the idea of an active co-producer of welfare;
- symbolically the term 'client' is being replaced by 'user'.

These are, of course, desirable changes because they mean that services can begin to better reflect the needs of older users and their informal carers. But the progress of change across the EU is patchy and it is still the case that the majority of older people who are fortunate enough to receive social care will not be aware of any new agenda or any push towards participation.

Shifting the Welfare Mix in Long-Term Care

The policy changes resulting from these combined pressures are beginning to be implemented in some EU countries, most notably the UK. There the traditional provider role of the state is being transformed by the introduction of a purchaser/provider split in the organisation of long-term care, with local government taking the lead purchasing role. Since this new approach is still in its infancy it is possible only to speculate about the implications of this change for the future of family care. This speculation takes the form of a series of seven questions, all of which may be applied to other countries contemplating similar changes in their welfare mix.

First of all, to what extent will the intended shift in the formal welfare mix — from public to for-profit and non-profit providers — maintain the existing relationship between the formal and informal sectors? The obvious danger is that the same 'taken-for-granted' assumptions that have helped to maintain the primacy of family care will be sustained in an unmodified form despite the fact that the nature of both the family and the care it provides is changing. Most importantly the new long-term intergenerational caring relationships require the adoption of longer term supportive strategies rather than short term casualty ones. Unless services adapt to this need for support on the part of informal carers the demand for long-term formal care is likely to increase as caring relationships are pushed to the limit. Thus the key question about the future interface between the formal and informal sectors concerns the ability of services to act in a supportive role to the family, a question which the debate about a mixed economy of care has so far signally failed to address.

Secondly, will it be assumed that more care can be squeezed out of the family? The danger here is that, faced with a severe shortage of resources, care managers may expect the informal sector to play a larger role in the provision of care. This would be a great mistake since all of the available evidence shows that the family is as fully committed as it can be to the task of caring and that there is no spare capacity. Indeed for the reasons outlined above, any attempt to push the family into providing more care may be counter-productive.

These first two questions indicate that policy-makers and service providers require a more sophisticated understanding of the dynamics of family care than they have at present. Such an understanding would form the basis for the more effective support of the family by services.

An important part of this new approach is the recognition of diverse family types, depending, for example on kinship network structures, family history and ethnic or racial background (Wenger, 1989; Finch, 1989; Twigg and Atkin, 1991). In other words the family itself is heterogeneous — a mixed economy if you like — and this requires flexible responses from service providers.

This raises a third question: to what extent will the purchasers of long-term care be able to determine the way diverse providers interact with the family? The main problem here is that there are conflicting pressures on purchasers: on the one hand they have to encourage the non-governmental sector of domiciliary care, while on the other they have to ensure the maintenance of standards of care and equity between different users. In the rush to contract new providers, purchasers may be tempted to compromise on the expectations that should properly be made of such services. With regard to the private sector there is always a conflict between the requirements of a contract and the need to ensure a commercial return on capital. Thus case managers' requirements concerning the operation of services may be regarded by private providers as unreasonable encumbrances on their ability to make a profit. In the absence of any system of regulation and inspection of domiciliary care once contracts are awarded the quality of provision may be compromised. This points to a fundamental weakness in the idea of the mixed economy of long-term care, at least as it is has been implemented in the UK. If diversity is seen as its greatest strength then the downside to diversity is the difficulty of ensuring certain standardised methods, approaches and quality levels on the ground when services are operating to different management rules and provider motivations. Any failure by new or existing domiciliary care providers to offer high quality support to family carers and to respond flexibly to the changes underway in the family is likely to have a severe impact on the supply of family care in the future.

Fourthly, therefore, will purchasers be able to encourage the growth of new domiciliary care providers? Obviously this will differ considerably from country to country and also within countries depending on the existing service infrastructure. And there is a supplementary question concerning the extent to which the process or pluralistic service innovation will result in widely different services being available to older people with similar needs in different parts of the country. This speculation can be answered to some extent by reference to the impact of innovations in the social services over the last decade or so.

While there are several very positive features of the many experiments in community care that have taken place in recent years, by definition the process of pluralistic service innovation has been haphazard and confined to very small local areas and, therefore, it has tended to reinforce territorial disparities in social services. The result of this fragmentary innovation is that people with similar needs in different parts of the same country, or sometimes local area, are experiencing very different forms of care, based on different assumptions, sorts of providers and, crucially, rights of access. Incidentally this also raises a fundamental issue of human rights. These sorts of innovations were not sought by the people concerned, nor did they have an equal voice to that of the service providers in the process of innovation — they were top-down innovations — though, of course, the honourable motives of those responsible for the new developments are not in doubt. But older people and other groups of people with disabilities have, in effect, being used as guinea pigs in the testing of service innovations.

This is an issue that those who argue against the standardisation associated with universalism must confront. At the same time it must be acknowledged that the universalism associated with the UK model of personal social services is a very minimal one indeed and one that is characterised by territorial injustice in the formal sector (Bebbington *et al.*, 1990). Thus long-term underfunding has created a growing 'care gap' with the result that most older (and younger) people with disabilities do not receive sufficient assistance to cover all of their care needs and many receive none at all. Moreover there is no evidence of a wide dissemination of innovatory approaches, such as paid neighbours, which instead remain largely confined to the demonstration projects. Yet these projects are sometimes quoted as examples of how the welfare mix has changed. In the research on older people living in the community and in residential care by Allen and her colleagues (1992, p. 302),

> There was little evidence of use by either sample of elderly people of private or voluntary sector community services. The organised use of 'paid neighbours' or of a recognised variety of helpers aiming to maintain elderly people at home, as found in the Kent Community Care Scheme and other schemes, was not found at all. Perhaps this indicates how difficult such schemes are to replicate without the resources of a 'demonstration' model.

Fifthly, how will the conflict between choice and rationing be resolved? The professed aim of increasing choice and sensitivity to user requirements is likely to be compromised by the process of assessment which is inevitably required to ration resources. The process of assessment is bound to limit individual choice and user influence while, conversely, enhancing the power of bureau-professionals acting as case managers. Moreover while service users do not have a right to elect to be assessed and while there are no safeguards — such as an appeals procedure — for those who disagree with professional assessments, choice will come a poor second place to rationing.

Sixthly, what financial contribution will the family be expected to make to the formal care of its older relatives? Increasing financial contributions are likely to be expected of older people and their families, both of which may create resentment and contribute to a weakening of the family care system. Successive generations have built up an expectation of financial and property inheritance, an expectation that was enhanced by the housing policies of the 1980s. Although the research evidence shows that such transfers are relatively small (Hamnett, 1992) the expectation continues to be present. Thus inheritance is part of the complex matrix of intergenerational relations and obligations on which the family care system is founded and policy-makers tinkering with it should exercise extreme caution. But caution does not seem to have been the guiding principle and the expectation of contributions from older people and, either directly or indirectly, from other relatives, may be counter productive in creating resentment on the part of family members. In a similar vein it is important for the policy-makers to recognise that increases in family poverty over the last decade, especially in the UK, have weakened the domestic economies of many families. If this continues it will affect the ability of the family to provide support, for example by constraining their opportunities to visit older relatives. Continuing poverty among a significant minority of older people is an important factor in limiting their ability to care for themselves. This harks back to discussions about the need to care *for* the community, or the family, if it is to be expected to go on being the primary source of care (Walker, 1982a).

The final question is, will the needs of older people and their family carers be taken fully into account in determining what *level* of service is needed and what *type* of provision is appropriate? In the UK and other EU countries there are few concrete proposals for empowering or, at least, involving older users and carers in decisions concerning social care. In the absence of clear guidelines for such involvement it is likely that professional opinions will continue to dominate. This is signalled to some extent in the prominence given to care (or case) management. This can be either administration centred or user centred. In the context of the pre-eminence given to the goals of value for money and economic efficiency the clear danger is that case management is likely to prove to be primarily an administrative tool for cost containment. If this happens it will constrain the potential of the care management role to orchestrate a truly supportive network for older people and will result in the perpetuation of the present situation of over-reliance on family carers.

There is a further contradiction between the goal of extending choice and other motivations behind the present policy of community care. The problem is not the desire to stimulate a range of providers but the premium placed on non-state or 'independent' forms of care and the mechanism chosen to encourage them. Thus purchasers are expected to employ competitive tendering or other means of 'testing the market' for the production of care. This gives a rather slanted meaning to the mixed economy of care. For example the 1989 UK White Paper suggested that one of the ways in which social services departments could promote a mixed economy of care is by 'determining clear specifications of service requirements, and arrangements for tenders and contracts' (DH, 1989, p.23). But evidence from the US indicates that competitive tendering may actually *reduce* the choice available by driving small producers out of contention (Demone and Gibelman, 1989). This is likely to effect specialist provision for some minority group needs, such as those for older ethnic minorities and particular disability groups.

These are the key questions concerning the policy that is currently evolving and it is on the answers to them that rests the future relationship between the formal and informal sectors of care and the viability of the new mixed economy of care. This shift in the welfare mix could have a very beneficial impact on the ability of the family to care for the next generation of older people, but only if the new system does not overburden the family with expectations and if traditional service provider assumptions about the nature and availability of family care are adapted to changed circumstances. If it fails to make this transition in thinking and approach the new system is likely to have a deleterious effect on the caring capacity of the family.

Towards Shared Care

The surest way in which a mixed economy of care can enhance the ability of the family to meet the needs of the next generation of older people with disabilities is for formal and quasi-formal service providers to work in partnership with families, in short, to share care. How might care be shared more effectively between the various providers in the mixed economy?

In the first place older service users/potential users and their family carers must be centrally involved in decisions concerning the need for and supply of care services. This chimes in unison with the increasing stress on user choice and involvement. Unfortunately, as I have indicated earlier, the dominant model of involvement is a limited form of supermarket-style consumerism which assumes that, if there is a choice between 'products', service users will automatically have the power of exit from a particular product or market. Of course even if this is true in markets for consumer goods, in the field of social care many older people are mentally disabled, frail and vulnerable, they are not in a position to 'shop around' and have no realistic prospect of exit. In other words the concept of 'active consumers' is not entirely appropriate with regard to the great majority of older people in need of care, whose voices are often too quiet to be heard in the marketplace.

The only way that frail and vulnerable service users can be assured of influence and power over service provision is if they or their advocates are guaranteed a 'voice' in the organisation and delivery of services. This would, in turn, ensure that services actually reflected their needs. In practice the weaker form of consumer consultation being pursued currently in the UK could consist of no more than an occasional survey among users together with minimal individual consultation at the point of assessment.

In contrast to the consumer-orientated model of care the user-centred or empowerment approach would aim to involve users in the development, management and operation of services as well as in the assessment of need. The intention would be to provide users and potential users with a range of realisable opportunities to define their own needs and the sort of services they require to meet them. Both carers and cared for would be regarded as potential service users. Where necessary the interests of older people with mental disabilities would be represented by independent advocates. Services would be organiscd to respect users' rights to self-determination, normalisation and dignity. They would be distributed as a matter of right rather than discretion, with independent inspection and appeals procedures, and would be subject to democratic oversight and accountability.

In order to realise the goal of user involvement service providers must develop explicit strategies to achieve it. The essential ingredients of such a strategy are positive action — to provide users and potential users with support, skills training, advocacy and resources — so that they can make informed choices, and access — the structures of both the facilitating and the providing agency must afford opportunities for genuine involvement. According to Croft and Beresford (1990, p. 24):

> Unless both are present people may either lack the confidence, expectations or abilities to get involved, or be discouraged by the difficulties entailed. Without them, participatory initiatives are likely to *reinforce* rather than overcome existing race, class, gender and other inequalities.

Thus user involvement must be built into the structure and operations of services and not bolted on.

Secondly, change is necessary in the organisation and operation of formal services. The concept of social support networks is particularly helpful in emphasising the need for formal and informal helpers to cooperate, share tasks and decision-making and 'interweave' with each other (Whittaker and Garbarino, 1983). This means that care would take the form of coordinated 'packages' in which both formal and informal carers would act as parts of a team. This purposive integration of informal carer and formal provider(s) has also been referred to as a 'care partnership' (Allen, 1983) and 'sensitive interweaving' (Bayley, 1980). According to Wenger (1984, p.192): "This approach calls for a more integrated perspective of service provision where the personnel of different agencies adopt a cooperative stance, sharing tasks and information in order to provide a cohesive support package."

Thirdly, there has to be an open policy of supporting informal carers and regarding their needs as having the same priority as those of users (recognising, of course, the frequent conflicts of interest involved). In the typology developed by Twigg and Atkin (1991) this would mean agencies shifting from regarding carers as 'resources', as part of the taken for granted context of care with only a marginal concern for the carers' well-being, to seeing them as 'co-workers' or 'co-clients'.

The most important method of supporting the carer is the level and quality of the services provided to the user (Twigg, Atkin and

Perring, 1990). Thus if it is possible to maximise the well-being and independence of the user this will relieve both the physical strain and the mental anxiety of the informal carer. This calls for increased domiciliary care provision, in which there are considerable 'care gaps' (Walker, 1985), rather than residential care which is now in excess supply in most countries.

Research by Levin and her colleagues (1983, 1985) indicates the enormous potential significance of domiciliary care in supporting the carers of older people with mental infirmity. As well as showing the inverse relationship between the burdens borne by carers and home care services received by their older relatives this research demonstrated the high relevance of these services to the needs of carers. Home care is the most appropriate form of service to address the problems carers face — such as the need for relief from household tasks, providing carers with a break and a chance for an ordinary conversation with the person they are caring for. Carers wanted more home care support. Most importantly though this research illustrated the beneficial impact of the home care service on the well-being of informal carers. Home helps considerably reduced strain among carers and improved their psychological health. Thus by listening to the needs of informal carers domiciliary care services can contribute enormously to enhancing the quality of the relationship between these carers and frail older people.

Fourthly, change must be initiated in professional values and attitudes within the formal sector so that cooperation and partnership with users is regarded as a normal activity. This does not mean that service provision must be deprofessionalised if shared care based around user involvement is to flourish. But rather that the role of professionals and para-professionals must change in order to share power with users.

Fifthly, the previous two points suggest a major transformation in training and re-training for service personnel. Thus the emphasis in training would shift away from autonomous expertise and individual diagnosis towards skills for working in partnership with users and encouraging community participation. The research by Allen *et al.*

(1992) on service provision and receipt by older people shows that home carers lack the skills to operate in a more flexible, open and empowering way.

Sixthly, a new approach to the provision of community care services is required. Thus it is important to reorientate policy-makers and formal service providers away from a short-term, casualty perception of need towards a longer-term strategy of prevention, for example the prevention of dependency and traumas such as carer breakdown. The function of responsible social care should not be confined to the management of stress but should also encompass prevention and rehabilitation.

Finally, shared care based on user-involvement is not a cheap option, it is usually time consuming and costly. Therefore there is a need for increased resources in the mixed economy of care not only to improve the choice and quality of services but also to ensure that they provide sufficient space for user-involvement. Again recent research by Allen *et al.* (1992) found that many Home Help Organisers were 'struggling' with the move from a service-led to a needs-led culture. They wanted to offer a person-centred approach to the delivery of care but this seemed to slip from their grasp as they recognised the overwhelming economic and political pressure to ration and prioritise services.

Thus the key components of an effective policy of shared care and user involvement are: resources, training, information, equal access, clear rights and entitlements, forms of redress, time and, if necessary, advocacy (Croft and Beresford, 1990, p. 42). In addition if specific local authority initiatives are to contribute to wider policy development then there must be research and evaluation and the dissemination of good practice.

Conclusion

'Empowerment' is an abstract term that must be turned into reality by a programme of practical action and innovation. This means commitment at all levels and the allocation of sufficient resources to put it into practice. The assessment process is crucial: do older people and their carers have a full opportunity to articulate their own needs in their own terms — not in service provider's pre-determined categories? Are they made to feel inferior to service providers/assessors or equal to them? If people cannot articulate their own needs are there advocates to help them? Do staff act like 'experts' or in a way that suggests that they have something to learn from the real experts? Is there scope for self or group assessment?

The changes necessary to enable participation and choice entail nothing short of a cultural revolution: the replacement of provider-led models of social care by a partnership in which users' needs are uppermost. This would bring benefits to both parties: older users seem to prefer a more flexible and open approach to service provision (Qureshi, Challis and Davies, 1989), while care staff would find their job more rewarding and, together, they may put a case for greater resources.

For their part governments must help to create the conditions for effective participation by ensuring that the social exclusion of older people is minimised and by enacting positive rights to consultation and involvement. The danger resides in the mixed economy being seen by policy makers purely as a mechanism to ensure economic (i.e. least cost) efficiency. The fact is that the family is the most efficient form of care in these narrow terms. But the family is changing along with the increases in the need for care. Thus, regardless of who provides, the size of the whole mixed economy must grow in order to compensate for the coexistence of these two phenomena. Since the family in many respects is already *over*-providing care to older people, other sources of care must be found. In other words there has to be a redistribution between providers and with it, the realisation of shared care. Because the period over which care is provided is getting longer it must be shared over time as well. Thus if a narrow cost efficiency imperative prevails it will constrain the ability of purchasers to encourage new more flexible forms of domiciliary care and will increase and extend the burdens falling on family carers.

Yet, if some of the commitments concerning user involvement being voiced by policy-makers in Europe are put into practice (which means adequately resourced) thus allowing the rapid expansion of user-orientated domiciliary services, they have enormous potential. In particular they could herald the development of shared care, in which the family is integrated in a mix of other care providers, including public ones. The creation of a genuine mixed economy regulated and coordinated by statutory authorities committed to user empowerment, would help to ensure that the growing care needs of older people into the next century will be met and in ways that increase the well being of both older users and their family carers.

Postscript

Since this chapter was written the General Election of May 1997 saw the installation of the new Labour Government in the UK. There has not been a radical shift in policy on long-term care so far mainly because the government was committed to establishing a Royal Commission to examine this issue, and it did so soon after coming to power. The Royal Commission is due to report in early 1999 and changes in long-term care arrangements are expected to follow. Meanwhile the new government has departed from the approach of its predecessor in several important respects, all of which make the prospect for shared care more optimistic. For example, public expenditure on social care has been increased; the government has halted the too rapid discharge of older people from acute hospitals without adequate preparation in the community; and considerable encouragement has been given to local health and social services departments to create partnerships and work more closely together. Finally, this is such a fast moving area of policy that, as I write, the government has announced a special package of measures to support family carers, including additional finance for respite care, encouragement to health and local authorities to take carers' needs fully into account and more 'carer-friendly' employment.

References

Allen, I. (1983) *Short Stay Residential Care for the Elderly*. London: Policy Studies Institute.

Allen, I.; Hogg, D. and Peace, S. (1992) *Elderly People: Choice, Participation and Satisfaction*. London, PSI.

Bayley, M. (1980) "Neighbourhood Care and Community Care: A Response to Philip Abrams", *Social Work Service*, No. 26, pp. 4–9.

Bebbington, A.; Davies, B.; Baines, B.; Charnley, H.; Ferlie, E.; Hughes, M. and Twigg, J. (1990) *Resources, Needs and Outcomes*. Aldershot: Gower.

Cicirelli, V. (1983) "A Comparison of Helping Behaviour to Elderly Parents of Adult Children with Intact and Disrupted Marriages", *The Gerontologist* 23: 619–25.

Croft, S. and Beresford, P. (1990) *From Paternalism to Participation*. London, Open Services Project.

Dalley, G. (1983) "Ideologies of Care: A Feminist Contribution to the Debate", *Critical Social Policy* 8: 72–81.

Demone, H. and Gibelman, M. (1989) *Services for Sale: Purchasing Health and Human Services*. London: Rutgers University Press.

DH (1989) *Caring for People*, Cm 849. London, HMSO.

Dooghe, G. (1991) *The Ageing of the Population in Europe*. Brussels, CBGS.

Evers, A. (1991) "Introduction", in R. Kraan *et al.*, *Care for the Elderly*, pp. 1–6.

Finch, J. and Groves, D. (1980) "Community Care and the Family: A Case for Equal Opportunities?", *Journal of Social Policy* 9: 487–514.

Finch, J. (1984) "Community Care: Developing Non-sexist Alternatives", *Critical Social Policy* 9: 6–18.

Finch, J. (1989) *Family Obligations and Social Change*. Oxford, Polity Press.

Fisher, M. (1989) (ed.) *Client Studies*. Sheffield, JUSSR.

Fisher, M. and Marsh, P. (1993) *Readiness to Practice*. York, Joseph Rowntree Foundation.

Hamnett, C. (1992) *Inheritance in Britain: The Disappearing Billions*. London: Lifetime PLC.

Harvey, D. (1989) *The Condition of Postmodernity*. Oxford: Blackwell.

Henwood, M. and Wicks, M. (1984) *The Forgotten Army: Family Care and Elderly People*. London, Family Policy Studies Centre.

Kraan, R. J.; Baldock, J.; Davies, B.; Evers, A.; Johansson, L.; Knapen, M.; Thorslund, M. and Tunissen, C. (1991) *Care for the Elderly — Significant Innovations in Three European Countries*. Frankfurt, Campus/Westview.

Land, H. (1978) "Who Cares for the Family?", *Journal of Social Policy* 7: 357–84.

Levin, E.; Sinclair, 1. and Gorbach, P. (1983) *The Supporters of Confused Elderly Persons at Home.* London, NISW.

Levin, E.; Sinclair, I. and Gorbach, P. (1985) "The Effectiveness of the Home Help Service with Confused Old People and Their Families", *Research, Policy and Planning* 3: 1–7.

Mayer, J. and Timms, N. (1970) *The Client Speaks.* London: Routledge.

Norman, A. (1980) *Rights and Risk.* London, Centre for Policy Studies on Ageing.

Oliver, J. (1983) "The Caring Wife", in Finch and Groves (eds.), pp. 72–78.

Phillipson, C. and Walker, A. (1986) (eds.) *Ageing and Social Policy.* Aldershot: Gower.

Qureshi, H.; Challis, D. and Davies, B. (1989) *Helpers in Case-Managed Community Care.* Aldershot: Gower.

Qureshi, H. and Walker, A. (1989) *The Caring Relationship.* London: Macmillan.

Sainsbury, E. (1980) "Client Need, Social Work Method and Agency Function: A Research Perspective", *Social Work Service* 23: 9–15.

Twigg, J. and Atkin, K. (1991) *Evaluating Support to Informal Carers* University of York.

Twigg, J.; Atkin, K. and Perring, C. (1990) *Carers and Services: A Review of Research.* London, HMSO.

Waerness, K. (1986) "Informal and Formal Care in Old Age?", Paper presented to the XIth World Congress of Sociology, New Delhi.

Waerness, K. (1990) "What Can a Promotive Orientation of Health and Care Services Mean for Women as Professionals and Family Carers?", Paper No. 8, Vienna Dialogue V, European Centre.

Walker, A. (1981) "Community Care and the Elderly in Great Britain: Theory and Practice", *International Journal of Health Services* 11: 541–57.

Walker, A. (1982a) "The Meaning and Social Division of Community Care", in Walker, A. (ed.) *Community Care: The Family, The State and Social Policy.* Oxford: Blackwell/Martin Robertson.

Walker, A. (1982b) "Dependency and Old Age", *Social Policy and Administration* 16: 115–35.

Walker, A. (1985) *The Care Gap.* London, Local Government Information Centre.

Walker, A. (1989) "Community Care", in M. McCarthy (ed.) *The New Politics of Welfare*. London: Macmillan.

Walker, A. (1990) "The Economic 'Burden' of Ageing and the Prospect of Intergenerational Conflict", *Ageing and Society*, 10(4).

Walker, A. (1992) "Towards Greater User Involvement in the Social Services", in T. Arie (ed.), *Recent Advances in Psychogeriatrics 2*. London: Churchill Livingstone.

Walker, A. (1993) *Age and Attitudes*. Brussels, Commission of the EC.

Walker, A. (1996) (ed.) *The New Generational Contract*. London: UCL Press.

Walker, A.; Guillemard, A-M. and Alber, J. (1991) *Social and Economic Policies and Older People*. Brussels, Commission of the European Communities.

Walker, A. and Naegele, G. (1999) (eds.) *The Politics of Old Age in Europe*. Buckingham, OUP.

Ward, D. and Mullender, A. (1991) "Empowerment and Oppression: An Indissoluble Pairing for Contemporary Social Work", *Critical Social Policy* 32: 21–30.

Warren, L. and Walker, A. (1992) "Neighbourhood Support Units: A New Approach to the Social Care of Older People", in C. Victor and F. Laczko (eds.) *Social Policy and Older People*. Aldershot: Gower.

Wenger, C. (1984), *The Supportive Network*. London: Allen & Unwin.

Wenger, G.C. (1989) "Support Networks in Old Age: Constructing a Typology", in M.Jefferys (ed.) *Ageing in the 20th Century*. London: Routledge.

Whittaker, J. and Garbarino, J. (1983) (ed.) *Social Support Networks*. New York: Aldine.

Wright, F. (1986) *Left to Care Alone*. Aldershot: Gower.

Chapter 5

Family Change and Family Bonding in Australia

Hal Kendig
The University of Sydney

Introduction

This paper provides an overview and interpretation of Australian experiences in intergenerational support and social change. While Australia shares a similar cultural heritage and economic development with many other English-speaking countries, its massive post-war migration and particular policy legacies have had distinctive impacts on generational relations. Australian gerontology has placed considerable emphasis on family relationships (Kendig, 1994), including a multidisciplinary Ageing and the Family Project which has provided the primary basis for this paper (Kendig, 1986a; 1988).

The paper suggests that there has been considerable stability of core family values in Australia over recent decades and rising labour force participation among women and increasing rates of marital dissolution. Some social groups — such as never married women and people with poor life-long economic prospects — continue to be disadvantaged. The growth of government support has ameliorated some inequalities and served to strengthen rather than supplant family ties. Inter-generational relations are changing, however, against a backdrop of reduced economic prospects for more recent cohorts and decreasing resources of the public sector.

The next section of the paper sets the context for these interpretations by reviewing changing social conditions in Australia. The following section turns to the social bonds which tie older people into Australian society and the expressive support received through them. Subsequent sections examine instrumental support from families and public policies. The conclusion argues that the future of elderly care remains finely poised. On the one hand, family values are unlikely to erode quickly and the resources of older people are increasing. On the other hand, younger family members are facing relatively worse lifelong economic prospects than their parents and Australians are reluctant to increase State support in line with the demands of an ageing society.

Aging and Social Change in Australia

Australia has 18 million people in a country the size of the continental United States. With 11% of the population now aged 65 years and over, it lags slightly behind most developed countries in its extent of population ageing. While Australia depends heavily on exporting natural resources and agricultural products, nearly 90% of the people are concentrated in urban coastal areas. Australia remains a nation of many first and second generation immigrants as was the United States at the turn of the Century. Social attitudes and institutions began in a British colonial past, were then heavily influenced by the United States, and with more Asian migration are now moving towards a distinctive multi-cultural society.

The Post-War Era

Population ageing in Australia has been gradual over recent decades because increasing life expectancy has been largely offset by massive immigration and a baby boom to the 1970s (Rowland, 1991). There has been increasing diversity among older people, however, with more men retiring before age 65 years and more disabled widows living into their eighties. Capacities for self provision among the current cohort of older people have been enhanced through home ownership (now 75%) and other resources accumulated over the post-war economic boom. Overall, Australia has yet to experience extensive population ageing and related demands on public expenditure.

A major feature of Australian aging has been increasing ethnic diversity as earlier post-war migrants have been growing older. Within the next few years 20% of older Australians will be migrants from Southern Europe and other non-English-speaking countries. Migration separated many now elderly Australians from their parents in the past. It also has led to cultural differences between parents from the 'old country' and children raised in Australia. Aboriginal people make up a few percent of the overall Australian population and many have living conditions comparable to those of people in poor developing countries.

The potential for family support among the current generation of very old people has been limited by relatively low marriage and childbearing rates during the Depression and Second World War (Rowland, 1991). The potential availability of family support has been rising, however, as a result of higher marriage rates and higher survival rates of spouses, siblings, and children. The proportion of women aged 35 to 55 years who have never married has fallen from nearly 15% to less than 5% over the last 35 years. The most sweeping change over this period has been the increase from 10% to 50% in the proportions of middle-aged women in the paid labour-force.

Social Values

The values and norms underlying family relations in Australia may appear weak and equivocal when viewed externally from another cultural perspective. From *within* Australian culture, however, family loyalty is widely held as a primary value which has strong personal, social and political significance. Australian attitudinal data (Kendig,1986a) and qualitative investigations (Day, 1985) show families as central arenas in which individuals strive to balance potentially conflicting cultural ideals of autonomy, emotional closeness, and practical support. A common tension in family care is between frail older people wishing to remain independent and concerned adult children who wish to meet obligations to help parents. These negotiations strike a very different tone from stereotypes of older people being abandoned by children and being left to nursing homes.

The concept of 'serial intergenerational reciprocity' (Sussman,1976) provides a sound basis for conceptualising the provision of informal support in Australian as well as American society. While spouses are central for support of married older people, filial ties are the primary avenue for intergenerational support. The relationships between older people and their adult children are characterised by relative permanence, bonds based primarily in affection, and the usual flow of support 'down' generations from parents to children (Litwak, 1985). A reverse flow of support 'up' the generations, from an adult child to an older parent, is a 'contingent risk' which in Australia is unlikely to ever be required and, if so, for a relatively brief period of a few years (Kendig, 1986a).

Household Arrangements

Older Australians and their adult children overwhelmingly prefer to live in their own households and generally do so. In 1992, more than half of the people aged 60 years and over lived with their spouse in their own household (Australian Bureau of Statistics, 1995a). A quarter of the total — and more than half of women aged 75 years and over — lived alone. The remainder have a variety of living arrangements including residence in another person's household or a health establishment or some other form of non-private housing. The substantial decline of co-residency over the past years has widely resulted more from the preferences and rising incomes of older people rather than any abandonment by adult children (Rowland, 1991).

Norms reinforcing the 'modified extended family' explain why only 9% of the Australian aged live in a child's home. In Australia, the concepts of family and households in most cases are very different, with family members having the financial resources, transportation, and telephones necessary for keeping in close touch while living separately. A move to a child's home is usually precipitated by widowhood, disability, low income, or cultural distance from the Australian mainstream (Rowland, 1991). The obligatory nature of two or three generational households is also shown by the tensions which can emerge particularly with co-resident in-laws (Day, 1985). Most such moves are initiated by adult children who are motivated by a sense of obligation and concern for the aged parent's needs.

Future Generations

The most notable demographic change presently underway is the doubling of the numbers of people aged 80 years and over from 1990 to 2010. Relatively more older people in the future will be widowed or divorced and there will be further diversity among ethnic groups and economic resources. The cohort which spawned the post-war baby boom, however, will potentially have more support from children. At the same time, more people in the middle generation will have very old parents in four and five generational families. Not until the baby boom generation fully enters old age, in 2020, will Australia reach the advanced population aging (15% aged 65 years and older) now found in many European countries.

The effects of the demographic changes are likely to be accentuated by economic and political change. The costs of meeting demands for income support and health and welfare services are likely to increase significantly (Office of Economic Planning Advisory Council, 1994). In marked contrast with earlier periods of Australian history, it is likely that the cohorts in old age after the turn of the century will have had, overall, better economic prospects than those who will follow in their wake. No longer is it likely that the older age groups will be relatively disadvantaged by their cohort of birth as well as position in the life span. Further, irrespective of the party in power, it seems unlikely that governments will be expanding redistribution from the young to the old on the basis of age irrespective of need. While the future is difficult to predict, the present trend is towards governments requiring that people pay more of their own way through old age.

Family Bonds of Older People

A substantial body of research in the 1980s showed that most older Australians were firmly embedded in rich but small personal support networks of people who provide and/or receive expressive and/or instrumental support. The Australian National University study found that a typical social network included three close relatives (a spouse, children, or siblings), several more distant relations, two friends, and a neighbour or another individual (Mugford and Kendig, 1986). Little evidence was found of social isolation of many older Australians in the community. While two-thirds of network members were relatives, one-fourth of close family did not provide or receive any expressive or other support, suggesting processes of individual selection and possible attenuation of some relationships.

The likelihood of exchanging support, given the availability of a relationship, was highest for spouses followed by children. These close bonds were also more likely, than other relationships, to involve complex expressive and instrumental exchanges. Kinship formed most intergenerational bonds while friends, spouses, and siblings were common ties between older people. Relatively little social support was exchanged with grandchildren or other young adults or children, notwithstanding the great affection felt for younger family members (Day, 1985).

There are major gender and family divides in the social relations of older Australians. Wives are more likely than husbands to have complex bonds with network members. When older parents have relatively more children, their networks tend to be larger but they also tend toward greater selectivity of ties with children and children-in-law. Older couples and single women generally maintain strong family bonds but many divorced men appear to have broken family ties and those who never married appear especially likely to be life-long 'isolates'. Widowhood appears to activate stronger ties with extended family and the onset of disabilities appears to weaken friendships and strengthen family bonds.

Expressive Support

The vast majority of older Australians' ties are entirely social in nature without any financial or instrumental dependency. When substantial instrumental support becomes necessary, it is usually forthcoming from close relations hitherto providing expressive support only.

The ANU study found that personal support networks generally met the expressive needs of older people (Gibson and Mugford, 1986). The availability of support was high for confiding, reassurance of worth, acceptance, and social participation. These ties were highly selective, suggesting that family and friendship circles provided the potential for bonds but that personal affinity and choice were equally essential. Those who had relatively little expressive support generally did not wish to have more social interaction and appeared to be 'isolates' rather than 'desolates'. Various kin were especially likely to serve as confidants, and reinforce a sense of personal worth, while friends tended to predominate in providing acceptance and joint social activities.

The findings reflect the long-term and deep attachments of some (but by no means all) close kin bonds, as compared to the mutuality and similarities of chosen friendships. Those who were without spouses or children generally were able to maintain alternative expressive bonds through the inclusion of siblings and more distant kin as well as more complex friendships. Overall, older people generally have expressive support even when they are frail or do not have close family. Those who had more kinds of expressive support had correspondingly higher levels of well-being (Gibson and Mugford, 1986).

The generally optimistic tone of these findings needs to be qualified. Some individuals, for reasons of personality or unfortunate circumstances, simply lead unsatisfying lives. Widowhood is a significant blow from which it can take many years to recover even when people have extensive social support (McCallum, 1986). Non English-speaking ethnic groups, particularly those who have arrived in Australia late in life with low levels of personal resources, are at high risk of experiencing social estrangement and low levels of well-being (McCallum and Shadbolt, 1989). Explanations appear to be language barriers, the lack of long-standing friendships from midlife, dependency on children, and the isolation of women confined to the home.

In the Australian cultural context, high dependency on a co-resident child can increase the chances of poor morale and depression (Kendig, 1986a). Co-residence in a child's home with his or her spouse and children violates strong norms for the modified extended family. Capable older widows having an unmarried child at home, however, generally have higher morale than do those who live alone. Nor do high levels of dependency on non-resident children appear to undermine morale. Demoralisation appears to be associated most closely with a combined losses of exchange power, dependent household arrangements, and lack of reciprocity in informal support.

Expressive Support and Social Change

A paradox emerges concerning the quality of emotional bonds of older people over the passage of the last generation. On the one hand, older people today have more of the material resources and independent households which are associated with well being. On the other hand, Day's (1985) qualitative study found massive discontinuities felt after a lifetime of change and the loss of independence in old age. Similar views were reported among the previous generation of older Australians (Hutchinson, 1954). While the status of older people may be eroding, it also may be that idealised views of the past emerge in each generation of older people out of complex wish fulfilments or attribution of life cycle losses to historical change.

The future of older people's expressive ties is difficult to predict but there is little reason to expect much attenuation of the strong emotional and social ties between the generations today. The emergence in old age of more divorced men could place many of them at risk unless they develop the skills to manage expressive relationships on their own. Increasing education levels and occupational advancement of children, however, do not appear to attenuate ties between the generations. Judging from present network patterns, greater financial resources and more favoured social class backgrounds of older people are likely to increase social cohesiveness among age peer friends without any attenuation of family ties.

Instrumental Support

The vast majority of individuals and couples are substantially independent over all but the last few years of life. The public sector now carries the primary responsibility for income support of older people (see below). Assistance with tasks of daily living is usually a matter of small amounts of reciprocal support between relatives and friends or paid help as conveniences rather than necessities. Instrumental support, even including shared household responsibilities, is usually provided by a few people with whom expressive bonds are also maintained (Kendig, 1986a).

Intergenerational Contributions

The ANU study showed that older people generally have already made substantial contributions within ongoing patterns of family support (Kendig, 1986a). Fully 80% have raised children and substantial numbers have provided significant financial support or housing to adult children during times of need. In old age, the majority of parents continue to be more likely to be providers than recipients of assistance.

Large financial gifts are rare but usually flow from the aged to their children. Older men help others particularly with transport while older women are more likely to look after grandchildren (Edgar, 1993). The high levels of home ownership in Australia mean that most adult children also will be substantial beneficiaries from their parents' estates.

Older people in the early 1980s reported that their own parents, when they were older in the 1940s to the 1960s, also were substantially independent. Only one-fourth of this last generation of older people had required care for a year or more prior to death and few more had lived with a child during old age. Even in those days before widespread availability of nursing homes, the provision of sustained parent care in midlife, and its possible receipt in old age, were unlikely. Most people who had supported their aged parents, or who later received this support themselves, do not have much previous experience in their immediate family (another instance of inadequate socialisation for old age).

Intergenerational Support

In contrast to the varied sources of expressive bonds, substantial instrumental support is generally restricted to close family members (ABS, 1995b). The marital bond involves strong attachments, and complementarity of gender-based skills, but remains vulnerable to disability of the partners and widowhood. High levels of instrumental support are overwhelmingly a matter for spouses and adult children. Friends and distant relatives seldom do more than provide modest assistance usually on a reciprocal or supplementary basis.

Particularly strong family support is received by most of the 16% of older Australians who are unable to manage independently with household tasks. Three-fourths of these people reside in the community rather than in institutions of any kind (Rowland, 1991). For those who become disabled, instrumental support networks remain small as a few ongoing expressive ties take on responsibility for providing considerable amounts of assistance.

Contrary to traditional gender expectations, husbands and wives are equally likely to provide extensive personal care for the other if necessary. When a husband is disabled, the distribution of household tasks generally remains unchanged except for outside support with transport, home repairs, and other tasks typically performed by men. When a wife is disabled, the men display considerable adaptability in sharing traditional female tasks with relatively little support from beyond the household. Older couples strongly resist the breakdown of the marital household or intrusion of assistance into the home. Spouse carers can pay a significant price, however, in reduced morale, higher rates of anxiety and depression, and lower levels of social activity.

There is a strong tendency for co-resident care of a disabled aged parent to be provided by a daughter or a daughter-in-law. Competing responsibilities of adult daughters to spouses, children, and employment generally add to the stresses of the carer rather than reduce their availability to care for parents (Kendig, 1986a). Unmarried sons and daughters live with able older parents but only daughters are likely to do so when a parent is disabled. The findings reflect the strong cultural assignment of caring responsibilities to women in Australia and the high price often paid by carers in loss of employment and reduced social life, health and life satisfaction (Braithwaite, 1990). There is increasing recognition that the intense stress can lead to abuse in the relationships (McCallum, 1993).

The importance of gender conditioning and family history is seen most directly in the case of older women living on their own. Never married women are much more self reliant than widows in both their attitudes and their actions. The current cohort of older widows had relied heavily on their husbands for typically 'male tasks' while never married women had generally learned to manage independently. Childless older people generally are able to secure more support from friends, other relatives, neighbours, and paid help with these tasks. The principle of 'hierarchical substitution' (Cantor, 1979) operates strongly but only up to the point of the very demanding tasks of aged care.

Some models of social change suggest that social mobility of children might attenuate family ties. The ANU study, however, found that middle class sons are much more likely than working class sons to support aged parents. They have more resources to fulfil traditional filial obligations and display greater likelihood of helping even with some traditionally female tasks such as housekeeping. To the extent that the middle classes may be at the forefront of social change, these patterns may suggest some relaxation of the strong assignment to women of support to aged parents.

Aged Care Services

Community services potentially can provide specialised services and amount of support which are beyond the capacities of families (Litwak, 1985). But only a third of the disabled Australian aged in the community make use of meals on wheels, home housekeeping, visiting nurses, or related services at home (Department of Health, Housing, and Community Services, 1991). Low usage of services is explained more by their limited availability and preferences for older people to remain independent (Davison, Kendig, Stephens and Merrill, 1993).

The primary impact of community services is to augment support through modified extended families. New forms of more intensive services, however, are providing genuine alternatives to people without family support as well as appropriate respite and other support for co-resident carers (Reynolds, 1995). The leading edge of community care practice recognises that often there are two clients, the older person and one or more carers, and the interests of all parties need to be taken into account in care planning.

The limits of informal support in the community are seen in the patterns of institutionalisation and the social processes in entering a home. Among women aged 75 years or over, the 1986 Census shows that proportions in institutions was 8% for those currently married, 19% for widows, and 27% for those never married. Minichiello's (1986) qualitative study showed that adult children initiate moves to nursing homes when co-resident care is not (or no longer) tenable as needs and stress increase — particularly after widowhood (when the elderly person is psychologically vulnerable) or when daughters or daughters-in-law feel they cannot give up employment. A small minority of older people actively initiate the move to a home. The impact of institutionalisation on older people's family ties varies from irreparable feelings of betrayal and abandonment, through to improved expressive ties as heavy instrumental burdens are lifted.

Life Span Inequalities in Family Support

The ongoing process of intergenerational support involves massive inequalities between groups over the life course (Kendig, 1988). Those who have never married, especially women, are more likely than their married counterparts to provide parent care in mid life and to not have any family support in their own old age. Older husbands are twice as likely as older wives to have the support of a spouse to death. It is women more than men who need to cast an eye forward to the day when intergenerational support may become a necessity.

The stresses and discontinuities in intergenerational exchange can be accentuated among older migrants from non-English speaking countries (Kendig, 1986b; Rowland, 1991). Those who arrived in midlife, while often coming from rural areas with strong cultural traditions of family support for the aged, have removed themselves from these chains of support. Yet their needs for intergenerational support, when they reach old age themselves, can be heightened by cultural barriers, lack of strong ties to others besides children, and reluctance to use services designed for the Australian mainstream. These difficulties are accentuated among those who arrive in old age to join adult children.

A new way of securing instrumental support in old age is emerging with the rapid growth of the retirement housing industry which now serves approximately 3% of the aged (Kendig, 1990). Older people put their wealth into a housing complex in exchange for some supportive services and, to varying degrees, access to long-term care.

This new form of care changes the balance of intergenerational exchange, for the more affluent aged, by decreasing reliance on family support while at the same time eroding the amount of inheritances. Surveys show that a retirement home is preferred by a margin of two to one over either co-residence with a child or a nursing home when people anticipated no longer being able to manage their own households.

Social Change

Overall, there is more evidence for continuity than for change in patterns of intergenerational support over recent decades. Longer life expectancy has probably increased the likelihood and duration of disability in old age but increased financial resources have enhanced capacities for self provision. While markedly fewer of the aged now live with children than in the past, the change is explained primarily by the rising economic fortunes and preferences of both generations (Rowland, 1991). The decreased availability of support from daughter housewives has in broad terms been matched by the increased availability of community and residential services. The general picture is one of continuity in the deeply-seated norms of intergenerational family support with some change in the means by which these obligations are fulfilled.

A continuation of these trends is anticipated for the future. While the vulnerability of the old will probably increase with a lengthening life span, capacities for self provision will rise as a wealthier cohort grows older. The potential availability of filial support will be high for the generation which produced the baby boom. Reducing age differences between the generations, and any continuation of trends towards earlier retirement, could well give rise to already emergent patterns of support between two generations of the elderly. The most significant change is that the minority of people who are called to provide parent support in middle age will increase appreciably. The outcome will depend crucially on two key factors. One is the extent to which gender limitations are reduced in the living skills of the aged and the caring responsibilities of those in middle age. Another is the capacity of the public sector to increase provision in line with demographic aging.

Public Policies and Generational Equity

There have been major improvements in policies for older people over the last 40 years (Sax, 1993). The means-tested, non-contributory old age pension has grown from a small supplement for a minority of the poor to an indexed payment providing most of the income for three-fourths of the aged. Pensioner health benefits introduced in the 1950s have been expanded and have been absorbed into a universal health insurance program. The past three decades also saw the introduction of subsidies for nursing home care, public housing, hostels, and community services. These policy developments have transferred some support responsibilities from individual family members to public services supported by the community.

Improved public provision has underwritten the greater independence and security of the present generation of older people. These policies have redistributed some of the benefits of the expanding post-war economy to individuals who lived most of their adult life in less advantaged times. They have reduced inequality between more and less advantaged groups of older people, and probably improved family relations by providing alternative support. However, major inequalities persist with the favoured tax treatment of retirement savings and inheritances and the inadequacy of pensions to lift private tenants out of poverty. It is not clear that the provision of aged care services will keep up with the growth of demand over the next decade.

Searching questions also arise concerning impacts on generational relations of future economic, social and political conditions. If real incomes remain stable or decline, older people as a group will no longer be disadvantaged by their cohort of birth as well as by the risks and losses of later life. Indeed, the aged will have continued wealth brought to old age through home ownership, superannuation, and other benefits from earlier economic boom days. A continuation of current policies would place a substantial burden on smaller and younger cohorts facing difficult employment and housing markets.

Significant intergenerational conflict seems unlikely, however, given the strong personal ties between the generations and Australian social values and institutions of government. Substantial movement is already underway for a transition towards policies based more on individual need rather than age rights. People now in mid life are likely to be a transitional cohort who in mid life pay twice for support of the aged: once through taxes for their parent's generation and again through private savings for themselves. The question most open to political uncertainty is the distributional impact of these adjustments between social classes, men and women, and other social groups over their entire life course.

Conclusions

Virtually every country seems to have a popular belief that social change is widening generation gaps and leading to increased isolation and abandonment of the aged. Australian findings, like those from other Western countries (Wenger, 1992), refute these stereotypes and indicate that ties between the age groups generally are deep and enduring. Relationships between the multiple generations of Western families are characterised by choice more than obligation, strong emotional ties, instrumental independence where possible, and residence in separate households (Bengtson and Achenbaum, 1993). Overall, the social position of older Australians has improved over recent decades due to increased lifetime incomes of successive cohorts and improved government policies.

The core of family ties in virtually all societies are deep attachments among family members grounded in values, affections, and interdependencies instilled since childhood (Hashimoto, Kendig and Coppard, 1992). Basic beliefs and orientations may be stressed by changing social and economic conditions but they are not easily changed. While there is great diversity among families, spouses and adult daughters continue as the primary caregivers should older people require support in the Australian community. Individuals' mid life investments in relationships, personal skills, and financial security generally provide a sound base for maintaining satisfying family relations in old age.

Family relations are likely to face further pressure in the next few decades as a result of both population ageing and the end of the post war economic boom. This historical watershed will see the emergence of parents in old age who will have experienced more favorable economic opportunities than did their children in midddle age. Concern for ageing in the future has its positive aspects in motivating personal and collective action which minimises future difficulties. Indeed, these concerns reflect the societal value placed on care of vulnerable older people, and the wishes of older people not to jeopardise the life chance of younger generations.

References

Australian Bureau of Statistics (1995a) *Focus on Families: Family Life*, Cat. No. 4425.0, Canberra.

Australian Bureau of Statistics (1995b) *Focus on Families: Caring in Families,* Cat. No. 4423.0, Canberra.

Bengtson, V. and Achenbaum, W.A. (eds.) (1993) *The Changing Contract Across the Generations.* New York: Aldine De Gruyter.

Braithwaite, V. (1990) *Bound to Care.* Sydney: Allen and Unwin.

Cantor, M.H. (1979) "Neighbours and friends", *Research on Aging* 1: 434–463.

Davison, B.; Kendig, H.; Stephens, F. and Merrill, V. (1993) *It's Our Place: Older People Talk About Their Homes.* Canberra: Australian Government Publishing Service.

Day, A. (1985) *We Can Manage.* Melbourne: Institute of Family Studies.

Department of Health, Housing and Community Services (1991) *Aged Care Reform Strategy Mid-term Review 1990–91 Report.* Canberra: Australian Government Publishing Service.

Edgar, D. (1993) "Family and inter-generational relations into the 21st century", in K. Sanders (ed.) *Ageing: Law, Policy, and Ethics Directions for the 21st Century.* University of Melbourne School of Social Work, pp. 220–227.

Gibson, D. and Mugford, S. (1986) "Expressive relations and social support", in H.L. Kendig (ed.) *Ageing and Families: A Support Networks Perspective*, pp. 63–84. Sydney: Allen and Unwin.

Hashimoto, A.; Kendig, H. and Coppard, L. (1992) "Family support to the elderly in international perspective", in H. Kendig, A. Hashimoto and L. Coppard (eds.) *Family Support to the Elderly: The International Experience*, pp. 293–308. Oxford University Press.

Hutchinson, B. (1954) *Old People in a Modern Australian Community: A Social Survey.* Melbourne: University of Melbourne.

Kendig, H. (ed.) (1986a) *Ageing and Families: A Support Networks Perspective.* Sydney: George Allen and Unwin.

Kendig, H. (1986b) "Informal support networks", in *Community and Institutional Care for Aged Migrants in Australia: Research Findings* (Australian Institute of Multicultural Affairs). Melbourne: Global Press.

Kendig, H.L. (1988) "Ageing and intergenerational support in Australia", in M. Bergener, M. Ermini and H.B. Stahelin (eds.) *Crossroads in Aging*, pp. 225–253. London: Academic Press.

Kendig, H. (1990) "Ageing and Housing Policy", in H. Kendig and J. McCallum (eds.) *Grey Policy: Australian Policies for an Ageing Society.* Sydney: Allen and Unwin.

Kendig, H. (1994) "Australian research on ageing and families: Developments and directions", *Australian Journal on Ageing* 13 (4): 157–160.

Litwak, E. (1985) *Helping Older People: The Complementary Roles of Informal Networks and Formal Systems.* New York: The Guilford Press.

McCallum, J. (1986) "Retirement and widowhood transitions", in H. Kendig (ed.) *Ageing and Families: A Support Networks Perspective*, pp. 129–148. Sydney: Allen and Unwin

McCallum, J. (1993) "Elder abuse: the new social problem", *Modern Medicine*, September, pp. 74–83.

McCallum, J. and Shadbolt, B. (1989) "Ethnicity and stress among older Australians", *Journal of Gerontology Social Sciences*, 44: S89–96.

Minichiello, M. (1986) "Social processes in entering nursing homes", in H.L. Kendig (ed.) *Ageing and Families: A Support Networks Perspective*, pp. 85–109. Sydney: Allen and Unwin.

Mugford, S. and Kendig, H. (1986) "Social relations: networks and ties", in H.L. Kendig (ed.) *Ageing and Families: A Support Networks Perspective*, pp. 36–80. Sydney: Allen and Unwin.

Office of Economic Planning Advisory Council (1994) *Australia's Ageing Society*. Canberra: Australian Government Publishing Service.

Reynolds, A. (1995) *People with Complex Needs; Effective Support at Home*, report prepared for the Aged and Community Care Division. Canberra: Australian Government Publishing Service.

Rowland, D.T. (1991) *Ageing in Australia*. Melbourne: Longman Cheshire.

Sax, S. (1993) *Ageing and Public Policy in Australia*. Sydney: Allen and Unwin.

Sussman, M.B. (1976) "The family life of old people", in R. Binstock and E. Shanas (eds.) *Handbook of Aging and the Social Sciences*. New York: Van Nostrand Reinhold.

Wenger, C. (1992) "The major English-speaking countries", in H. Kendig, A. Hashimoto and L. Coppard (eds.) *Family Support to the Elderly: The International Experience*, pp. 117–137. Oxford University Press.

Chapter 6

Care and Social Support —
The Example of Ageing Migrants

Ken Blakemore
University of Wales, Swansea

Introduction

In the introduction to this book the editors identify key aspects of the international context of ageing and care-giving, noting in particular the impact of 'westernization'; the demographic revolution and rapid ageing of many societies, especially in the East; changes associated with industrialization and, more recently, the emergence of post-industrial society. These significant trends are manifesting themselves in somewhat different ways in the family life and care-giving arrangements of different societies.To the above list we might add another key influence on the family and care of older people — the impact of international migration. This is the subject of this chapter.

There are several reasons for including a perspective on international migration in East-West comparisons of care-giving. Firstly there are the lessons to be learned from the experience of ageing migrants from Eastern societies in a Western society and culture. It is an example of this experience, the ageing of older migrants from South Asian countries (India, Pakistan and Bangladesh) in the United Kingdom, which forms the main part of the discussion here. Older Asians' experiences in Britain raise many questions about the durability of 'traditional' Asian family patterns of care-giving and have implications for understanding processes of 'Westernization' elsewhere. Problems of either a significant lack of care or of *perceptions* of a decline in care and caring values are evident to a significant degree in the West and, as the editors remind us, are also of growing concern in rapidly ageing societies in the East, such as Japan.

Secondly, migration is of wider significance to our understanding of ageing and care because international migration has become an increasingly common experience in the past century. However, earlier theories of ageing which informed thinking about the status of older people neglected these realities. Modernization theory (Cowgill and Holmes 1972; Cowgill 1986), activity theory (Lemmon *et al.* 1976) and disengagement theory (Cumming and Henry 1961) fostered views of ageing against a background of social stability, even where (as in the case of modernization theory) processes of social change were an intrinsic part of the theory. They were essentially a historical theories which could be used to make generalizations about Western, Eastern or any other types of society, but were limited by their lack of reference to significant historical events or to specific examples of political and economic change, including the pressures which have precipitated international migration. These theories were based primarily upon research on ageing in Western (specifically, American) society and they sought to answer the questions raised by problems of ageing in a Western cultural context.

More recent theories of ageing and of the relationship between the generations, including political economy and structured dependency perspectives (Phillipson 1981, Phillipson and Walker 1986) have succeeded in illuminating a much wider range of influences on the ageing process and in particular, the impact of inequalities in material resources and in access to care services. These theories have tended to focus on ageing in capitalist and market-based societies in the West, but they have not included a perspective on international migration and its impact on these societies.

Thus the main theoretical perspectives which have guided research in social gerontology have tended to neglect international migration and of large-scale population movements. Yet certain features of migration in the twentieth century are of great significance in any estimation of the care needs of older people.

For example, there have been considerable movements of refugees in the past century. Forced migration has taken place on a large scale in some parts of the world as a result of wars, inter-ethnic violence and other forms of conflict on a scale unimaginable in previous centuries. The full effects of the fall of state communism upon rates of migration from, or within, the former Soviet Union and eastern Europe have yet to be seen, while in China the rapid pace of economic and political change seems to be resulting in momentous rises in rural-urban migration and to the special economic zones of South and Eastern cities. All these examples, whether of international migration or large-scale movement within one country, have serious implications in terms of family disruption and consequent problems such as a potential lack of relatives or care resources for older people.

In addition, economic migration in the twentieth century has been closely associated with European colonialism, which reached its zenith by mid-century and then collapsed. As a result of colonialism, extensive groups of people in developing countries were granted residence rights in Europe, only to find that these rights have been qualified or withdrawn later (as with Hong Kong and rights to residence in the UK). The recent tightening of residence and immigration rules in European Union countries and the construction of a 'Fortress Europe' policy poses problems, not only for younger migrants and relatives who might wish to join families already settled in Europe but also for older migrants who fear re-entry will be difficult if they leave to visit their old countries.

Thus, in addition to the political upheavals which have led to forced migration and the refugee experience for many millions of people, there is also the legacy of economic migration to contend with. Only now are developed or industrialized societies in the West and the East coming to terms with the reality that migrants age, and that their elderly populations are becoming increasingly diverse in terms of 'race', ethnicity, religion and family structure.

Migration and Ageing — A Typology

In order to advance understanding of the impact of international migration on ageing it is clearly necessary to develop some way of breaking down the 'big picture' sketched above. As outlined, there are many different experiences of migration and each major type poses different hypotheses about the possible impact upon ageing and support in later life.

For instance, migration which takes place relatively early on in life, is a choice and represents a search for better prospects can be contrasted with migration which is forced, such as refugees, or at least in which there is little choice, and which might take place relatively late in the life course. Not all refugees, for instance, are children and young people. In addition to elderly refugees, there are examples of grandparents and other older people who migrate later to join their grown-up children in 'new' countries. They arrive as dependents and might be expected to adapt to an unfamiliar culture in a country in which they cannot understand or speak the majority language. These factors will have far-reaching implications for the ability of older migrants to fend for themselves, to maximize life satisfaction and keep their health and mobility.

However, it is important not only to contrast younger migrants who have enjoyed a degree of choice in their re-location with older migrants who might have been forced or at least strongly pressured to uproot themselves. It is equally important to reverse these comparisons — for instance, between relatively affluent older people who choose to migrate internationally (for instance, British and other older northern Europeans who settle in southern Spain) and younger people who are forced or pressured to move (for instance, young refugees from 'ethnic' conflicts in south-east Europe, or young Asian women who are pressured to migrate to fulfil arranged marriage agreements between families).

Also there are yet other aspects of the migration experience that could have a permanent effect on the direction of a person's life course and subsequently upon that person's economic and social resources, the strength of his or her social network and community support, and upon his/her identity and psychological wellbeing in later life. For instance, there is the dimension of 'permanence' to add to the aspects of 'chosen' vs. 'forced' migration mentioned above. How permanent is the migrant's stay in the 'new' or host country, either from the point of view of the migrant him/herself or that of the 'host' community, and what impact does either the real prospect of return or the myth of return have upon preparation for later life?

As can be seen from these illustrative questions, the relationship between migration and ageing in later life is an extremely complex one. The purpose of the typology of migration (see below) is to offer a framework for identifying common experiences among different groups of ageing migrants, or at least points of comparison between two or more groups that might share similar orientations or aspirations.

However, the typology presented here is a descriptive rather than an analytical scheme. The categories included in the typology are not intended to generate specific hypotheses or research questions about the impact of international migration upon ageing. Nor does the typology contain a hidden agenda about possible links between types of migration in earlier and later periods of the life course. On the other hand, the typology could be seen as a ground-clearing device and as a way of reaching the stage of preliminary identification of possible research questions. For instance there is the central question of care-giving and social support in later life. Do those who migrate internationally, either at younger or older ages, experience loss of support and care from family and friends, relative to their counterparts in the old country or to older people in the society to which they have migrated? How robust are the bonds of 'traditional' family support among older migrants from Eastern societies and in what ways do different patterns of migration and settlement affect those bonds? It is to these questions that this chapter will now turn, using the illustrative example of South Asian migrants and other migrant or minority communities in Britain.

Ageing Migrants — The Example of South Asians in Britain

In one sense the experience of older South Asian (Indian, Pakistani and Bangladeshi) migrants in Britain presents only a limited range of examples of the wide variety of migration experiences indicated in the typology. Most of these migrants' experience is of only one 'new' or adopted country, Britain, and migration for almost all of them took place within a limited historical period, between the mid-1950s and mid-1960s. Therefore caution must be exercised in drawing lessons from these particular examples.

On the other hand, however, the category 'South Asian' is an umbrella term covering a wide variety of regional, national, cultural and religious differences, together with marked differences within and between communities in terms of family structures and housing. Also, there are sharp differences between the migration histories of Asian men, most of whom migrated to Britain without wives or fiancees in the late 1950s and early 1960s, and those of Asian women, most of whom joined the men a few years later as 'dependent' relatives. Furthermore, although most South Asian men originally travelled to Britain as economic migrants with relatively short-term expectations of staying in the country, a substantial minority — the so-called 'African' Asians from countries such as Uganda — arrived as refugees.

Therefore these distinct minority communities in one Western country represent a relatively wide range of experiences of migration and ageing and their experiences provide valuable and instructive lessons. Perhaps the most important lesson of all, as far as the example of ageing Asian people in Britain is concerned, is that each of the minority communities has stabilized in Britain. This was always going to be the case in respect of the African-Asian community because of

Typology of Migration in the Life Course: Implications for Care and Family Support

Migration Category	Greater risk of disruption to family support	Care costs and needs in: 'new' country	old/third country
Earlier in the life course			
a. Economic/labour migration		x	
b. As a dependent:			
– Child		x	
– Spouse/fiancee			
– Older relative		x	
c. As a refugee:			
– Remaining or becoming dependent	x	x	
– Becoming self-supporting			
Later in the life course			
1. Intending to stay:			
– Legally entitled to stay		x	
– Cannot stay, or insecure	x		x
2. Uncertain			
– Planning to visit old country	x	x	
– No plans, no visits	?	?	?
– refers new country, visits old country to meet obligations	x		
– Prefers old country	x	x	?
3. 'Circular' migration visits			
– Prefers new country		x	
– Prefers old country	x	x	x
– Permanent return intended	x		x
4. Return to old country			
– Permanent return intended	x		x
– Permanent return not intended	x	x	
– Permanent return forced (eg immigration rules, family duties)	x		x
5. Move to another, third, country			
– Permanent move intended	x		x
– Permanent stay not intended		x	
– Permanent move forced	x		x
6. Move within new country			
– Moving with younger relatives		x	
– Seeking better conditions		x	
– Avoiding family ties	x	x	
– Evading residence controls	x	x	

their status as refugees; at the time of arrival there was no prospect of a return to Africa and, for most families, ties to their original communities and families in the Indian subcontinent had weakened to the point that they offered little prospect of settlement there. For a variety of reasons including relatively high levels of education and aspirations, this community has enjoyed considerable economic and educational success in British society, and these achievements have been shared to some extent by the wider Indian community that migrated directly from India to Britain (Modood 1991, Jones 1993).

As a result, older people in African-Asian communities and to some degree in the Indian community are ageing in a context in which their sons, daughters and younger relatives are tending to do relatively well in higher education and professional or managerial employment. Problems of racism and discrimination remain, but in economic and status terms these communities are upwardly mobile.

For different reasons, older people in the other South Asian minority communities, Bangladeshis and Pakistanis, also face a future in which most will continue to age and eventually will die in Britain rather than in the old country. This outcome contrasts with the original intentions of most of the men who initially migrated to Britain who, as pointed out above, had envisaged a relatively short stay of a few years in which to save some money before a permanent return to the home community in Pakistan or Bangladesh. Many migrants in these communities continued to cling to a 'myth of return' (Anwar 1979), but in practice have found that return to the old country is either not desirable or feasible. In the first place the older 'grandparent' generation now has an established and extended family structure in Britain and, as with all ageing migrants, often finds that the prospect of return and of leaving one's immediate descendants and grandchildren behind too difficult. In the second place, these communities, unlike the Indian and African-Asian communities, have experienced considerable social exclusion, poverty, unemployment and limited economic success (Jones 1993). As a result it would be difficult for many to return to the old country with sufficient capital or resources to enjoy the lifestyle they had once envisaged.

Whether or not permanent return is feasible, however, the overwhelming preference among all the South Asian communities is to continue with life in Britain. In some ways the maintenance of strong links with families and communities in the old countries has added to the stabilisation effect rather than weakening the older migrants' resolve to stay in Britain. Because international travel is now relatively affordable and convenient, compared with its cost in the 1960s and 1970s, a considerable number of older Asian people engage in 'circular migration' (see typology). Both older men and women spend considerable periods of time visiting their former home districts; the women might be involved in lengthy family discussions about arranged marriages or inheritance matters, for instance, while men might re-visit the home community to boost their status by contributing to the construction of a mosque or a local school.

There are some similarities in these respects with another important minority community, those who migrated from the Caribbean to Britain at approximately the same time as the majority of South Asian men (though Caribbean migration began to increase earlier in the 1950s than migration from the Indian subcontinent). Older African-Caribbeans have also retained extensive links with the island communities from which they originated. However, unlike the South Asian examples, there is growing evidence that a substantial number of older black migrants are returning to their 'home' countries in the Caribbean. This is a racially sensitive issue and there is a danger that racist opinion could seize upon it as a justification for the view that black and Asian people do not 'belong' in a predominantly white society. There is certainly no evidence that a majority of older or middle-aged black people are contemplating either a return to the Caribbean or re-settlement in another, third country such as the United States. However, out-migration statistics reveal considerable falls in the total of African-Caribbean people living in Britain (Peach 1991) and it is this trend which contrasts so markedly with the South Asian communities, among whom there is little sign of return.

One way of interpreting this difference between the Asian and African-Caribbean experience is to see it as a difference between

'Eastern' and 'Western' patterns of family structure and of the ties which support care-giving and receipt of care. This is a little misleading, in that African-Caribbean family and community structures do not neatly correspond with their social class equivalents in 'western' British society (and in any case there are significant variations in family life within British regions and class groups). For instance, there are more households headed by a single woman in the African-Caribbean community than in the white majority — a feature which is paralleled in the United States by significant numbers of female-headed black households there, and which — as in Britain — raises interesting questions about the distinctive ways in which older black people both seek and provide care in later life (Coke and Twaite 1995).

Nevertheless, and despite distinctive characteristics of family and community life in the African-Caribbean community, there are some basic similarities between Caribbean and majority British families and household structures. For instance, British population census data show that approximately similar proportions of the majority white and the African-Caribbean population live in 'single adult, no children' households (OPCS 1992). In British cities such as Birmingham, Coventry and Leicester, where there are sizeable black communities, between 25 and 30 per cent of households are of the single adult variety. Some of these 'single adult, no children' households are younger people living alone, though most younger black and white people live in other types of household such as 'single parents with dependent children' or households shared with other single adults. Thus a significant proportion of 'single person, no children' households in the African-Caribbean community are middle-aged and older people living alone — a 'Western' and increasingly post-modern pattern which contrasts strikingly with the family structures in which older Asian people live.

In all the minority South Asian communities living in Britain, larger households are much more common. For instance, while the proportions of Asian families living in households comprised of 'three or more adults with dependent children' (an indicator of joint family living and/or multi-generational households) is often between 25 and 40 per cent (OPCS 1992), the proportion among white and black or African-Caribbean families is only a few per cent. These are, of course, only rough and ready indicators of household and family structure and they tell us nothing about levels of family support and care-giving between households, which might be more extensive among older people in the Caribbean community than appears to be the case from the picture portrayed by large numbers of single adults living alone. However, it remains the case that all but a few older South Asians live with family members and a substantial proportion of these continue to live in relatively large, three-generation households which are in turn surrounded by extensive networks of kin.

South Asian Families — The Prospects for Care-Giving

This brief portrayal of the circumstances of family life among ageing South Asian migrants, together with the nature of their relationships with their old countries or 'home' communities, suggests that a 'persistence of tradition' or an 'Asian family values' model best explains the distinctiveness of their family and community characteristics when they are compared either with the white 'Western' majority among whom they live and work, or with a black 'Western' minority who have shared the same urban, economic and welfare state context with the South Asians, and have experienced similar forms of racial oppression and disadvantage.

However, there are dangers in drawing conclusions which are based too readily on a 'strength of culture' or 'Asian values' argument. Equally, it would be dangerous to draw the conclusion that, if Asian family patterns and traditions of care-giving to older people are robust in a British or strongly Western context, they could have a similar level of resilience or persistence in other communities of migrant Easterners.As indicated in the typology, patterns of migration vary considerably from one context or country to another, and the migrant experience of Britain might not be applicable to other Asians' experiences elsewhere — those of Chinese or Korean migrants' experiences in the United States, for instance.

As far as the example of ageing in a minority 'Eastern' context in Britain is concerned, there are several reasons for exercising some caution when interpreting the apparent strength of Asian families as a persistence of tradition or as an intrinsic cultural feature. By the same token it cannot be taken for granted that older Asian people in the 'migrant' situation will always be well cared-for in a supportive, extended family. This latter perception is as much a Western myth as the view that all older people in the white majority live alone and are not cared for by relatives.

Firstly, there are clear signs that the 'traditional' Asian extended family in Britain is on the brink of major changes. Stopes-Roe and Cochrane's (1990) survey found that, while there is still considerable support in the various Asian communities for extended or joint family living, a surprisingly high proportion of middle-aged couples revealed questioning and critical attitudes towards living in a large family group. This shows that it is no longer only the younger, British-born generation who expect to live in 'Westernized' nuclear families (Stopes-Roe and Cochrane found that two-thirds of young Asian women want this), but also that a considerable number in the pre-retirement age group neither want to live with their ageing parents or in-laws nor expect to live with their own children. There are other signs of a search for extra-familial ways of meeting housing and care needs. For instance, new inner-city schemes to provide sheltered housing for older Asian people have met with strong demand (Blakemore and Boneham 1994). If traditional Asian values were still holding sway with almost all Asian families, one would expect only lukewarm demand for housing for older people to live on their own.

As trends towards smaller households and separate living arrangements for older people gain ground in Britain's Asian communities, this does not necessarily entail less actual support for older people, nor a weakening of the care-giving relationship between younger and older generations. The extended family will be able to provide some daily care at a distance, and the development of a network of voluntary sector care organizations will in part take over some of the family's obligations and will also offer an avenue for middle aged and younger Asian volunteers to help frail elderly people who no longer live with their children (Ahmad 1996). However, a shift in expectations of what the family could and should do for, or with, elderly relatives has undeniably taken place. This sea-change is perhaps most clearly observed in the more affluent and increasingly 'Westernized' Indian and African-Asian communities. Younger people in these communities increasingly see themselves as 'British Asians' and, though their attitudes towards family life and the status of older people are still distinctly different from those of younger people in the white majority (Stopes-Roe and Cochrane 1990), it is likely that social mobility and changing aspirations will lead them towards a more 'Westernized' and partly extra-familial set of solutions to problems of care for their parents and grandparents.

A second reason for scepticism about the 'persistence of tradition' view of Asian family values and care-giving patterns is that, for a variety of reasons, family support in South Asian communities has never matched the myth of warm, inclusive care for all older people. The author's research revealed that in one British city, Birmingham, almost a quarter of older Asian men were not living with close relatives or wives (Blakemore and Boneham 1993). Living in a large household of two or more generations might mean that one is living with more distantly-related people or with people who originate from the same 'home' village or district, but the support that can be expected from such co-residents will usually be much less than from immediate relatives.

Another point to bear in mind is the highly gendered nature of the power and status relationships in many South Asian families. Though older women are not without power and influence in Asian families (Bhachu 1985, Werbner 1989), they are more at risk than men from problems of isolation, neglect and even physical or mental abuse. It is important not to overstate these problems, about which little is known and in respect of which more research is needed. On the other hand, if such problems are only at levels found in the majority community they should be recognized as such. Older Asian women's needs are easily neglected when few can speak or understand English, and when traditions of male responsibility for matters outside the family have restricted their access to welfare benefits, social services and other forms of community life and enjoyment.

Thirdly, the quality and level of care that Asian families can give to their elderly relatives is significantly affected by the economic and social resources at the disposal of the family and of the community as a whole. The housing occupied by Pakistani and Bangladeshi families, for instance, is more likely to lack the amenities and improvements that make it easier to care for frail elderly people. In the English West Midlands, for instance, a third of white residents and under a quarter of Indian residents occupy houses with no central heating, but just over half of the Bangladeshi and 58 per cent of the Pakistani households lack this amenity (OPCS 1992: 326).

Rather crude indicators of well-being such as car ownership, home ownership (by older people in their own homes) and facilities in the home will matter a great deal as the migrant generation ages. In most respects it is the Pakistani and Bangladeshi communities that are most disadvantaged. Unemployment, for example, reaches levels of between 25 and 30 per cent among the economically active in these communities, compared to an unemployment rate of 8 per cent in the white community and 12 per cent among the Indian community (ONS 1996: 46).

Family care in most Pakistani and Bangladeshi homes is warm and supportive, but the point is that it is not inevitably so. As in any community, severe tension and conflict erupt in some families from time to time. If the family is already struggling with problems of racism, poor health, poverty, high rates of unemployment, inadequate housing and overcrowding, such tensions are likely to impair the care-giving role of the family. They underline the importance of blending a little realism into the rose-tinted view of the 'traditional' Asian family and its supportiveness, and equally the need to qualify the impression of a decline from a situation in which unconditional support was always given unquestioningly.

Conclusion

Increasing proportions of older people in the East and the West will be migrants. They will have moved from one country to another in their lifetimes, or they will have experienced significant long-distance migration. Yet the question of migration and its impact upon the ageing process is a seriously neglected topic in social gerontology. This chapter has focused on the theme of international migration in an attempt to show, firstly, how we might begin to separate out different kinds of relationship between migration and ageing and, secondly, how the examples of Asian communities in a western country, Britain, illustrate the possibilities of different kinds of outcome from the migration experience and its impact on the well-being and care of older migrants.

The combined experience of South Asian older people in Britain seems to show, in some respects, a surprising amount of stability in terms of the rootedness of older migrants in their 'new' or adopted country, and in terms of the apparent resilience of Asian family structures, relationships and norms of care-giving which are still largely based upon the practice of living in relatively large family groups which often comprise three generations. Despite problems of 'racial' discrimination and additional problems of social exclusion and disadvantage, especially in the Pakistani and Bangladeshi communities, it would seem as though Asian family traditions and priorities in caring for elderly relatives are surprisingly resilient.

However, some care should be exercised in the interpretation of these conclusions. Though several decades have passed since the main groups of Asian migrants arrived in Britain, it is still rather too early to draw firm conclusions about likely future patterns of care-giving and the more general role and status of older people. Cultural, economic and employment changes are likely to result in the gradual 'Westernization' of family life and patterns of care, especially in the better-off Asian communities, though it is also likely that some distinctly 'Asian' attitudes towards the care of older people — mirroring, perhaps, the distinctiveness of other minority ethnic groups' approach to care-giving, such as that of the Jewish community in Britain or the United States.

Thus the impact of a wave of international migration from Asia, which took place between 30 and 40 years ago, continues to influence the ageing of the migrant generation and the nature of the family life of those migrants' descendants. While this is but one of many different examples of the impact of migration, it reminds us of the significance of historical events and specific social changes in understanding the nature of ageing, and the need to temper wide-range, ahistorical theories about family life and care-giving with evidence of the migrant experience.

References

Ahmad, W.I.U. (1996) "Family obligations and social change among Asian communities", in Ahmad, W.I.U. and Atkin, K. (eds.) *'Race' and Community Care,* Buckingham, Open University Press, pp. 51–72.

Anwar, M. (1979) *The Myth of Return: Pakistanis in Britain,* London, Heinemann.

Bhachu, P. (1985) *Twice Migrants. East African Settlers in Britain,* London, Tavistock.

Blakemore, K. and Boneham, M. (1994) *Age, Race and Ethnicity,* Buckingham, Open University Press.

Cowgill, D. O. (1986) *Aging Around the World,* Belmont, Calif.,Wadsworth.

Cowgill, D.O. and Holmes, D. (eds.) *Aging and Modernization,* New York, Appleton-Century-Crofts.

Cumming, E. and Henry, W.E. (1961) *Growing Old: the Process of Disengagement,* New York, Basic Books.

Jones, T. (1993) *Britain's Ethnic Minorities,* London, Policy Studies Institute.

Lemmon, B.; Bengston, V. and Peterson, J. (1976) "An explanation of the activity theory of aging", in Bell, B. (ed.) *Contemporary Social Gerontology,* Springfield, Illinois, Charles Thomas.

Modood, T. (1991) "The Indian economic success: a challenge to some race relations assumptions", *Policy and Politics,* 19, 3: 177–89.

Office for National Statistics (ONS) (1996) *Social Trends,* London, HMSO.

Office for Population Censuses and Surveys (OPCS) (1992) *1991 Census, County Report: West Midlands (Part 1),* London, HMSO.

Peach, C. (1991) *The Caribbean in Europe,* Research Paper No.15, Centre for Research in Ethnic Relations, University of Warwick.

Phillipson, C. (1981) *Capitalism and the Construction of Old Age,* London, Macmillan.

Phillipson, C. and Walker, A. (eds.) (1986) *Ageing and Social Policy,* Aldershot, Gower.

Stopes-Roe, M. and Cochrane, R. (1990) *Citizens of this Country: the Asian-British,* Clevedon, Bristol, Multilingual Matters.

Werbner, P. (1989) *The Migration Process,* New York, Berg.

Chapter 7

The Value of Old Age in Modern Society: Social Responses to 'Elder Abuse'

Richard Hugman
Edith Cowan University

Introduction: Old Age in Human Society

Evidence for the diversity of human responses to the later stages of adult life is provided by a range of sources. Historical and anthropological material reveals an array of ways in which different cultures have dealt with old age and the changes within specific societies over time (de Beauvoir 1972; Silverman and Maxwell 1982; Minois 1989; Hazan 1994). In Europe, and in other western countries, there is a common view of ancient European society, whether of the north or the south, that a veneration of older people combined with gerontocracy (literally, rule by old men) to create a pattern of social relations and institutions in which elderly people were highly valued and powerful. This perspective purports that the devaluing of old age is a relatively recent phenomenon. However, as historians point out, this is a partial grasp of history (Laslett 1977; Quadagno 1982; Minois 1989). For example, there was a long period in classical Greece when elderly people were frequently ridiculed and excluded from public life: it was only under foreign influence that old age became less stigmatised (Minois 1989, pp. 75–6). The 'elders' who exercised authority in this time were 'senior' in a social sense rather than old chronologically. Similarly, in the northern Teutonic and Scandinavian cultures the older person was likely to be highly valued to the extent that he (or sometimes she) was a triumphant survivor against the odds, or even took risks more usually associated with the social roles of younger adulthood (Minois 1989, pp. 190–1). The old people who became infirm or lost their faculties were as much the object of pity or denigration as elsewhere. In the mediaeval period and more recently in rural communities, the hold of older people on property (and hence the lives of younger kin) was often resented (Quadagno 1982).

The cultural heritage of Europe, in this respect, has parallels with old age in other parts of the world. Silverman and Maxwell noted (1982, pp. 66–7) that in twenty of the ninety-six pre-industrial societies on which they reviewed evidence the socially sanctioned active killing of frail or infirm elderly people had been observed, while in more than half the remainder forms of passive neglect and low status were seen as normal and acceptable. In some cases such euthanasia took a festive of ceremonial form (Victor 1987; Hazan 1994). It appears that in some instances the older person might be expected to take part willingly in their own death, and some historical or anthropological evidence suggests that where this happened it was supported by powerful social norms in which the honour of acceptance was contrasted with the ignominy of resistance (de Beauvoir 1972). Indeed, Keith (1992, p. 16) notes that in many instances such euthanasia was consistent with the high status of old age, even supporting it, as the elderly person herself or himself would play an active role in decisions about being killed or abandoned. So, it may be concluded that such practices gave social support to older people *where they were able to make an appropriate contribution to the society.*

Europe, therefore, may share with much of the rest of the world a sense that traditionally old age might be highly regarded in certain prescribed circumstances, while in others it was regarded negatively. A common factor between such otherwise different cultures was the extent to which elderly people were perceived as a threat to the well-being of the society, for example by posing a burden to one where a high level of mobility was necessary for survival. This might be countered by the elderly person fulfilling a role which contributed to survival in a social sense, through the preservation of culture, the fulfilling of religious observance and other forms of authority (Victor 1987; Hazan 1994). In summary, therefore, it must be said that the diversity of the ways in which societies have responded to old age, and the value ascribed to elderly people, is to be understood by examining the inter-relationship between social structures, institutions, cultures and patterns of belief.

Two Forms of 'Value'

Two approaches have developed with contemporary social gerontology which offer competing explanations for the nature of elderly people's lives in (post-) industrial western society. The first of these may be termed the 'modernisation thesis' (Cowgill and Holmes 1972; Fischer 1978). In brief summary, this position argues that as societies industrialise and urbanise ('modernise') so the numbers of older people increase. This in turn leads to a decline in the 'scarcity value' of being old, which, along with other very rapid shift in social values and forms of knowledge, effectively makes the older person 'culturally redundant' with regard to the positive aspects of the value of old age.

The critiques of the modernisation theory together identify several serious weaknesses. Achenbaum and Stearns (1978, pp. 307–8) point to the ethnocentricity of some modernisation analysis. Although in social science terms it may be reasonable to equate 'modernisation' with 'westernisation', neither should be seen as synonymous with 'development'. The theory contained an implicit social evolutionism which assumed that all societies would follow a similar path as they developed. By challenging this, critics pointed to the possibility that 'modernist' patterns of old age would also themselves been seen as historically and culturally specific (Achenbaum and Stearns 1978; Gruman 1978).

In Europe, the critics of the 'modernisation' theory identified more clearly that the historical context is that of industrial *capitalism* (Walker 1981; Phillipson 1982; Guillemard 1983). The political economy approach which they developed argues that old age is a product of the social structures within which people live. Under industrial capitalism (and in other industrial societies) the reality of old age is defined by exclusion from the labour force. Later life comes to be seen as unproductive, a time at which people are regarded as no longer capable of making a 'useful' contribution to society, in which 'useful' is equated with paid employment. From this perspective it becomes clear that the apparent decline in the value of older people is not simply cultural, but has a strong economic component. Indeed, the 'age war' proponents, who argue that the cost of social welfare for elderly people is undermining the opportunities for younger cohorts to experience prosperity, typify older people as 'unproductive' and therefore a 'burden' which society cannot 'afford' (if others are to have the good life) (Callahan 1986). Although this type of argument has been criticised widely as a form of ageism (age related discrimination), as well as ignoring the active contribution older people make to society (for example through unpaid voluntary work), it has subtle parallels in social welfare policy in most western societies (Estes 1986; de Jouvenal 1988; Torres-Gil 1990). The justification for rethinking welfare systems throughout the western world is largely driven by a perception of rising costs that are attributed to the rapidly growing numbers of older people and their demographic proportion relative to other age groups (de Jouvenal 1988).

Where older people do have value it is likely to be as consumers (Fennell *et al.* 1988; McCallum 1993; Hugman 1994). In the public discourse of politicians, professionals, academics and the media, respect is shown towards older people as of inherent social value.

For different reasons, including war, political upheaval and economic recession, the cohort which forms the current generation of older people may still be seen as having 'made sacrifices' or 'struggled against the odds' and therefore as 'triumphant survivors' who should be respected for overcoming difficult life circumstances. Nevertheless, the older person who can afford to travel, to live in good housing and to eat well, in other words who has an adequate income, will have a greater social status than the older person who depends entirely on the state for a subsistence standard of living (Fennell *et al.* 1988). Elderly people are only valued when they are able to act independently as consumers of goods beyond the subsistence level. The emergence of 'grey power' thus does not reflect so much the social valuing of older people *per se*, but rather their spending and voting capacities. This situation then mirrors that discussed above, in rural agrarian or early industrial periods, in which such power might be viewed ambivalently by other social groups because of differences of interest.

Debates about the primacy of cultural or economic explanations for social structures and relations have characterised the social sciences through the twentieth century. In this area of social gerontology it is possible to become enmeshed in a version of these debates. For the purposes of this paper, however, I want to avoid the problems of polarised theorising. Rather, my concern here is to examine some aspects of the relationship between the cultural value and the economic value of elderly people. The commodification of both these facets of older people in industrial society is an important element in the lives older people live, even though life for those who are wealthy will be different from that of those who are poorer. 'Industrial' society is emphasised, rather than 'capitalist', because there is evidence that the process of industrialisation in other socio-economic systems is co-related to changing circumstances for elderly people that parallel those of the capitalist west (for example, in China or in India) (Chuanyi and Qin 1992; Fang *et al.* 1992; Gore 1992).[1] In such situations also the economic circumstances of older people will have an impact on their life-styles (although in China this might be the wealth of the local community rather than the individual or family). A central feature of the lives of older people in contemporary eastern societies is a devaluation which can be identified as an issue much as it is in western society.[2]

The significance of the social value of old age and older people for a discussion of 'elder abuse' is that the very widespread ambivalence about later life, and those people who have reached it, revealed in the literature is a key element in understanding the contemporary emergence of 'elder abuse' as a topic for public, political and professional concern. In the following sections of the paper the notion of value will be used to consider responses to 'elder abuse' and to examine the possibility that such responses might be more *social* in their focus.

The Emergence of 'Elder Abuse'

'Elder abuse' as a term appears to have developed from the work of Baker (1975), following which it has steadily gained a presence in the fields of health and social welfare as well as academic social gerontology. There is a degree of consensus concerning the meaning of the term to refer to the harm or neglect of an elderly person (Council of Europe 1992), yet there is also a substantial disagreement over what counts and what does not count as instances of 'abuse' (Hugman 1995). Although those who argue that the phenomenon does not exist at all are few in number, there is widespread variation in the extent to which 'elder abuse' is said to occur. Alongside this debate, there is also controversy over whether 'elder abuse' has recently increased in prevalence, if it has been occurring for a long time but only just come to the attention of professionals and academics (who are now more attuned to the issue, or less prejudicial towards the needs of elderly people), or even whether it has emerged as a product of professionals and academics creating new areas of expertise for themselves (Callahan 1988; Kosberg 1988; Leroux and Petrunik 1990; Kurrle *et al.* 1991).

Elsewhere (Hugman 1994, 1995) I have argued that all the available indicators point to the 'discovery' or 'emergence' of 'elder abuse' as a social issue or problem, rather than its rapid onset within advanced industrial societies. The historical evidence from European countries is that the ambivalence towards older people, which was noted above, was and is sometimes expressed in acts which are now being understood or defined as abusive. The perception of those older people who are dependent on others for aspects of ordinary daily living as a 'burden' is neither new or confined to western culture. So, it is not the occurrence of violence or neglect which is new, but the language utilised to define and respond to these events which has changed (cf. Hazan 1994). What is perhaps more remarkable is that at the same time as the issue of 'elder abuse' has entered the public domain so too there has been a resurgent legitimation in some respects of the view of elderly people as a 'burden', within social policy as well as at the common-place level. 'Elder abuse', it would seem, has become an issue at a time when the contradictions between the respect and the denigration of old age has become much sharper.

Contradictions of 'Elder Abuse' as an Issue

One of the reasons why it may appear that professionals have focused on 'elder abuse' for their own interests is that the health and social welfare professions, along with the societies of which they are a part, do not have a history of great concern for elderly service users. Indeed, specialising in work with older people may often be seen as a low-status branch of medicine, nursing, social work or remedial therapy (see, for example, Slevin 1991). Callahan's argument (1988) that we should beware of creating a band-wagon effect that promotes careers without helping service users is pertinent, at least to this extent. However, at the same time, the work of professionals in this area has established the 'fact' of violence or neglect towards elderly people who are dependent on others for some aspect of daily life. Arising from the same social forces as the shifts in public discourse about other forms of domestic violence, 'elder abuse' perhaps took longer to establish within the prevailing discourse precisely because of the widespread ambivalence towards older people. In this sense, it may be that the greater professionalisation of work in this field has benefited those dependent elderly people who are at risk of violence or neglect.

The contradictions contained within the greater awareness of and responsiveness to 'elder abuse' are to be seen in two respects. First, there is the realm of policy, in which the vulnerable elderly person at risk from 'abuse' is also the older member of society for whom current levels of services 'cannot' be sustained through the present arrangements. Second, the powerlessness of the 'abused' person emphasises their membership of the 'dependent' sub-group of older people, thus reinforcing their marginality. For both reasons, the social value ascribed to elderly people remains highly ambiguous, subject to a division of older people on grounds of socio-economic class, gender, race and ethnicity, disability and so on.

Demographic projections, showing growth in the numbers and proportions of older people in western societies are now the driving force of social policy (de Jouvenal 1988; Kaplan 1989; Australian Institute of Health and Welfare 1995). The reasons for this are partly that the costs of retirement pensions are paid by the current cohort of workers, and the falling birth rate is assumed to mean a declining pool of economically active citizens to provide for those who are retired. Partly, also, the need for health and social care rises markedly over the age of 75, and it is this age group in which the demographic growth is most rapid. The thrust of social policy in response has been to seek changes in the basis for the provision of health and welfare. The perceived greater wealth of many people among the older generations, and therefore their ability to pay directly for care services, has become the rationale for various forms of privatisation or quasi-market models of health and welfare. While such a process may enhance the value of those older people who have the economic capacity to be consumers of services it may devalue others precisely because it will emphasise their relative lack of access to resources. The latter are those people who, by definition, are most likely to need the public provision of these very services. Where such services are reduced, or more difficult to access, there is a probability that the additional pressure on family carers may result in an increase in the incidence of violence or neglect towards the older person (Phillipson 1993). The evidence is that situations where people do not have private resources to gain access to supportive services will be at greater risk of 'abuse' (although there are several other contributory factors, to which this discussion will return below) (Glendenning 1993).

There is also the second possibility, that those older people who are most at risk of 'abuse' will find their dependency emphasised by the very processes established to provide protection. They are likely to be those older people who are more marginalised within their communities and who are not often the most compelling for professionals. The reformulation of professional interest around the notion of 'abuse', because of its focus on incapacity, simultaneously may ensure that they receive appropriate assistance while reinforcing their membership of a marginalised and highly dependent social group. As the provision of care to adults, and hence dependence, in contemporary western culture does resonate with experiences of childhood, it is very difficult to avoid patterns of action and relationship which do not increase the powerlessness of the person receiving care (Hugman 1994; Biggs 1995).

It is in this context that the political and professional concern with 'abuse' must be understood. One outcome, evident in the USA and the UK, is that some professionals appear to take on a role in which 'elder abuse' becomes a campaigning issue. The politicians and policy makers, fellow professionals, and the wider public who question the existence or the extent of the problem (and who, in other words, suggest it is not a problem) become the objects of a concerted effort to generate concern and provide the basis for a social response to deal with 'abuse'. The widespread ambivalence about old age, older people and the idea of 'elder abuse' may appear to create a resistance to the idea that this is 'a problem' with the result that professionals who in their work see people who have been subject to violence or neglect think it necessary to become campaigning on behalf of others who are less powerful. Not to take such action would run counter to the ethics of most professions; some countries (or regions within countries) now have mandatory reporting.

For these reasons the main thrust of much of the discussion about 'elder abuse' has focused on the need to have workable definitions and good professional knowledge, supported by adequate policies and general awareness (Glendenning 1993). However, as Glendenning's comprehensive summary of available research demonstrates, not only is there continuing definitional uncertainty but also there is a tendency to focus on individual attributes, on symptoms and indicators, while paying less attention to the context of social policies and the social values they embody within which 'elder abuse' is perpetrated.

Privatising Values: The Definition of 'Elder Abuse'

There are three reasons why it might be expected that the risks faced by older people would be of common social concern:

1. western society, for the most part, is more wealthy than in previous periods, so that the use of wealth to support those who cannot *or are required* not to work is a political choice and not a matter of literal survival;
2. although the rapid increase in the number of older people means that old age has lost its scarcity value, it is more likely that most people will experience it, so that there is a greater sense of shared interest in how old age is valued;
3. the privatised nuclear family, so prevalent in industrial society, may have been part of the loss of status for older people, but at the same time can give new opportunities for older people to gain a sense of meaning by making a contribution, as well as continuing to form the basis for most direct care (Hugman 1994, pp. 76–7).

However, in most research and analysis of 'elder abuse', as well as most practical responses to instances in which 'abuse' is judged to have occurred, it is the individual characteristics of perpetrators and victims to which primary attention is given. The growing literature is focused around typologies of the predisposing factors identifiable among those who are involved in 'abusive' acts or relationships (Glendenning 1993). In part, this may be a consequence of the extent to which this field is led by health and social welfare professionals, who, after all, may reasonably wish to develop their knowledge in order to assist the individuals with whom they work.

Knowledge concerning individual older people and their carers who are involved in instances of 'abuse', and the skills which are based on it, undoubtedly is necessary for appropriate intervention. However, as a consequence of the focus on individual situations, the idea that 'elder abuse' is a private matter of personal values and behaviour may be reinforced. In the location of the issue in the private domestic sphere the acts and relationships which constitute 'abuse' are taken out of their social context and given the semblance of being set in a social and cultural vacuum. Yet however one chooses to interpret issues such as the moral responsibility of perpetrators, the value of old age or the motivations of health and social welfare professionals, it is clear that the 'problem' of 'elder abuse' has a social dimension. How these factors are addressed is related to the broader understanding of society which is brought to the question; that is, it has a theoretical and an ideological component.

First, as I have argued at some length above, negative images of old people are widespread in western industrial society. Where older people are abused by carers they do so within a culture which emphasises that youth, strength, health and independence are to be prized. Definitions of beauty, success and attraction to others frequently are defined in relation to these factors. Their opposites (age, frailty, illness and dependence) are seen as undesirable and by implication associated with ugliness, failure and rejection by others (cf. Covey 1989). Although few people would chose to be ill, it might be unavoidable, as might age, frailty or dependence, and these latter aspects of life are given meaning within social structures and cultures. In particular, ageing is normal in biological terms, but in western society increasingly is seen as pathological. We may subscribe to the aphorism, usually attributed to Samuel Johnson, that 'when I consider the alternative, I am pleased to be growing old', but around us are all the indicators that such a belief is unreasonable. 'Abuse' against older people in such circumstances has all the social and cultural supports that have been identified for other forms of domestic violence within patriarchy (Phillipson 1993).

Second, it must be asked if family carers commit violence or neglect, whether they were providing care in isolation. The contradiction of a growing concern with 'elder abuse' at the same time as social policy is being developed around the idea that older people are a 'burden' on the economy and the state has been discussed above. The practical implication of this contradiction is that it tends to over-emphasise private individual pathology as against a more careful analysis of the contribution of supportive services to older people who are dependent for daily needs on informal carers. Although most care is provided by families, who are willing to undertake the task, other aspects of society make this more difficult without support (Finch 1989; Graycar and Jamrozik 1989). Isolation and fatigue are common experiences of carers, to which public provision of community or institutional services is often the only alternative. Where such services are reduced *relative to the overall level of need* then the personal and the political meet in an increased risk that 'elder abuse' may occur.

Third, it is important to recognise that not all violence or neglect is age related. Clear and careful definition of the issue remains a crucial task (Glendenning 1993; Hugman 1995). There appears to be a tendency in some discussions of the issue to equate all violence toward or neglect of elderly people as 'abuse'. For example, some case examples of abusive situations appear to blur the distinction between those instances where violence or neglect occur as a consequence of frailty or infirmity in old age and those which are the continuation of life-long patterns of relationship (Pritchard 1992; Decalmer 1993). This is not to argue that such situations can be ignored, either by the professionals involved or the wider society, but that to typify them as 'elder abuse' may lead to further difficulties. At the value level it may be ageist, albeit unintentionally, because it further separates older people as a distinct social group by emphasising vulnerability and incapacity. At a practical level it can lead to professionals responding in prescriptive or stereotypical ways. Indeed, it may be more appropriate in some instances to understand some situations as criminal acts against an adult and to respond accordingly, even though this may be difficult for the elderly person (and so action may not be possible) (Leroux and Petrunik 1990; Kurrle *et al.* 1991; Hugman 1995).

Fourth, another outcome of an overly private domestic view of 'elder abuse' is that abusive formal care may be ignored. Increasingly this is coming to be recognised as an area to which attention must be paid (Pritchard 1992; Glendenning 1993). Again, there may be a tendency to understand such a situation in terms of the individuals involved, the 'bad apple' approach to what is a form of bad practice. To the extent that this is an appropriate response, then recourse to law might be the logical outcome. However, to characterise this as 'elder abuse', even though the older person might be using an age-related service, emphasises the *age* dimension when, were the victim younger, it would be said that a crime had been committed. Where the issue of 'elder abuse' might be relevant is in looking at the circumstances in which elderly people are provided with formal care services. They are often relatively low in status, with more limited training opportunities for staff than other health and social welfare services (and with fewer qualified professional staff) (Hugman 1995). The social context, in which the formal care of elderly people appears not to be highly valued, then staff too can feel vicariously devalued. Moreover, as members of the wider society even staff who choose to work with older people may have ageist attitudes which they bring to the workplace, and there are some people working in these services who are there because they have failed to get into a career path which they (and many others) regard as more prestigious. This is the social background to violence or neglect in formal care, which reflects the wider social value of old age and older people.

Interpretations of 'elder abuse' which focus only on the individual characteristics of perpetrators and victims, therefore, miss the important point that it occurs within a social and cultural context that may appear if not actually to legitimate 'abuse' then at least to provide a partial condoning through the ambivalence that permeates policies, organisations and wider attitudes. Both older people who require care and those who provide that care, whether informal or formal, are subject to the way in which the ageism endemic to western society underpins all aspects of old age.

Conclusion: Developing Social Responses

Recognising the social dimension to the phenomenon of 'elder abuse' leads to the conclusion that if it is to be dealt with then social responses must accompany the careful definition of risk factors in individual situations. This is not to argue that individual people do not have moral responsibility for their own actions, but to emphasise that unless the context is also addressed then intervention at the individual level will always be only a partial response. Two elements of the social context that have been identified in the preceding discussion are of particular importance. The first is the type and quantity of social supports provided to carers of dependent older people, the second is the general social and cultural background against which the lives of dependent older people and their carers live. Following from these elements it may be seen that a more precise definition of 'elder abuse' will assist in the provision of practical assistance and developing social policy.

Appropriate supports for dependent older people and their carers include a range of types of health and social welfare provision (Hugman 1994). The aspects of services which have been identified as important in this area are similar to those which relate to services for elderly people generally. They include services which support informal care rather than taking over (preventive rather than substitutionary wherever possible), involving elderly people and their carers in planning and decision making, giving elderly people and their carers choice and providing care with dignity (Jamieson 1991; Howe 1992; Hugman 1994).

At a wider level, social policies to deal with 'elder abuse' are in conflict with social policies that typify older people as a 'burden'. To respond fully to 'elder abuse' requires that this policy background is debated and the ageism implicit in policies being developed throughout western society challenged. Building a stronger professional base from which to assist dependent elderly people and their carers necessitates a commitment to valuing older people as part of society, irrespective of whether they have needs for care. Such an approach requires professionals to be involved in discussions around resources and the goals of policy. This is legitimate precisely because it is not possible (even were it desirable) to separate the 'political' from the 'professional' or the 'personal': all are part of the social fabric.

Following from these two key elements, it is necessary also for greater precision to be reached in the definition of 'elder abuse'. Two specific examples illustrate the importance of this. The first can be seen in the way that some analysis has characterised policies as 'abusive' because they are discriminatory. Certainly older people are discriminated against in various ways, but in addition to age-related disadvantage, there are also various ways in which the lives of older people are affected by other forms of oppression, including gender, race and disability (Walker 1987). The connections must be grasped for an effective policy analysis, and to emphasise the age-related component may be (unintentionally) unhelpful because it emphasises a social division which should be set in context.

The second area in which greater precision is required can be seen in the inclusion of all forms of inter-personal violence towards older people, for example in the intimidation or assault of older people by gangs of youths for the purpose of theft (Pritchard 1992, pp. 60–1). Such events may satisfy the criteria outlines by Kosberg (1988) of ageism (selecting older people because they are seen as acceptable targets) and threat (the personal risk of harm), but they separate elderly people as a social category in situations in which younger people might also find themselves. Ageism is perpetuated, even though again it is unintentional.

To overcome these terminological difficulties, it would seem that the idea of 'elder abuse' should be reserved for those situations in which Kosberg's criteria are satisfied and there is an 'obligation of care' between the perpetrator and the victim (Hugman 1995). This would support both the individualist clinical frameworks which have been successfully used in the field and at the same time provide a basis for engaging with social policy debates. Policies should be examined in terms of the extent to which they recognise and support the 'obligation of care' which exists in most caring relationships; those which weaken these obligations could then be challenged as creating the potential for 'elder abuse' to increase. Such precision would also permit the avoidance of the band-wagon effect against which Callahan (1988) warned.

The greatest challenge, however, is to undertake such tasks in a cultural and social environment in which old age and older people are regarded as of social value only to the extent to which they can be 'consumers'. Meeting this challenge is not only the task of dependent elderly people and their carers or professionals and academics. It is the responsibility of the society at large, through educational, religious, cultural and political institutions. This is a task to which all those who are concerned with the health and social welfare of our older fellow citizens must be committed if progress is to be made in more concrete and practical ways.

Notes

1 Chuanyui and Qin (1992, pp. 72–6) and Fang *et al.* (1992, p. 258) also point to the 'emergence' of 'elder abuse' by family in these circumstances. In addition, current analysis relates the growth of 'elder abuse' to the impact of the 'Cultural Revolution', thus placing it clearly in the realm of ideology as well as of political economy.

2 There is an irony, given the history of western anthropology, that some recent Asian studies propound the generalised view that families in the west do not care for their elderly members, even though the 'indigenous' research provides evidence that most care is provided directly by immediate close family members (cf. Fang *et al.* 1992, p. 253; Finch 1989, p. 84; Knipscheer 1992, p. 153). Similarly, Gore (1992, p. 262) quotes a large over-estimate of the proportions of older people living in institutions in the west (cf. Hugman 1994, p. 125).

References

Achenbaum, W. A. and Steams, P. N. (1978) "Old age and modernization", in *The Gerontologist*, 18: 307–12.

Australian Institute of Health and Welfare (1995) *Australia's Welfare 1995*. Canberra: Australian Government Publishing Service.

Baker, A. A. (1975) "Granny bashing", in *Modern Geriatrics*, 5: 20–4.

de Beauvoir, S. (1972) *Old Age*. Harmondsworth: Penguin.

Biggs, S. (1995) *Understanding Ageing*. Buckingham and Philadelphia: Open University Press.

Callahan, D. (1986) "Adequate health care and an ageing society", in *Daedalus*, 115: 247–67.

Callahan, J. J. (1988) "Elder abuse: some questions for policy makers", in *The Gerontologist*, 28: 453–8.

Chuanyi, Z. and Qin, X. (1992) "China: changes and problems", in J. I. Kosberg (ed.) *Family Care of the Elderly*. Newbury Park: Sage.

Council of Europe (1992) *Violence Against Elderly People*. Strasbourg: Council of Europe Press.

Covey, H. C. (1989) "Perceptions and attitudes toward sexuality of the elderly during the Middle Ages", in *The Gerontologist*, 29: 93–100.

Cowgill, D. O. and Holmes, L. D. (1972) "Summary and conclusions: the theory in review", in D. O. Cowgill and L. D. Holmes (eds.) *Aging and Modernization*. New York: Appleton-Century-Crofts.

Decalmer, P. (1993) "Clinical presentation" in P. Decalmer and F. Glendenning (eds.) *The Mistreatment of Elderly People*. London: Sage.

Estes, C. (1986) "The aging enterprise: in whose interests?", in *International Journal of Health Services*, 16: 243–51.

Fang, Y.; Chuanbin, W. and Yuhua, S. (1992) "Support of the elderly in China", in H. Kendig, A. Hashimoto and L. Coppard (eds.) *Family Support for the Elderly: The International Experience*. Oxford: Oxford University Press.

Fennell, G.; Phillipson, C. and Evers, H. (1988) *The Sociology of Old Age*. Milton Keynes: Open University Press.

Finch, J. (1989) *Family Obligations and Social Change*. Cambridge: Polity Press.

Fischer, D. H. (1978) *Growing Old in America*. New York: Oxford University Press.

Glendenning, F. (1993) "What is elder abuse and neglect?", in P. Decalmer and F. Glendenning (eds.) *The Mis-treatment of Elderly People*. London: Sage.

Gore, M. S. (1992) "Family support to elderly people: the Indian situation", in H. Kendig, A. Hashimoto and L. Coppard (eds.) *Family Support for the Elderly: The International Experience.* Oxford: Oxford University Press.

Gruman, G. J. (1978) "Cultural origins of present day 'age-ism': the modernization of the life-cycle", in S. F. Spicker, K. M. Woodward and D. D. van Tassel (eds.) *Aging and the Elderly: Humanistic Perspectives in Gerontology.* Atlantic Highlands, N. J.: Humanities Press.

Guillemard, A.-M. (1983) "The making of old age policy in France", in A.-M. Guillemard (ed.) *Old Age and the Welfare State.* London: Sage.

Hazan, H. (1994) *Old Age: Constructions and Deconstructions.* Cambridge: Cambridge University Press.

Howe, A. (1992) "Participation in policy making: the case of aged care", in H. Gardner (ed.) *Health Policy.* Melbourne: Churchill Livingstone.

Hugman, R. (1994) *Ageing and the Care of Older People in Europe.* Basingstoke: Macmillan.

Hugman, R. (1995) "The implications of the term 'elder abuse' for problem definition in health and social welfare", in *Journal of Social Policy,* 24: 493–507.

Jamieson, A. (1991) "Home-care in Europe: background and aims", in A. Jamieson (ed.) *Home Care for Older People in Europe: a Comparison of Policies and Practices.* Oxford: Oxford University Press.

de Jouvenal, H. (1988) *Europe's Ageing Population.* Paris and Guildford: Futuribles and Butterworths.

Kaplan, G. (1989) "Ageing in Australia", in R. Kennedy (ed.) *Australian Welfare.* Melbourne: Macmillan.

Keith, J. (1992) "Care-taking in cultural context: anthropological queries", in H. Kendig, A. Hashimoto and L. Coppard (eds.) *Family Support for the Elderly: The International Experience.* Oxford: Oxford University Press.

Knipscheer, K. C. P. M. (1992) "The Netherlands in European perspective", in H. Kendig, A. Hashimoto and L. Coppard (eds.) *Family Support for the Elderly: The International Experience.* Oxford: Oxford University Press.

Kosberg, J. I. (1988) "Preventing elder abuse", in *The Gerontologist,* 28: 43–50.

Kurrle, S. E., Sadler, P. M. and Cameron, I. D. (1991) "Elder abuse — an Australian case series", in *The Medical Journal of Australia,* 155: 150–3.

Laslett, P. (1977) *Family Life and Illicit Loves in Earlier Generations: Essays in Historical Sociology*. Cambridge: Cambridge University Press.

Leroux, T. G. and Petrunik, M. (1990) "The construction of elder abuse as a social problem: a Canadian perspective", in *International Journal of Health Services*, 20: 651–63.

McCallum, J. (1993) "Australia", in J. I. Kosberg (ed.) *International Handbook on Services for the Elderly*. Westport: Greenwood Press.

Minois, G. (1989) *The History of Old Age*. Cambridge: Polity Press.

Phillipson, C. (1981) *Capitalism and the Construction of Old Age*. London: Macmillan.

Phillipson, C. (1993) "Abuse of older people: sociological perspectives", in P. Decalmer and F. Glendenning (eds.) *The Mis-treatment of Elderly People*. London: Sage.

Pritchard, J. (1992) *The Abuse of Elderly People*. London: Jessica Kingsley Publishers.

Quadagno, J. (1982) *Ageing in Early Industrial Society*. New York: Academic Press.

Silverman, P. and Maxwell, R. J. (1982) "Cross-cultural variation in the status of old people", in P. N. Steams (ed.) *Old Age in Pre-Industrial Society*. New York: Holmes & Maier.

Slevin, 0. (1991) "Ageist attitudes among young adults: implications for a caring profession", in *Journal of Advanced Nursing*, 16: 1197–205.

Steinmetz, S. K. (1988) *Duty Bound. Elder Abuse and Family Care*. Beverley Hills: Sage.

Torres-Gil, F. (1990) "Seniors react to the Medical Catastrophe Bill: equity or selfishness?", in *Journal of Aging and Social Policy*, 2: 1–8.

Victor, C. (1987) *Old Age in Modern Society*. London: Chapman Hall.

Walker, A. (1981) "Towards a political economy of old age", in *Ageing & Society*, 1: 73–94.

Walker, A. (1987) "The poor relation: poverty among old women", in C. Glendinning and J. Millar (eds.) *Women and Poverty in Britain*. Brighton: Wheatsheaf.

Wolf, R. S. and Pillemer, K. A. (1989) *Helping Elderly Victims: The Reality of Elder Abuse*. New York: Columbia University Press.

PART TWO
The Eastern Perspectives

Chapter 8

The Social Psychological Perspective of Elderly Care

Ying-Yi Hong
The Hong Kong University of Science and Technology
and William T. Liu
East Asian Institute, National University of Singapore

Introduction

Because caregiving is a form of social interaction, it is subject to the same process of theoretical analysis as other types of dyadic interactions. Furthermore, the nature of such caregiving relationships can be a function of the caregiver's social role *vis-à-vis* the role of the recipients. For example, if care is rendered by professional health providers, the primacy of the relationship is focused on its functional specificity and affective neutrality. On the other hand, if care is given by a member of the primary family of the elderly, the relationship is expected to be marked by affective mutuality as in the case of spousal care, or lineal affection as in the case of an adult child being the caregiver. The relationship may be mixed and largely contingent upon idiosyncratic interpersonal chemistry if relatives, neighbors, and paid servants provide primary care. In such non-primary relationships, even if the caregiving may be functionally specific, there exists a range of caring relationships that transcend specific functional assistance. Furthermore, the onset of a state of impairment of the elderly invariably alters his/her spousal or filial relations. The processes of familial role relationship evolve around passage of time throughout the individual's life course and family life cycle.

In spite of the complexity of such dynamic relationships in the caregiving system, the dominant research paradigm has placed elderly care in the framework of a simple, unqualified Exchange Theory. First, we discuss how the exchange theory lies at the heart of the debate between the proponent and opposition of family as the primary care provider for the elderly. We discuss critically the basic assumptions Exchange Theory holds about caregiving relationships. Second, we argue that focusing on the perceptions and expectations between the elderly and caretaker may instead be more valuable in understanding the caregiving relationship. Research on "secondary baby talk" is a case in point. Third, we discuss how such an approach may provide insight into a range of culturally variant behaviors for family members caring for the elderly.

The Debate

Our first task is to narrow the range of a finite number of social ties between the caregiving dyad in order to limit the range of observable behaviors that are modified by the disabling condition of the elderly. The range of social ties include children taking care of their parents, spousal assistance, other relatives such as in-laws, siblings, and relatives beyond these close kindred, neighbors, and friends. In addition, there are professional caregivers who have no prior relationship with the elderly. The literature points to overwhelming evidence that care for the elderly by adult children and spouses is universal (Shanas, 1968). Furthermore, in the field of family studies, there is the established explanation for the universality of family care of its young, elderly, and infirm. Empirical evidence of the universal emphasis on care of the elderly by primary relatives is certainly important in that any exception, if ever one existed, should be carefully examined. In an epoch in which there is a considerable debate in every post-modern society on whose responsibility it is to provide major care for the fastest growing cohort of the aging population, one might ask what significance such a universal family caregiving tendency might have on social policy decisions. On the one hand, proponents of *family care* policy argue that inasmuch as elderly care by adult children is universal, the *prima facie* evidence of the necessity to use the family as the locus of elderly care is already demonstrated by the very absence of exceptions. On the other hand, opponents of the *family care* policy argue that there has not been sufficient time to confirm a universal tendency in human history since population aging as a world-wide phenomenon did not begin until only one generation or so earlier in the present century. Prior to the 1960s, transfer of elderly care from the family to community facilities was not necessary even in most developed countries. This argument implicitly suggests that the change of elderly care from family to community is expected to take hold after community facilities become widely available; but the change of elderly care sentiment may be delayed, to follow the famous Cultural Lag theory (Ogburn, 1922; Ogburn and Nimkoff, 1955).

The most convincing argument brought forth by opponents of family care policy came from two sets of writings. The first pertains to survey evidence indicating that in a number of developed countries, the elderly themselves preferred not to be cared for by their adult children, if possible, because of the extra burden they might inflict on their children (Ingersoll-Dayton & Antonucci, 1988; Kendig, 2000). Second, there is the argument, mixed with emotional and ideological overtones, that family care is really about unmarried middle-aged women caring for their elderly mothers (Brody *et al.*, 1984; Brody and Schoonover, 1986), and frequently requires the caregivers to alter their life situations, including career plans and life styles, in order to discharge their filial duties. In other words, the message suggests that family care would inflict an unwanted burden on adult children caregivers and that such a care burden is often heavily loaded on daughters rather than sons.

Yet, not preferring care by one's adult children seems incomprehensible in the context of the intergenerational caregiving role reversal. That is, the child who was cared for by the parents in turn takes care of the parents when they age and need to be cared for. Though obstacles to family care of the elderly have been discussed, including the financial burden of the middle generation which must bear the cost of elderly care and care of their own children, the underlying rationale seems to center around the fact that prolonged care for one's elderly parents requires personal sacrifice that is not consistent with the values of individualism and pursuit of personal happiness and goals. A more concrete explanation — one which can be empirically tested directly — lies in the center of a well-known and often-quoted *Exchange Theory.*

Exchange Theory

Social exchange theories (Blau, 1964; Burgess & Huston, 1979; Emmerson, 1990; Kelley & Thibaut, 1978) have been employed widely as a theoretical framework to guide research on family care for the elderly (e.g., Walker & Allen, 1991; Shi, 1993; Brackbill & Kitch, 1991). The social exchange perspectives assume that people keep track, though not literally, of the costs and benefits involved in a relationship. Although people may not explicitly or consciously calculate costs and benefits, they may be aware of them in the long term. In general, people strive to maximize benefits and minimize costs in relationships with others (Thibaut & Kelley, 1959).

When applying the social exchange framework to caregiving of the elderly, the focus has been on the costs incurred on the caregiver. Significant costs to adult child caregivers include emotional costs, such as feeling of burden and frustration (e.g., Abel, 1986; Archbold, 1983), financial costs (e.g., Archbold, 1983), and costs due to changes caregivers have had to make in their lives (e.g., Archbold, 1983; Montgometry, Gonyea & Hooyman, 1985). There are, however, a few exceptions who reported no such care burden (Matthew, 1985; Shi, 1993; Stueve, 1982). However, seldom did researchers pay attention to the potential rewards to caregivers provided by the elderly except a sense of the elderly appreciation of their assistance. On this issue, Walker and Allen criticized seemingly unbalanced views by saying that "such a restricted perspective exaggerates the strain of caregiving and understates the contributions that elderly family members make in their relationships with their children..."(Walker & Allen, 1991:389).[1] A major flaw of the social exchange theory, we submit, is that the exchange theorists postulate that cost to benefit ratio is the *unqualified key factor* in determining the satisfaction outcome of a relationship. That is, the costs paid by a caregiver would probably cause dissatisfaction and emotional distress (e.g., see Ingersoll-Dayton and Antonucci, 1988). Most fundamentally, the social exchange theory fails to distinguish between affective and instrumental aspects of social relationship, and thus ignores the communal nature of the primary group in family caregiving.

Based on research reports thus far available to us, we wish to point out that the social exchange model in the case of elderly care relationships must be modified in two major areas. First, we contend that these models often focus on costs and benefit calculations and neglect the fact that *in communal relationships, which are characteristic of close-kin relationships, motivation to meet the needs of the other partner exceeds the desire to weigh costs against benefits.*

Second, we wish to suggest that the modification of equal exchange of mutual benefits can vary considerably from one culture to another. In other words, we propose that *culture* can shape the norm that applies to certain dyads more stringently than other dyads in the same social system relative to the rules of reciprocity. In general, we submit that *the more equal the perceived status between the dyad, the greater the expectation of the norm of reciprocity that can be applied to the relationship.* For example, the relationship between two friends is normally considered to be on equal terms with respect to social status. It is then not surprising that in their usual social interchange, the norm or reciprocity is applied over time, if not immediately. However, the relationship between an adult and a child is not based on equal status; the adult is viewed as being more capable of doing things and commands more social resources. It is then expected that not all that an adult does for the child can be equally repaid by the child until the latter is able to command resources equivalent to what is to be reciprocated.

Reciprocity of Dependency and Caring

Earlier writers on the theoretical importance of reciprocity in social relations can be attributed to Malinowski in anthropology (1999), Goulder in sociology (1960), and Walster in psychology (Walster, Walster & Berscheld, 1978). More specifically focused on the reciprocity of help in recent years have been Fisher & Nadler (1976), DePaul & Fisher (1980), Greenberg & Shapiro (1971), Keith & Schafer (1985), Kessler, McLeod & Wethington (1985), and Rook (1987), to mention a few. In a capsule, these authors argue that people feel obligated to help someone whom they have received help from. However, it should be noted that this seminal theoretical work has been done on friendship patterns and network of social support studies. In these studies, largely centered around friendship, the relationship is supposed to be equal, non-obligatory, and even transitory. Friendship ties last when the relationship is mutually beneficial. It ceases when one partner of the dyad feels exploited and taken for granted. In contrast, kinship relations can best be described as a network of responsibilities and obligations; and the gradations of kin-obligations are culturally determined. Thus, extrapolating from helping patterns found among peers to those among kins may overlook differences in role obligations. The claim that the elderly would not wish to ask for help from their children because of their inability to reciprocate is perhaps in need of further clarification against cultural norms.

Culture, Communal Cohesion and Exchange Theory

The second issue we raise concerns the norm of reciprocity among the unequal. Caregivers' concern for the needs and welfare of care receivers may be especially characteristics of intergenerational caregiving in most Asian cultures where lineal relations take precedence over collateral relations as in Anglo-American cultures. Kluckholm and Strodtbeck (1960) showed that in all cultures, value orientations can be distinguished in a number of dimensions, including *time* and *relational values*. Briefly stated, people in different cultures are differentially oriented towards the past, present or future. In relational values, people in one culture may endorse *lineality*, according to which decisions are handed down from elders to young members of the group, whereas other people may choose to make decisions by majority preference (democracy), or by total consensus (collatorality). In cultures where lineality is the priority, obedience to parents continues to hold even when the son is an adult as is emphasized in the *virtue of filial piety* under Confucianism. Age, then, in this case, as a *variable*, has no particular bearing on relation, a *constant*. Anthropologist Hsu (1971), although approaching the issue from a quite different perspective, reached a similar conclusion. Specifically, he argued that in any society, there is one dominant dyad over other seven dyadic relations in the primary family. In China and Japan (presumably all Confucian societies) the dominant dyad is the father-son relation, and in India, it is the mother-son dyad (Hsu, 1971: Chapter 1). In contrast, the dominant dyad in Anglo-American culture is the husband-wife dyad. The characteristics of the dominant dyad tend to shadow other dyadic relations. The father-son dyad emphasizes asexuality, volition, discontinuation, and exclusiveness in relationship. Taken together, these theoretical postulates support our contention that cultural values can greatly alter the specific manner in which one takes care of one's parent at any age. Inasmuch as filial piety is deemed core familial norm, caring for one's parents in times of need is considered only one aspect of filial relations. This view contrasts sharply and fundamentally with the notion of inequality exchange in caring for elderly as espoused in the social exchange theory.

In addition to specific areas of cultural value orientation, the communal and urban impersonal cultures may also be used to show contrast with the best-fit meaning of elderly care. On the one hand, the *gemainschaft* described by Tonnies (1855–1936) as *communal* is characterized by a high degree of within-group cohesion resulting from mutual identification of purpose and history among members of primary groups. On the other hand, the exchange of interests and benefits described by Tonnies as *gesellschaft*, or associational relationship, often occur among people bonded only through specific purpose rather than through common kinship or primary group ties. Similar distinctions have been proposed by psychologists when attributes of relationship in exchange are described. Clark and Mills (1979), as psychologists, distinguish between exchange and communal relationships in exchange encounters. They argue that, although exchange processes operate in both types of relationships, the rules governing the giving and receiving of benefits differ significantly. Exchange relationships occur most often with stranger or casual acquaintances in business transactions and professional-client relations. To the extent that the family caring relationship is best described as a caregiving relationship within the context of the family, the attributes of such a dyad relationship are expected to vary from one culture to another. In societies where intergenerational dependency throughout the course of life is valued, younger kin often volunteer their services as an affective gesture and an act of filial piety even though the elderly are entirely capable of doing such chores independently, a situation we called *socially desired dependency* or SDD. SDD tends to increase cohesion and provide mutual satisfaction and interdependency. Viewed from this perspective, we submit that *differential expectations shaped by cultural norms might be the key to the dynamics of the caregiving relationship.*

An Alternative Approach: The Role of Expectations

Based on the paradigm of lineal relationships between the caregivers and the elderly, we have argued that equity of exchange is neither a requisite for satisfactory caregiving, nor does it necessarily produce caregiving as a burden even if it failed to measure up to an equitable exchange of benefits. Consequently, costs and benefits should not be useful constructs in understanding the caregiving relationship. What are the alternative constructs? We submit that expectations and perceptions may play important roles in caregiving relationships. Research on "secondary baby talk" is a case in point.

Secondary Baby Talk

Sociolinguists have shown that people define a caring relationship frequently through their displays of verbal expressions and the use of languages and signs. That is to say, the verbal discourse between the caregiving dyad may serve as a window through which the meaning of caregiving can be examined.

One common speech pattern observed is that the caregivers simplify their speech when talking to the elderly. Asburn and Gordon (1981) reported that, in comparison to speech patterns with peers, utterances to the elderly tend to be shorter, less complete, and containing more imperatives, interrogatives, and repetitions, and indication that caregivers often associate physical impairment with the loss of cognitive comprehension. Similarly, Caporeal and her associates (Caporeal, 1981; Caporeal, Lukaszewski & Culbertson, 1983) show that caregivers and adult speakers modify their speech when talking to the elderly. More importantly, they found a sizable proportion of utterances addressed to institutionalized elderly have the prosodic features of high and variable pitch. Both the morphemes and paralinguistic features of the modified speech were found to be similar to those of speech directed to young children (Ashburn & Gordon, 1981; Caporeal, 1981). Caporeal and her associates thus described such speech patterns as "secondary baby talk" (Caporeal *et al.*, 1983).

The use of secondary baby talk is reported to be most frequent when caregivers think that the elderly are mentally inept. Specifically, Caporeal *et al.* (1983) found a significant association between the caregiver's expectations of impairment and the likelihood of using secondary baby talk when speaking to the elderly. Caregivers with low expectations of the elderly's functioning were more likely to believe that baby talk would increase communicative efficiency and that "baby talk" would also be preferred by the elderly relative. Yet, secondary baby talk is not used exclusively with the mentally impaired elderly. It is also widely used to address institutionalized elderly, regardless of their mental status. This evidence suggests that secondary baby talk may indicate something more than the perception of communicative difficulties with cognitively impaired elderly (Tamir, 1979). It is also likely that by using secondary baby talk the caregiver attempts to restructure status relations and to reduce the level of the elderly to that of a small child, similar to nurses in a hospital ward addressing a patient needing help.

Ashburn and Gordon (1981) examined structured relationship by comparing the speech patterns of paid caregiving staff at a rest home and those of volunteers who visited the elderly frequently. They found that staff-caregivers displayed a speech pattern similar to baby talk when communicating with the elderly, but that volunteers did not. They concluded that the differential use of language reflected the different roles of the two groups of individuals. Only the caregivers who took the role as persons in charge of other persons professionally would employ the secondary baby talk speech pattern. These "differences between the speech of the staff member group and the volunteer group suggest that not just attributes of the addressee elicit modified speech. Instead, speaker and addressee attributes, as well as the function of the interchange, combine with the relationship of the speaker and addressee to account for the modifications made by the speaker" (Ashburn & Gordon, 1981:28). We interpret these findings to indicate that the caregiving relationship is a modified adult relationship in which an equal status protocol has been made unequal in order to change the care receiver's status to that of a helpless child.

How would the elderly respond to secondary baby talk? Research has shown mixed responses. Some elderly perceived the secondary baby talk as demonstrating affection and nurturance, yet others felt that this speech accommodation was unnecessary, if not insulting. Henwood and Giles (1985, as reported in Ryan, Giles, Bartolucci & Henwood, 1986) interviewed 33 elderly community women (aged 65–94 years) who lived alone in England while using Home Care Assistance. They found that secondary baby talk was used quite frequently when the Home Care Assistants talked to the elderly women. More than one-half of the elderly women responded favorably, feeling that the secondary baby talk signaled affection, warmth, nurturance and liking. Yet about 40% claimed that they had been the recipients of what they felt to be demeaning talk. The same authors reported in a separate and large sample of upper working class elderly people who did not require Home Help Assistance that more than 50% felt that baby talk was demeaning.

One clear indication as to whether an elderly person would respond positively to secondary baby talk depends on the elderly's mental functioning level. Specifically, Caporael, *et al.* (1983) found that elderly people who were functioning at a lower level and who needed a significant amount of attention in their day-to-day living responded positively to secondary baby talk. Perhaps the use of secondary baby talk was perceived by the elderly as communicating reassurance and nurturance. For the elderly at a higher level of functioning, normal patterns of speech were more likely to be preferred. To these elderly, secondary baby talk could mean they were perceived as being in need of personal care beneath their functional status. More generally, it appears that "whether baby talk communicates pejorative or nurturant affect is in the ear of the target and not just any listener" (Caporael *et al.*, 1983:752).

Caregivers with lower expectations for the elderly also tended to view secondary baby talk more positively than do those with higher expectations. Similarly, the elderly with poorer functional status enjoy secondary baby talk more than do those with greater functional ability. These findings suggest that the dynamics of the caring relationship could be an interaction of the caregiver's expectations and the care-receiver's attributes.

Social Consequences of Secondary Baby Talk

The significance of our proposed framework with respect to the caregiving relationship lies in the social consequences that the expectations may render. Consider secondary baby talk as an illustration. Using secondary baby talk may communicate to the elderly that they are not competent in understanding sophisticated speech. This recurrent experience of demeaning speech in face-to-face interaction may then lead to a belief that old age is a time of dependence and sharply declining abilities. To the extent that these beliefs about old age are used to form the bases of self-definitions, elderly people may behave in ways that fulfill the expectations of the caregivers (Robing and Langer, 1980; McPherson, 1983). As such, low expectations which are originally formed by the caregivers could be communicated to the elderly through interactions which in turn affects the elderly's self-concepts. Inasmuch as the elderly's self-concepts affect his/her behavior, the caregiver's low expectations can easily be self-fulfilling (see Synder, 1981).

In language accommodation research, communication breakdown is predicted to occur when the elderly reject the low expectations that the caregivers communicate to them through secondary baby talk. This again suggests that the elderly are motivated to maintain autonomy and independence. Being talked to in a way that implies dependence is detrimental to the elderly's self-esteem. Lowered self-esteem would then lead to withdrawal and helplessness. Indeed, Brackbill and Kitch (1991) reported that one of the major dilemmas American elderly faced is that, on the one hand, they want to be cared for by their children. On the other hand, they are afraid that this would be perceived as being dependent, which is not socially desirable.

A contrasting picture, however, is revealed in Chinese culture. Lui *et al.* (in preparation) interviewed caregivers and elderly in Shanghai and Hong Kong. Findings from both studies consistently revealed that the elderly expected their adult children to take care of them if they needed to be cared for, such as when they were ill. More importantly, elderly parents reported that they would feel proud if they have offspring who would take care of them. In contrast to the elderly in

Anglo-American societies, the elderly in Chinese culture would gain social approval and social status through being dependent on their adult offspring. As a result, the elderly in Chinese culture in general accept, if not anticipate, becoming dependent on their offspring. Data collected in Shanghai and Hong Kong did not suggest that the Chinese community elderly have the same kind of dilemma which their American counterparts face. They do not need to strike a balance between obtaining assistance when needed on the one hand and avoiding being viewed as losing their autonomy on the other.

Cultural Variant Expectations

Filial responsibility originates from Confucianism, which prescribed conduct in basic familial relationships. Accordingly, filial piety clearly spelled out the proper way that sons and daughters should relate to their parents, a relational norm not subject to negotiation. On the contrary, the rationale for the social exchange principle lies in the interpretation of a fair exchange principle, the latter of which can only be assessed subjectively. Filial piety is thus not an act of reciprocity for the care and love offered by the parents. As an ideal norm, it is motivated by genuine care and love for the parents.

Filial responsibility has created a standard for younger generations in relating to the elderly. Younger generations are expected to provide the bases for dependence. Problems would arise if the adult children are not able to provide support or assistance for elderly parents. Because filial responsibility is prescribed by the Chinese culture as a moral obligation, adult children, especially sons, are vulnerable to shame and guilt feelings if they do not carry out their filial duty as expected. Indeed, the guilt ridden behaviors resulting from omission of filial duties have been well reported by Vogel (1962) and DeVos (1973) when they studied mental illness and child-rearing behavior in Japan some three decades ago.

Similarly, elderly parents could feel frustrated and even depressed when they perceived their children falling short of the filial duty they expect them to fulfill. This could then create tension in intergenerational relations as it is reported by Hu and Chou (this volume) in the tension-ridden relationships between elderly Taiwan women and their daughters-in-law.

Conclusions

In caregiving literature, we noted that a promising, though perhaps theoretically questionable, approach came from the social exchange tradition in which the concept of equality of reciprocal benefits was deemed important in such a relationship. We argued that the simple, unqualified exchange theory is inadequate in explaining family caregiving relationship. Specifically, we submit that the family caring relationship is a kind of communal relation, in which meeting the needs of the care receivers takes precedence over reducing the costs and maximizing the equity of benefits. Furthermore, we further posited that culture may shape the norms of exchange and provide symbolic meaning of care and its social consequences. As a result, a family caregiving relationship had different meaning in different cultures. Despite this, the roles of the perceptions and expectations of the adult child caregivers and the elderly care recipients are the psychological mechanisms through which the meaning of such a relationship is shared by the caregiving dyad.

In the absence of direct testing of our assumptions, we employed results from studies on language accommodation. The use of baby talk, for example, provides a usable indicator of the care-provider's evaluation of the elderly's declining mental abilities. We assumed that what a caregiver thinks an elderly person is able to manage in his or her daily life, such as the activities stated in the Activities of Daily Living, could set up some behavioral expectations for the elderly. These expectations could differ from the elderly person's own assessment of his/her capabilities. These differential expectations may have significant effects on the caregiving relationship. If the caregivers' expectation of elderly functioning is lower than the elderly person's own expectation, caregivers may offer more assistance than the elderly person needs. This might not create a feeling of resentment in the elderly person in Chinese culture because assistance from younger generations is often interpreted as an act of affective respect. In contrast, if the elderly's expectation of their own functioning is lower than that of the caregiver's, they may demand assistance such that the caregiver may think it is not justified and exploitative. We are led to believe that the mismatch between expectation and reality is the source of frustration and care burden on the part of the caregiver, and of elderly abuse and/or neglect on the part of the needy elderly. More direct empirical confirmation of these assumptions is needed.

In summary, the present chapter is an attempt to modify the social exchange theory to better explain the family caregiving relationship. The dynamics involved in such relationships may be related systematically to the expectations and perceptions between the caregiving dyad.

Note

1 There is a general misconception that the elderly, being economically inactive, can provide relatively little in return for being cared for by their younger family members. Empirical evidence suggest that such an assumption has no factual foundation. In fact, a recently published account in Japan suggested that, like the People's Republic of China, the opposite is true, namely, the older generation commands more material goods than younger members of the family.

References

Abel, E. K. (1986) "Adult daughters and care for the elderly", *Feminist Studies*, 12: 479–497.

Archbold, P. G. (1983) "Impact of parent-caring on women", *Family Relations*, 32: 39–45.

Ashburn, G. & Gordon, A. (1981) "Features of a simplified register in speech to elderly conversationalists", *International Journal of Psycholinguistics*, 8: 7–31.

Blau, P.M. (1964). *Exchange and Power in Social Life*. New York: Wiley.

Brackbill, Y. & Kitch, D. (1991) "Intergenerational relationships: A social exchange perspective on joint living arrangements among the elderly and their relatives", *Journal of Aging Studies*, 5: 77–97.

Brody, E. *et al.* "What Should Adult Children Do for Elderly Parents" *Journal of Gerontology*, 39 (6): 736–746.

Brody, E. and C. Schoonover (1986) "Patterns of parent-care when adult daughters work and when they don't", *The Gerontologist* 26(4): 372–381.

Brody, E. M. (1981) "Women in the middle and family help to older people", *The Gerontologist*, 21: 471–480.

Burgess, R. L. & Huston, T. L. (eds.) (1979) *Social Exchange in Developing Relationships*. New York: Academic Press.

Caporeal, L. R. (1981) "The paralanguage of caregiving: Baby talk to the institutionalized aged", *Journal of Personality and Social Psychology*, 40: 876–884.

Caporeal, L. R.; Lukaszewski, M. P. & Culbertson, G. H. (1983) "Secondary baby talk: Judgments by institutionized elderly and their caregivers", *Journal of Personality and Social Psychology*, 44: 746–754.

Clark, M.S. & Mills, J. (1979) "Interpersonal attraction in exchange and communal relations", *Journal of Personality and Social Psychology*, 37: 12–24.

DePaulo, B. M. & Fisher, J. D. (1980) "The Cost of Asking for Help", *Basic and Applied Social Psychology*, 1: 23–35.

DeVos, G. A. (1973) *Socialization for Achievement*. Berkeley, University of California Press.

Emmerson, R. M. (1990) "Social exchange theory", in M. Rosenberg & R. H. Turner (eds.), *Social Psychology: Sociological Perspectives*. New Brunswick: Transaction Publisher.

Fisher, J. D. & Nadler, A. (1976) "Effect of Donor Resources on Recipient Self-esteem and Self-help", *Journal of Experimental Social Psychology*, 12: 139–150.

Gouldner, A. W. (1960) "The Norm of Reciprocity: A Preliminary Statement", *American Sociological Review*, 25: 161–178.

Greenberg, M. S. & Shapiro, S. P. (1971) "Indebtedness: An Adverse Apect of Asking for and Receiving Help", *Sociometry*, 34: 290–301.

Henwood, K. & Giles, H. (1985) *An Investigation of the relationship between stereotypes of the elderly and interpersonal communication between young and old.* Final report to the Nuffield Foundation, London.

Hsu, F. L. K. (1971) *Kinship and Culture.* Chicago: Aldine.

Hu Yow-Hwey & Chou Yah-Jong (2000) "The Cultural Politics of the Asian Faculty Care Model: Missing Language and Facts" (in this volume).

Ingersoll-Dayton, B. & Antonucci, T. C. (1988) "Reciprocal and nonreciprocal social support: Contrasting sides of intimate relationships", *Journal of Gerontology: Social Sciences*, 43: 568–573.

Keith, P. M. & Schafer, R. B. (1985) "Equity, Role Strains, and Depression Among Middle-Aged and Older Men and Women", pp. 37–49, in W. A. Peterson and J. Quedagno, *Social Bonds in Later Life.* Beverly Hills: Sage.

Kelley, H. H. & Thibaut, J. W. (1978) *Interpersonal Relations: A Theory of Interdependence.* New York: Wiley-Interscience.

Kendig (2000) "Family Change and Family Bonding in Australia" (in this volume).

Kessler, R. C.; McLeod, J. D. & Wethington, E. (1985) "The Costs of Caring: A Perspective on the Relationship between Sex and Psychological Distress", pp. 491–506, in I. G. Sarason and B. R. Sarason (eds.), *Social Support: Theory, Research and Application.* The Netherlands: Martinus Nijhoff, Dordrecht.

Kluckholm & Strodtbeck (1960) "Variations of Value Orientation". New York: Van Nostrand.

Liu, W. T. (in preparation) "Notes on thirty intensive elderly interviews in Shanghai" (unpublished material, 1996).

Malinowski, Bronislaw (1999) "On Phatic Communion", in Adam Jaworski and Nikolas Coupland (eds.), *The Discourse Reader.* New York: Routledge.

Matthews, S. H. (1985) "The burdens of parent care: A critical evaluation of recent findings", *Journal of Aging Studies*, 2: 157–165.

McPherson, B. D. (1983) *Aging As a Social Process.* Toronto: Butterworth.

Montgomery, R. J. V.; Gonyea, J. G. & Hooyman, N. R. (1985). "Caregiving and the experience of subjective and objective burden", *Family Relations*, 34: 19–26.

Ogburn, William F. (1922) *Social Change*, New York,

Ogburn, William F. and M.F. Nimkoff (1955) *Technology and Family Change.* Boston: Houghton Mifflin.

Rodin, J. & Langer, E.J. (1980) "Aging labels: The decline of control and the fall of self-esteem", *Journal of Social Issues*, 36: 12–29.

Rook, K. S. (1987) "Reciprocity of Social Exchange and Social Satisfaction Among Older Women", *Journal of Personality and Social Psychology*, 52: 145–154.

Ryan, E. B.; Giles, H.; Bartolucci, G. & Henwood, K. (1986) "Psycholinguistic and social psychological components of communication by and with the elderly", *Language & Communication*, 6: 1–24.

Shanas E., P. Towsend *et al.* (1968) *Old People in Three Industrial Societies.* London: Routledge & Kegan Paul.

Shi, L. (1993) "Family financial and household support exchange between generations: A survey of Chinese rural elderly", *The Gerontologist*, 33: 468–480.

Stueve, A. (1982). "The elderly as network members", *Marriage and Family Review*, 5: 59–87.

Synder, M. (1981). "On the self-perpetuating nature of social stereotypes", in D. Hamilton (ed.), *Cognitive processes in stereotyping and intergroup behavior.* Hillsdale, N.J.: Erlbaum.

Tamir, L. M. (1979) "The older person's communication needs: The perspective of developmental psychology", in Dunkie, R. E., Haug, M. R. and Rosenberg, M. (eds.), *Communications Technology and the Elderly.* New York: Springer.

Thibaut, J. W. & Kelley, H. H. (1959) *The Social Psychology of Groups.* New York: Wiley.

Vogel, E. (1962) "From Friendship to Comradeship", *China Quarterly.*

Walker, A. J. & Allen, K. R. (1991) "Relationships between caregiving daughters and their elderly mothers", *The Gerontologist,* 31: 389–396.

Walster, E.; Walster, G. W. & Berscheld, E. (1978) *Equity: Theory and Research.* Boston: Allen and Bacon.

Chapter 9

Values and Caregiving Burden: The Significance of Filial Piety in Elder Care

William T. Liu
East Asian Institute, National University of Singapore

Problems of Explaining Caregiving Burden

There is a general consensus that the modern nuclear family is incapable of taking care of an ever-growing number of elders in the future. It is on the basis of such consensus that prompted social welfare professionals and academic researchers to suggest that the government, or the community should lend greater assistance to take care of the old and frail. The role of the government in elder care has already been well accepted in Western European countries. In East Asia, however, the government takes a limited responsibility, leaving the family to bear much of the burden.

The European model has been supported by the concept of the welfare state, where entitlement to care at old age is an individual right, a social value which is deeply embedded in individualism. It is, for example, not fair for other members of the primary family to sacrifice in order to take care of an older relative. Related to this line of thinking, there are several propositions that support the consensus of researchers in the West. First, there is a general agreement that women bear a heavier burden than men as caregivers. This is so because the traditional domestic role dictates that caring of the young and the infirmed are accepted responsibilities of women worldwide. Second, there is the demographic fact that women live longer than men. If spousal elder care is the most common and valued caring relationship, who is going to take care of the growing number of widows after their husband had left them? This situation leads to the next proposition, which states that if the widow depends on her grown children to provide the care, the literature also points to the fact that the typical intergeneration elder care rests mainly on the daughter, who is most likely middle-aged. If married, she has an extra burden of taking care of both her own children and her aged parent(s). If unmarried, the situation fits well what has been written about the middle-aged unmarried daughter, who has to sacrifice her own life and plans in order to assume the caregiving responsibilities. Because of these important gender differences in an aging society, most studies on the burden of caregiving focused mainly among women caregivers.

However, there remain some unanswered questions about the "extra" burden felt by women presumably compared with men as caregivers. There are additional questions about the causes, if not etiologies, of caregiving burden. Furthermore, a related assumption that suggested the caregiving relationship is a function of the balance between cost and benefit. When the cost is too great and benefit too little, frustrations and burden would result in caregiving relationships. Both propositions on extra "women burden" and on "balance sheet" of the exchange theory applied to the caregiving relationship may deserve further examination, if only in the context of cross-cultural comparisons.

With respect to the extra burden reported by women, for example, we need to find out if it is because women normally are given, or assuming, more care chores than men? Is there a commonly accepted division of labour in caregiving that is linked to the gender of caregiving as well as to the division of domestic labour? This is apparently a legitimate question, since division of labour is shaped by norms of social institutions. A second important question: is it possible that women in general are more emotionally committed to the caring relationships than men? This question could be biological, hormonal, or socio-cultural in nature, or both. If that is the case, deeper emotional attachment could bring about higher degrees of stresses and strains in the context of caregiving. We also need to know if emotional attachment, rather than gender, is the precursor of emotional burden regardless of the objective assessment of the duties of caregiving (for example, number of hours given to caregiving chores, and the nature of such chores, and the like). Conversely, it is not at all clear whether men in general are more emotionally detached from such relationships, and if so, can this assumption stand the test cross-culturally? Does the nature of social ties and specific kin-relations help to explain the varying degrees of caregiving burden? Would adult children have higher caregiving burden than neighbours as caregivers simply because of a greater emotional commitment to the elder on the part of elder children and a more detached tie in the case of the neighbour? Would children experience greater burden in caregiving than a spouse, because married couples share common life styles and because of closer age gaps? Can it be the other way around because spouse care burden is largely determined by prior patterns of conjugal relationship? Would caregivers for cognitively demented patient in general experience higher burden in caregiving than those who provide care to physically dependent but mentally alert elders?

In order to answer these questions, we need to set forth some fundamental sociological and psychological principles about human societies. We need to assume that caregiving relationship is a specific form of social interaction. In the context of care, the attributes of social interaction ranges from functional specific interchange of duties and expectations, to rather diffused and affective gestures, which convey positive and supportive messages. The whole process should be objectively tested and coded for comparative analysis on both the form and content, and on different kinds of caregiving tasks. Psychology is the major discipline wherein micro-processes of inter-personal encounters are observed, analysed, and interpreted. A cursory survey showed that the (psychological) literature has paid surprisingly little attention to the problem of caregiving as a type of inter-personal relations (for an extended discussion, see Hong and Liu, 1999, in this volume).

Caregiving as a Commodity in the Context of Exchange Theory

A second type of writing pertains to the theory of social change. It is accepted that industrialisation requires standardisation, and the use of technology requires that large-scale economic infrastructure be established in place of traditional small and informal groups to accommodate the efficient use of technologies. By analogy, as societies become fully-aged, to provide care for an expanding number of elders would require efficient administrative apparatus, and the delivery of services must be standardised in order to be efficient, and personnel needs to be trained to assure uniformity of standards. All these mean the formalisation of care is inevitable.

Perhaps more important to the needed professionalism and the requirement of standardisation as efficient means to use scarce resources in elder care is the fact that formal and professional care fits well into the classic economic theory of services to be measured by exchange values. It is one way to take the "burden" out of a personal care situation, which is said to be unfair to women. If the caregiver is paid for the service in the same way as a nurse is paid for her work in taking care of patients in a formal setting, the equity issue can then be reduced to the cash value of such care, and outside the realm of a measure that is based on the concept of "burden".

But obviously elder care goes much beyond functional assistance, and high technology probably could satisfy some, but not all, aspects of elders' need. There are other needs for which impersonal technological devices could not possibly satisfy. This is evidenced by the fact that surveys repeatedly showed that in both the developed and developing societies; members of the elder's primary family are the most frequently and universally identified caregivers (Shanas, 1979). Furthermore, policymakers throughout the world seemed to express the same sentiment that elder care should be given in their own homes, or a home-like environment, with increased reliance on the family and other informal sources of support (Davis, 1995; Dooghe, 1992; Nolan, Grant and Keady, 1996).

The Need for Primary Group Informal-Care and Support

It does become clear that the field of caregiving faces a contest between an efficient and socially justified programme of formal and standardised caregiving in institutional settings on one hand, and, on the other hand, small informal group care in homes or home-like environment on the other. If home-care were deemed unfair and impractical, the answer, insofar as elder care policy is concerned, obviously would have to lean heavily upon formal and community care.

Experts argued that modernity, by definition, is associated with the declining importance of kinship ties in that society. It then follows that the need for increased state intervention of care is precisely due in part to the declining functions of the family. The home-like environment as the locus of care for the elder, therefore, could best be designed by social engineers in an effort to re-create the human family as a prototype of elder care without the pitfalls of the family, or the inflexibilities of a modern urban nuclear family.

Let us imagine that such an artificially contrived human group is like a small cottage type of residential facility that houses individuals young and old like a natural family. Would those younger members who presumably were to take care of the older ones be free of caregiving burden regardless of gender? The fact is that there had been such experiments in the past, to the image of an artificial domestic group. In order to satisfy sexual needs, economic co-operation, and care of the child and the old, small groups of people of varying ages embraced one another to form a commune. These commune-like domestic groups, developed in the vision of utopian self-sufficient communities, never worked well nor long enough to sustain the formation of multi-generation institutions. Similarly, domestic groups were formulated in the 1970s during the Woodstock generation referred to then as *extended families* where unrelated adults shared the care of children and the elder, as well as household budget. These 1970s "extended families", too, discontinued shortly before the decade was over. History has shown that all such idealism had died within a brief period for a variety of reasons, the longest survived for twenty years.

On the other hand, history and anthropology showed that the nuclear unit of the human natural family is never known to be absent in any society, past and present (Murdock, 1949) . Would it still be possible to create a primary group in place of the family for the efficient and appropriate care of an ever-growing size of the old population, and at an affordable cost?

The Family is a Non-Substitutable Primary Group

There are two good reasons why this should not be done and could not work even if it were possible to re-create the family. First and foremost is that the chief reason for the elder to be cared in the home or home-like environment is the very nature of the family. There are basically eight sets of interacting familial dyads and each is different from the other. These eight sets are: husband-wife, father-son, mother-son, father-daughter, mother-daughter, sister-sister, sister-brother and brother-brother. The possibility that father-son relationship exist is because there is the husband-wife relationship; and for the same reason there is the relationship of the brother-sister relationship. All eight-sets of nuclear familial dyads are *interdependent,* and are universal in all human families.

Perhaps the question should be rephrased to say: "why bother to re-create the family when there is the natural family about which the state can help to strengthen rather than to re-create a set of artificially conceived relationships (and for which we do not even have vocabularies to designate such relationships?)" The fact that family dyads are interrelated, caring for father by the son compels the daughter to think her kin-obligations. Caregiving to the mother is a way to help the father to do his spousal caregiving chores. It is quite possible that in some cases the daughter does not really bother to take care of the mother if that were the only dyadic relationship in the family. In short, the relationship of one dyad does not operate in a vacuum; it is unavoidable that other dyads serve as the context. The intimacy and complexity of such relationships cannot be duplicated in an artificially contrived human group.

Cultural Values, Kinship Structure and Caregiving Relations

Human families vary according to cultural values and relationships with other social institutions in a given society. If the family is still regarded as the most ideal locus for elder care, it follows that elder care burden may also somehow reflect attributes of dyad relationships that also vary from one society to another.

In the absence of data specifically collected to test this assumption, we used data collected in the Shanghai Epidemiological Survey. Detailed methodological descriptions of the survey were published elsewhere and no repetition is warranted here (see Zhang *et al.*, 1990; Yu, Liu *et al.*, 1989; Levy *et al.*, 1989). In spite of the fact that China is a socialist society, Confucian percepts still have strong influence on the way people think about their family obligations. It is essentially a patriarchy that defines gender-specific filial obligations, argument to the contrary notwithstanding. There is neither sweeping generation about uniformity of family values in contemporary China, nor how little or how much deviations have been created from the ideal norm. The fact is that Confucian concept of family relations provided the cultural frame of reference for individual families to adapt to the social and political realities that may demand change.

1. We had a priori assumptions about caregiving burden in Shanghai. First, we predicted that there would be a gender difference. As a corollary of this assumption, we also predicted that the reported subjective burden would be higher for daughters because of the asymmetrical loading of duties required in filial piety in a patriarchical society. Here we used the objective burden as a control variable to show that the subjective and objective burden may operate independently. The higher subjective burden for women therefore may have nothing to do with the objective allocation of time one has to devote to caregiving duties.

2. A second hypothesis posited that when the caregiver was a daughter-in-law, employment outside the home provided relief and it contributed positively to the caregiving relationship. In other words, filial responsibilities do not have the same weight on the daughter-in-law as they are on the son. An escape from such duties can considerably lessen the burden. On the other hand, if the relationship was between the father and the son, employment seemed to have contributed negatively to the subjective burden, since the son is under the pressure to perform both duties with equal degrees of seriousness and commitment.

3. Hypothesis 3 has to do with the age of the caregiver. We predict that the older the caregiver (normally the spouse), the closer the caregiver is to the elder in terms of shared experience, the higher level of objective, but the lower the subjective level of reported caregiving burden. The high objective burden can be explained by extra efforts needed (because of age) for an older person to assist another older person. A lower subjective burden is explained by the fact that the older caregiver can empathised the feelings of an older person needing help, and therefore has more patience and understanding of a special caregiving relationship with the elder.

4. The fourth hypothesis has to do with the caregiver's position in the family. Caregivers having no filial obligations would report higher burden of subjective caregiving burden compared to those who have direct filial obligations. To put in more concretely, sons would have lower subjective burden than daughters as caregivers.

These four major predictions are based on the assumption that structural characteristics of the family as an institution, and the element of filial piety as a cultural value, may have significant impact on burden felt as a result of taking care of an elder relative in the family.

The Result of Data Analysis

Figure 1 represents average z-scores of measures of tolerance, objective and subjective burden, and clinical depression. A mean z-score below 0 suggests that the specific stratified group is below the average of the entire sample.

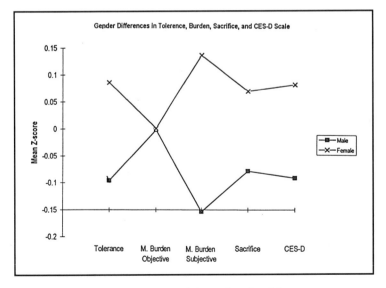

Figure 1. Gender and Care-burden Measures

For example, in this figure, under tolerance scale, the average score for male on tolerance is lower than the overall average score for both genders. A lower tolerance score mean a higher degree of tolerance when the elder care recipient behaves badly. The higher the score, on the other hand, the less one is able to tolerate.

Figure 1 therefore suggests that female caregivers are less able to tolerate their elder's bad behaviour than male caregivers. The same graph shows that though both sexes had similar profiles of objective burden scores, meaning female caregivers did not commit more hours than male caregivers, they differed most significantly on the subjective burden scores. We predicted depressive symptoms and sacrifices in providing care differently depending on the gender.

Employment outside the home seemed to have had a diversion on all measures. Caregivers who had regular jobs were most likely to tolerate the elder's unreasonable behaviour. They are also reported to have both lower objective and subjective caregiving burden. This is shown in Figure 2.

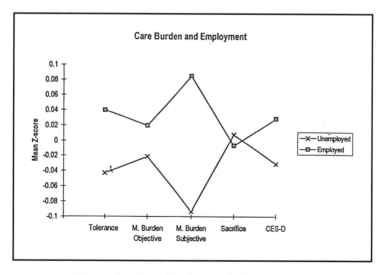

Figure 2. Care Burden and Employment

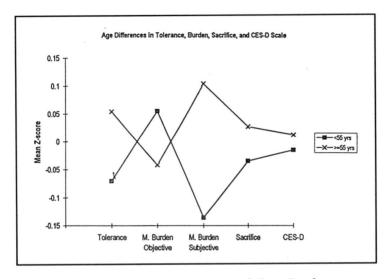

Figure 3. Age of Caregiving and Care Burden

Figure 3 confirmed our prediction that older caregivers (55 years of age and older) were more tolerant than younger ones with respect to having to cope with the recipient's bad behaviour, though the difference is barely discernible. Younger caregivers had much lower CES-D scores (measuring depressive symptoms) than older caregivers, though from previous research we know that depressive symptoms were more prevalent among older people in the general population. The result may be the artefact of age rather than being caused by caregiving burden. Older caregivers, however, had lower objective burden score than younger caregivers, but the opposite was true on subjective scores. The data suggested that older caregivers spent less time in caregiving, had higher subjective burden scores, and reported to have more depressive symptoms. Without data on the type of social ties, it is difficult to interpret the meaning of such comparisons.

We found that male spousal caregivers had a lower subjective burden score than female spousal caregivers. The reverse was true if the recipient was a non-specified extended kin-relative. In the event

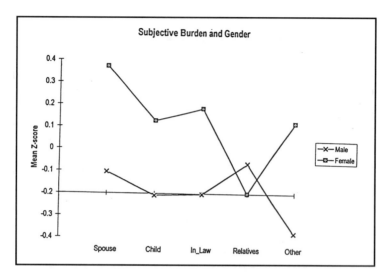

Figure 4. Gender and Subjective Care Burden

that the caregiver was a daughter or daughter-in-law of the elder, the
subjective burden was the second highest of any family dyadic
relations; the wife has the highest subjective burden score. This is
shown in Figure 4. The high subjective score of other relatives cannot
be explained clearly, since it is a mixture of unspecified female
relatives. But the unspecified male relatives have the lowest subjective
score, gender is obviously a factor along with the factor of social
relations.

Finally, Figure 5 shows that between sons and daughters, the son,
occupying a role in the family most clearly and directly expresses the
value of filial piety, had the lowest tolerance score, which means have
the highest tolerance level when parents did not seem to act rationally.
Having to show intolerance would be contrary to the expression of
filial piety. On the other hand, the daughter-in-law, if providing elder
care, does so because of her relations with her husband and not out of
affection and a sense of gratitude. In fact, the nature of the patriarchy
most likely suggests that the mother and daughter-in-law relation is

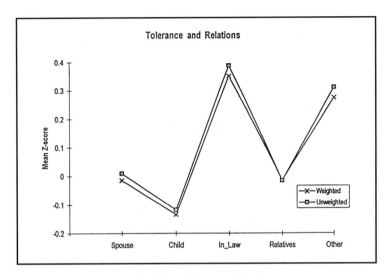

Figure 5. Social Ties and Tolerance

embedded in the structural tension in the family system. It is not surprising that a high tolerance score (low tolerance) is revealed.

Discussion

This paper touches upon three major questions at a time when the issue of elder care is called to question for Asian and for Western societies.

In the West, existing policies of elder care based on the social values of the welfare state is currently facing challenges. At a time when individual responsibility is valued, and a cost prohibitive programme of the government is under review, the challenge is particularly significant. In reducing the burden of the state, increasing emphasis has been placed on the family and on compulsory individual investment portfolio to provide old-age care. It is unclear whether it is politically feasible to provide care to old people at home, given the multitudes of research literature that focused on women's caregiving burden, presumably aggravated by conflicting role demands on caregiving to both their aged parents and their own young families. The family, experts argued, is no longer capable of taking care of their aged members with declining functions and reduced size.

In the East, except Japan, the problem of full-fledged status of ageing society has not yet reached the stage that needs immediate crisis intervention. Most demographers, however, agreed that the fully ageing crisis can no longer be avoided or delayed in the next thirty to forty years in Asia as well. Japan already had experienced the full impact of being an aged society.

At present, most of the Asian societies, including Japan and China, rely on the family to provide care to the elderly, reflected by both written governmental policies and tax provisions that encourage the younger family to keep their old parents nearby. Even without such provisions, co-residence as a form of elder care practice seems to be a statistical fact in Asia. However, more Western scholars and some Japanese scholars have begun to question the durability of such government policies and the family's ability to continue to provide care for longer periods of time.

It is at this crossroad, and during the past decade, that some important publications have begun to document the dynamic nature of caregiving among close relatives, neighbors and friends. Some (e.g. Sussman, 1992) even suggested that intergenerational transfer of wealth be formalised in the form of a family contract as an incentive to unload government burden to younger members of the family. Provocative as Sussman's idea may be, it is difficult to see just how such a contract can be drawn when the child is small, and could not fully understand what the contract means later in his life. If the contract is signed when the elder is in need of care, it is doubtful that many of his adult children would sign, if the element of affection does not work in the first place. Even if we could assure the adult child would sign because of the promised inheritance and other material rewards, the system would benefit the haves, and not the have-nots. Sussman clearly had in mind that a contractual relationship would work in some families. In that context, it is worth exploring.

A major objective of this paper is to show that subjective burden in caregiving must be understood in the context of relationships and gender differences. Similarly, the meaning of individual freedom and independence should be interpreted in the context of kinship structure.

Our Shanghai Epidemiological Survey of Alzheimer's Disease gave us an opportunity to examine more carefully the impact of social values that explains the differential subjective burden in caregiving reported by sons and daughters — and other relatives — in the context of filial piety. The empirical reference of the impact of filial piety in a Confucian society seems clear.

References

Abel, E.K. (1986) "Adult Daughters and the Care for the Elderly", *Feminist Studies*, 12: 479–97.

Archbold, P.G. (1983) "Impact of Parent-Caring on Women", *Family Relations*, 32: 39–45.

Blau, P. (1964) *Exchange and Power in Social Life*. New York: John Wiley.

Brody E. (1981) "Women in the Middle and Family Help to Older People", *The Gerontologist*, 21: 471–80.

Burgess, R.L. and T.L. Huston (1979), *Social Exchange in Developing Relationships*. New York: Academic Press.

Cho, B.E. (forthcoming) "Middle-Aged Women's Supporting Behavior to Elderly Parents: The Comparison of Parents-in-Law and Own Parents", in W.T. Liu and H. Kendig (eds.) *Social Change, Human Values, and Elder Care*.

Davis, B. (1995) "The Reform of Community and Long Term Care of Elderly Persons, An International Perspective", in T. Scharf and G.C. Wenger (eds.) *International Perspectives on Community Care for Older People*. Aldershot: Avebury.

Dooghe, G. (1992) "Informal Caregiving of Elderly People: A European Review", *Aging and Society*, 12: 369–80.

Emerson, R.M. (1990) "Social Exchange Theory", in M. Rosenberg and R.H. Turner (eds.) *Social Psychology: Sociological Perspectives*. New Brunswick: Transaction Publisher.

Goode, W.J. (1963) *World Revolution and Family Patterns*. New York: The Free Press.

Gubrium, J. (1995) "Taking Stock", *Qualitative Health Research*, 5 (3): 267–69.

Hong, Y.Y. and W.T. Liu (2000), "The Social Psychological Perspective of Elderly Care" (in this volume).

Hu, Yow-hwey (1995) "Elderly Suicide Risk in Family Contexts: A Critique of the Asian Family Care Model", *Journal of Cross-Cultural Gerontology*, 10: 199–217.

Ingersolol-Dayton, B. and T.C. Antonucci (1988) "Reciprocal and Nonreciprocal Social Support: Contrasting Sides of Intimate Relationships", *Journal of Gerontology: Social Sciences*, 43: 568–73.

Kelley, H.H. and J.W. Thibaut (1978) *Interpersonal Relations: A Theory of Inter-Dependence*. New York: Wiley-Interscience.

Levy, P.S.; E.S.Y. Yu; W.T. Liu; *et al.* (1989) "Single-Stage Cluster Sampling with a Telescopic Respondent Rule: A Variation Motivated by a Survey of Dementia In Elderly Residents of Shanghai", *Statistics in Medicine*, 8: 1537–44.

Liu, W.T. *et al.* (1987) "The Shanghai Survey of the Elderly and the Epidemiology of Alzheimer's Disease", in W.T. Liu (ed.) *A Decade Review of Mental Health Research, Training and Services*, University of Illinois.

Mathews, S.H. (1985), "The Burdens of Parent Care: A Critical Evaluation of Recent Findings", *Journal of Aging Studies*, 2: 157–65.

Montgomery, R.J.V.; J.G. Goinyea and N.R. Hooyman (1985), "Caregiving and the Experience of Subjective and Objective Burden", *Family Relations*, 34: 19–26.

Murdock, G.P. (1949) *The Social Structure*. New York: The Free Press.

Nolan, M.R. and K. Caldock (1996) "Assessment: Identifying the Barriers to Good Practice", *Health and Social Care in the Community*, 4(2): 77–85.

Nolan, M.R.; G. Grant and N.C. Ellis (1990) "Stress is in the Eye of the Beholder", "Reconceptualizing the Measurement of Carer Burden", *Journal of Advanced Nursing*, 15: 544–55.

Poulshock, S.; A. Walker and G.T. Deimling (1984), "Family Caring for Elders in Residence: Issues in the Measurement of Burden", *Journal of Gerontology*, 39: 230–39.

Shanas, E. (1979) "Social Myth as Hypothesis: The Case of the Family Relations of Old People", *The Gerontologist,* 19: 3–9.

Shi, L. (1993) "Family Financial and Household Support Exchange Between Generations: A Survey of Chinese Rural Elderly", *The Gerontologist,* 33: 468–80.

Stueve, A. (1982), "The Elderly as Network Members", *Marriage and Family Review,* 5: 59–87.

Sussman, Marvin (2000), "Family Change and Family Bonding: Conceptual and Policy Issues" (in this volume).

Walker, A.; J. Albert and A.M. Guilemard (1993) "Older People in Europe: Social and Economic Policies", the 1993 Report of the European Observatory, Brussels: Commission of the European Communities.

Yu, E.S.H.; W.T. Liu, *et al.* (1989) "Cognitive Impairment among Elderly Adults in Shanghai, China", *Gerontology: Social Sciences,* 44: S97–S106.

Yu, E.S.H.; W.T. Liu and Wong, Z.Y. *et al.* (1993) "Caregivers of Cognitively Impaired and the Disabled in Shanghai, China", in S.H. Zarit, L. Pearlin and K.W. Schaie (eds.) *Caregiving Systems: Informal and Formal Helpers,* Lawrence Erlbaum Associates, Inc.

Zhang, M.Y. *et al.* (1990) "The Prevalence of Dementia and Alzheimer's Disease in Shanghai, China", *Annuals of Neurology,* 27: 428–37.

Zarit, S.H.; K.E. Reever and J. Bach-Peterson (1980) "Relatives of Impaired Elderly: Correlates of Feelings of Burden", *The Gerontologist,* 20: 649–55.

Chapter 10

Filial Piety, Co-residence, and Intergenerational Solidarity in Japan

Wataru Koyano
Seigakuin University

Introduction

During the last 50 years, Japan has experienced drastic social changes. She arose from the ruin of world war and accomplished remarkable economic growth. However, economic growth was not the only change that Japan experienced, though it made possible and facilitated other social changes covering almost all facets of living and thinking. As the result of changes, the lives of today's Japanese are more Westernized than before. For instance, most contemporary Japanese rarely or never wear *kimono* (traditional ethnic clothes) and do not know how to dress. Much traditional Japanese equipment in houses has been replaced by Western things or new Japan-Western mixtures: for example, *shoji* (sliding doors with rice paper) have been replaced by aluminium sash or *shoji* placed inside the sash; *tatami* (matting with grass) and *zabuton* (sitting mattress on *tatami*) have been partly replaced by wooden floor and sofa but, in most cases, people do not wear their shoes inside the house.

The family life of the elderly and elderly care have also changed and are still changing. The traditional living arrangement of the Japanese elderly is the patri-lineal, patri-local stem family. Typically, co-resident family provided all kinds of support. Even if the elderly were completely dependent, their lives seemed secure because the co-resident family members were "protective" (Hashimoto, 1996). Factors motivating family members to be supportive of the elderly seem complex, including affection, social norm, and necessity. The Confucian norm of filial piety was a normative factor regulating intergenerational solidarity. Filial piety was repeatedly taught as the most important moral virtue. Even a legend of *ubasute* (deserting the elderly) was used to teach the grace of parents and filial piety, like other legends of respect for the elderly.

Confucianism developed in ancient China and spread to Asian countries. Therefore, the Confucian norm of filial piety has been shared by the Chinese, Korean, and Japanese but with unique historical and cultural deviations (Tsai, 1996). In Japan, the norm of filial piety was the moral aspect of co-residence under the *ie* ideology. The *ie* ideology was established and propagated by the Imperial Government in pre-war Japan, and then intentionally denied after the war.

In this paper, the author outlines the Japanese version of filial piety, changes occurring since World War II, and social relationships of the elderly observed in contemporary Japanese society, with special attention given to the difficult situation of daughters-in-law living with their elderly parents-in-law.

Changes in Filial Piety and Co-residence

Filial Piety and Elderly Support Under the Ie Ideology

The Japanese word *ie* has several meanings, including family, lineage, home and house. In the *ie* ideology, however, the word exclusively means lineage, which is conceptualized as continuously succeeding from generation to generation.

The *ie* ideology consisted of two elements: conception of *ie* (lineage) and paternalism within the family. Since the existing family was conceived as a small link in the long chain of lineage, family name, assets, social status, and occupation should be inherited by the eldest son. The tomb and home Buddhist altar (in which mortuary tablets of ancestors were placed) should be bequeathed also to the eldest son in order to continue the ancestor worship of lineage. If there were no son, the adoption of successor should be undertaken through or not through marriage. If there were no son, but only daughters, adoption through marriage with the eldest daughter should be arranged.

As typically found in adopting a successor, marriage was conceived as a means of continuation of lineage. Thus, marriage should be carefully arranged in order to fit the main purpose of marriage — maintenance of lineage — and should not be made freely by the couple without the permission of the heads of both families.

In the existing family, inequality among family members is taken for granted in terms of importance, power, and privileges. There is an order of importance and power among family members. Typically, the father was the household head having the supreme position and legal power to predominate over other family members. The position, power and privileges of the household head were means of fulfilling his obligation: to maintain family name, social status, and all assets of the lineage, and to pass them to the next household head (ideally, his eldest son). The wife of the household head should serve and be obedient to her husband but could have superior position as a parent. Among children, the eldest son was given a superior position as the future household head.

The obedience of children to their parents or parents-in-law was regarded as an expression of filial piety. Filial piety was an extremely important moral virtue corresponding to the infinite grace of parents, including the grace of bearing, nurturing, and allowing marriage. Filial piety was repeatedly taught in moral education; for example, children were instructed to obey parents absolutely and never resist them. They were not even to stretch their feet in the direction of their parents while sleeping.

The norm of filial piety was propagated by the Imperial Japanese Government in combination with loyalty to the Emperor. Ideally, only family and nation were regarded as "formal" organizations, and the nation was conceptualized as a big family consisting of real families, headed by the Emperor. Then, filial piety and loyalty to the Emperor were tightly interwoven in the Imperial Japanese ideology.

The life of the elderly under the *ie* ideology was typical of a retired household head who had already transferred the headship to his eldest son, his wife, or the widow of the household head. The elderly person lived with the successor, his wife, and children. For the successor, co-residing and sharing all assets with elderly parents was not only an obligation but also an actualization of filial piety. Therefore, the successor and his nuclear family should provide support with gratitude and respect for elderly parents. In moral education in pre-war Japan, it was praiseworthy to serve parents while neglecting wife and children.

Changes after World War II

After World War II, as part of the democratization of Japan, the *ie* ideology was officially renounced, and the conception of *ie* was completely removed from the constitution and civil law. For example, the constitution declares that agreement between the couple is the only basis of marriage, and civil law gives the highest priority of support to the wife and children rather than to elderly parents. Filial piety is no longer taught in classrooms, at least in its original and extreme form found in pre-war Japan.

Changes in people's attitudes toward the conception of *ie* and support for elderly parents can be traced in opinion polls. Matsunari (1991) reviewed nationwide opinion polls and found a gradual decline of positive attitudes toward the *ie* ideology. For both adoption of successor and dependence on children in old age, the percentage of people showing positive attitudes decreased from over 60% in the 1950s to less than 30% (Table 1). For the dependence on children in old age, Matsunari commented that the percentage of people with positive and negative attitudes reversed in the 1960s when old age pension became effective.

In the later half of the 1980s, Takahashi (1987) scrutinized the factorial structure of the attitudes of elderly persons toward the *ie* ideology and detected four factors. He reported that, among the factors he found, "decision of marriage made by the household head" and "inequality among family members" were no longer accepted even by elderly persons who had been socialized in pre-war Japan, while

TABLE 1

Changes in Attitudes toward *Ie* Ideology

(a) Adoption of Successor

	Positive	Negative
1953	73%	16%
1958	63	21
1963	51	32
1968	43	41
1973	36	41
1978	33	48
1983	27	51
1988	28	52

(b) Dependence on a Child in Old Age

	Will Depend On	Will Not
1950	59.1%	16.6%
1959	43.8	23.3
1969	28.6	50.5
1979	24.3	54.5
1990	17.5	61.7

NOTE: Reconstructed from Matsunari (1991).
DK, NA, and "Uncertain" are excluded from the table.

"co-residence and support provided by children" was still accepted (Table 2). For the extent of support and intergenerational solidarity in old age, an opinion poll conducted in 1986 found that a relatively small portion of the Japanese people aged 20 to 59 preferred to have economically close ties with children. The percentage of persons willing to have economically close but not emotionally close ties was only 4.0%, and 19.4% preferred to have both emotionally and economically close ties. The remaining 37.4% preferred to have emotionally close but not economically close ties, and 31.2% preferred to keep their independence.

Changes in people's attitudes toward the *ie* ideology appeared gradually in the actual living arrangements of the elderly. Since the elimination of the concept of *ie*, co-residence with elderly parents was no longer an obligation of their children. Nevertheless, the percentage of the elderly co-residing with adult children was very high for several decades and started to decrease only in the 1960s. During a 30-year period from 1960, the frequency of co-residence decreased from 86.8% to 60.6%, while that of living alone and living only with spouse increased from 3.8% to 10.9% and from 7.0% to 24.1%, respectively (Table 3). The frequency of co-residence is generally lower in urban areas, among employees and younger generations, and is expected to decrease further.

TABLE 2

Attitudes toward *Ie* Ideology among the Elderly

	Positive	Negative
Co-residence and Support	59.5%	32.8%
Continuity of Lineage	48.3	34.0
Inequality among Family Members	35.6	45.4
Decision of Marriage by Household Head	22.2	65.3

NOTE: Calculated from Takahashi (1987).

TABLE 3

Changes in Living Arrangement of the Japanese Elderly

	Living Alone	Only With Spouse	With Children	Other
1960	3.8%	7.0%	86.8%	2.4%
1965	4.6	9.1	83.8	2.5
1970	5.3	11.7	79.6	3.4
1975	6.6	15.1	74.4	3.9
1980	7.8	18.1	69.8	4.3
1985	9.2	20.6	65.5	4.7
1990	10.9	24.1	60.6	4.4

SOURCE: Population Census.

The decrease of co-residence is usually taken seriously by many Japanese observers as an indication of the weakened informal support system and filial piety because co-resident family members, especially adult children and children-in-law, are considered as the most important source of social support. However, co-residence itself is a very poor indicator of social relationships, for it merely indicates a level of geographical proximity. In order to scrutinize the intergenerational solidarity of the contemporary Japanese elderly, as well as relationships with others outside the household, a survey focusing on dyadic interpersonal relationships was conducted in two communities with high and low frequency of co-residence.

Social Relationships of the Contemporary Japanese Elderly

Data

The survey was carried out in Setagaya Ward, Metropolitan Tokyo, and Yonezawa City, Yamagata Prefecture, in 1993. Tokyo is the most urbanized area in Japan and has the lowest percentage of elderly living together with their adult children in the same household. Yonezawa City is not a rural village but a provincial city with a high percentage of co-residence.

The sampling frame consisted of 1,200 elderly community residents (600 in Setagaya and 600 in Yonezawa, respectively), aged 65 to 79 years, randomly selected through stratified two-stage probability sampling from the residents' registration. Home visit interviews were completed for 882 of the sample (425 in Setagaya and 457 in Yonezawa). The average age of the respondents was 70.5 years in Setagaya and 71.1 years in Yonezawa.

The respondents were asked to name all the family members living together, all the children and children-in-law, up to five siblings and relatives, up to five neighbors, and up to five friends, and to report interactions with them. Three items respectively indicating the different aspects of social relationships of the Japanese elderly were adopted (see Asakawa, *et al.*, in press). They were emotional closeness ("make relaxed"), instrumental support received by the respondents ("run errands"), and perceived availability of long-term care. The measurement was performed for the dyadic relationship between the respondent and each of the others listed by him or her. For example, the respondent was asked to evaluate whether a person made him/her relaxed, ran errands, or seemed to be a dependable source of long-term care. The responses were dummy-coded, respectively. The others were divided into 16 categories of relationships (see Table 6), and the percentages of others who had each of these three types of interactions were compared across the relationships.

Co-residence with Married Children

Table 4 shows the distribution of the living arrangements of the respondents. The percentage of co-residence with married children was significantly higher in Setagaya than in Yonezawa, both for men and women.

TABLE 4
Living Arrangement of Respondents

		Living Alone	Only with Spouse	With Un-Married Children	With Married Children	Other	Total (n)
Setagaya	Men	2.5	44.4	29.9	19.7	3.5	100.0 (198)
	Women	15.4	26.4	22.5	29.5	6.2	100.0 (227)
	Total	9.4	34.9	25.9	24.9	4.9	100.0 (425)
Yonezawa	Men	0.6	24.4	15.6	58.3	1.1	100.0 (180)
	Women	5.1	12.6	12.3	64.2	5.8	100.0 (277)
	Total	3.3	17.3	13.6	61.9	3.9	100.0 (457)

NOTE: Figures are unweighted percentages.

When cases without a married child and those co-residing with unmarried children were excluded, in Yonezawa the percentage of co-residence was significantly higher for the respondents having sons than those without a son, while no significant difference was found in Setagaya (Table 5). For respondents having both sons and daughters, the percentage of co-residence with a daughter was slightly higher in Setagaya than in Yonezawa, though in both areas a majority co-resided with a son. Consequently, among the respondents co-residing with daughters, 59% in Setagaya and 91% in Yonezawa did not have a male offspring.

For the elderly living in Yonezawa, co-residence with married children almost exclusively means co-residence with a married son, and the lack of male offspring is likely to lead to a life without a co-residing child in the same household. The findings indicate that the traditional pattern of family life established under the *ie* ideology is still alive more strongly in Yonezawa than in Setagaya.

Interactions with Others

Table 6 shows the percentages of others who had the three types of interactions with the respondents. For emotional closeness ("make relaxed"), the highest percentage was found for wives, followed by husbands, daughters, sons, siblings, and friends. For instrumental support received by the elderly ("running errands"), however, the order was different: the highest percentage was also found for wives but was followed by co-resident daughters and daughters-in-law, and the percentage was very low for siblings, neighbors, and friends. For the perceived availability of long-term care, the highest percentage was found for wives, followed by co-resident daughters and daughters-in-law. Differences between the cases in Setagaya and Yonezawa were small.

For most categories of the others, the percentage to whom the elderly felt emotionally close exceeded the percentage of others who provided instrumental support. Also, the percentage of others being felt as emotionally close by the elderly exceeded the percentage of others who were perceived as available sources of care.

TABLE 5

Gender Composition of Children and Co-residence

	With Married Son		With Married Daughter		Without Child		Total	(n)
Setagaya								
Son only	31.1	[25.7]	–	–	68.9	[25.3]	100.0	(61)
Daughter only	–	–	32.3	[58.8]	67.7	[25.3]	100.0	(62)
Both son and daughter	36.4	[74.3]	9.3	[41.2]	54.3	[49.4]	100.0	(151)
Total	27.0	[100.0]	12.4	[100.0]	60.6	[100.0]	100.0	(274)
Yonezawa								
Son only	76.5	[27.3]	–	–	23.5	[21.3]	100.0	(85)
Daughter only	–	–	56.9	[91.1]	43.1	[33.0]	100.0	(72)
Both son and daughter	78.7	[72.7]	1.8	[8.9]	19.5	[45.7]	100.0	(220)
Total	63.2	[100.0]	11.9	[100.0]	24.9	[100.0]	100.0	(377)

NOTE: Cases without a married child and those who co-resided with unmarried children were excluded. Figures are unweighted percentages. Figures in [] were column percent.

TABLE 6

Percentages of Others Having Interactions

| | Setagaya | | | Yonezawa | | |
	Make Relaxed	Running Errands	Availability of Care	Make Relaxed	Running Errands	Availability of Care
Wife	94.1	81.6	91.9	88.4	55.5	93.1
Daughter Living Together	67.0	57.8	56.9	41.2	52.9	67.6
Daughter Living Apart	64.4	34.7	53.9	60.4	30.6	43.2
Daughter-in-law Living Together	31.6	53.2	67.1	33.1	44.8	68.1
Daughter-in-law Living Apart	33.1	18.4	28.2	23.3	8.8	19.3
Sister	53.7	12.8	15.7	41.7	10.3	17.5
Neighbor (women)	40.8	12.2	8.0	37.5	9.2	6.1
Friend (women)	59.6	14.0	6.8	41.9	8.6	5.1
Husband	77.6	44.8	49.6	83.8	48.0	39.9
Son Living Together	37.3	36.0	24.7	39.1	29.4	18.7
Son Living Apart	51.2	24.7	27.5	42.9	11.9	20.4
Son-in-law Living Together	26.5	23.5	23.5	15.6	20.0	2.2
Son-in-law Living Apart	20.3	9.7	9.7	18.2	7.8	6.4
Brother	45.1	7.8	6.9	37.0	9.3	10.2
Neighbor (men)	37.2	11.2	3.2	35.1	8.9	3.5
Friend (men)	56.2	11.8	3.0	42.8	11.3	4.0

NOTE: Figures are unweighted percentages.

The excess of emotional closeness over the exchange of instrumental support seems a natural consequence of interpersonal relationships, because emotional closeness and its expression are the most common basic rewards exchanged in interpersonal relationships. An unnatural pattern was found only for daughters-in-law living with their parents-in-law. Elderly parents do not feel emotionally close to their daughters-in-law, but they receive instrumental support from daughters-in-law. Further, elderly parents think their daughters-in-law are (or should be) a dependable source of long-term care though they do not feel emotionally close to the daughters-in-law. Such unnatural relationships seem to indicate the difficult situation of daughters-in-law living together with their in-laws and to explain the well-known conflict between mothers and daughters-in-law.

Differences between Children and Children-in-law

To explicate further the difficult situation of daughters-in-law, multiple logit analyses were conducted for the dyadic ties between parents and their children/children-in-law. Characteristics of elderly parents and children/children-in-law were simultaneously used as independent variables. They were age, gender, functional capacity, years of education, marital status, years of residence, and co-residence with other children of elderly parents, relationship (either child or child-in-law), gender, age, birth order, and geographical proximity of children/children-in-law. Functional capacity was measured by the TMIG Index of Competence (Koyano, *et al.*, 1991). Gender, marital status, co-residence with other children, and relationship were measured in dummy variables and scored 1 for women, the currently married, the co-residents, and children. Age, birth order, and geographical proximity of children/children-in-law were measured as categorical variables, and categories of "aged 50 years and over", "3rd or younger", and "2 hours or more driving time" were used as the basis of comparison.

The analyses indicated significant differences between children and children-in-law, differences between men and women, and significant effects of geographical proximity upon instrumental support both in Setagaya and in Yonezawa (Table 7). When the effects of other variables were controlled, children were more likely than children-in-law, and women were more likely than men, to be felt emotionally close by elderly parents, to provide instrumental support, and to be seen as a dependable source of long-term care. Children or children-in-law living nearer to their parents were more likely to provide instrumental support and to be seen as available sources of long-term care than those living farther away.

Table 8 shows odds ratios calculated from the results of multiple logit analyses, corresponding to gender, geographical proximity, and differences between children and children-in-law. The effects of other variables were held constant. The basis of comparison (valued 1.0) was daughters living well apart (2 hours or more driving time) from their elderly parents. For emotional closeness, those most likely to be felt emotionally close by elderly parents were daughters living far apart from them, followed by co-resident daughters. However, those most likely to provide instrumental support and to be regarded as dependable sources of long-term care were co-resident daughters. Co-resident daughters-in-law provided instrumental support as frequently as daughters living far apart, and only in Yonezawa were seen as dependable sources of long-term care as daughters living apart. However, they were far less likely to feel emotionally close to elderly parents than daughters either co-resident or living apart.

Again, the differences between daughters and daughters-in-law are apparent. Elderly parents feel emotionally close to their daughters whether they provide instrumental support or not, and either as co-resident or not, while they seldom feel emotionally close to co-resident daughters-in-law who actually provide instrumental support. The data clearly show the sad and difficult situation of co-resident daughters-in-law.

Direction of Change

The Japanese word for informal support provided by adult children to elderly parents is *fuyo*. Although *fuyo* may include any kind of

TABLE 7

Predictors of the Intergenerational Solidarity

	Make Relaxed	Setagaya Running Errands	Availability of Care	Make relaxed	Yonezawa Running Errands	Availability of Care
Characteristics of the Elderly						
Gender (women/men)	−0.475**	−0.146	−0.020	0.237*	0.321*	0.285*
Age	−0.064**	0.013	−0.002	0.000	−0.005	−0.005
Functional Capacity	0.147**	0.031	0.53	0.059**	−0.016	0.047*
Years of Education	−0.030	0.024	−0.003	0.051**	0.103**	0.059**
Marital Status (married/not married)	−0.508**	0.245	−0.025	−0.268*	−0.111	−0.235
Years of Residence	0.005	−0.006	−0.006	0.000	−0.003	−0.006*
Co-residing with Other Children	−0.302*	−0.415**	−0.345**	−0.180	−0.434**	−0.461**

TABLE 7 (continued)

Characteristics of Children						
Relation (child/child-in-law)	1.324**	0.817**	0.822**	1.282**	0.766**	0.634**
Gender (women/men)	0.742**	0.855**	1.372**	0.684**	1.097**	1.971**
Age (-39/50+)	-0.132	-0.180	0.160	-0.169	0.172	-0.218*
(40-49/50+)	0.102	-0.160	0.067	-0.023	0.095	0.035*
Birth Order						
(1st/3rd+)	-0.026	-0.114	0.181*	0.104	0.053	0.071
(2nd/3rd+)	0.053	0.043	0.070	0.084	0.087	0.112
Proximity						
(co-residence/2h+)	-0.225*	0.793**	0.335*	-0.231*	0.781**	0.586**
(>29 min./2h+)	0.293**	0.636**	0.282*	0.157	0.504**	0.339**
(>119 min./2h+)	0.013	-0.382**	0.004	0.236*	-0.402**	-0.459**
Constant	2.398	-3.162*	-2.215	-2.460*	-2.750*	-2.744*
Model Chi-square (d.f.=16)	242.0**	234.1**	247.4**	260.9**	352.8**	463.3**

NOTE: Figures are unstandardized logistic regression coefficients and constants. Subjects were dyadic ties between parents and their children or children-in-law.
* p<.05, **p<.01.

TABLE 8

Comparison among Children and Children-in-law: Odds Ratios of Having Interaction with Elderly Parents

	Setagaya			Yonezawa		
	Make Relaxed	Running Errands	Availability of Care	Make Relaxed	Running Errands	Availability of Care
Daughter Living Together	0.799	2.209	1.398	0.794	2.183	1.796
Daughter Living Apart */**	1	1	1	1	1	1
Daughter-in-law Living Together	0.213	0.976	0.615	0.220	1.015	0.952
Daughter-in-law Living Apart**	0.266	0.442	0.440	0.277	0.465	0.530

TABLE 8 (continued)

Son Living Together	0.380	0.940	0.354	0.400	0.729	0.250
Son Living Apart**	0.476	0.425	0.253	0.504	0.334	0.139
Son-in-law Living Together	0.101	0.415	0.156	0.111	0.339	0.133
Son-in-law Living Apart**	0.127	0.188	0.111	0.140	0.155	0.074

NOTE: Figures are odds ratios, calculated from the results of multiple logit analyses (Table 7), corresponding to gender, geographical distance, and differences between children and children-in-law. The effects of other variables were held constant.

   * Basis of comparison (valued 1.0)

  ** Children or children-in-law living well apart (2 hours or more driving time) from their elderly parents.

support, the nuances of the word suggest instrumental support, especially financial aid and long-term care. Instrumental support was greatly emphasized as the actualization of filial piety in pre-war Japan. Gratitude and respect were attached to instrumental support, not to emotional closeness or affection.

The life of the elderly in pre-war Japan described earlier is an ideal deduced from the *ie* ideology. Since there is no empirical data indicating the actual lives and attitudes of the people, reality might have been different from the ideal. However, during several decades after the war, the Japanese people changed their attitudes toward *ie* ideology and intergenerational solidarity. At the end of the 20th century, the majority of Japanese people prefer to keep emotionally close ties with adult children in old age, but they do not want to depend on children. Based on the results of opinion polls, it seems possible to say that emotional closeness becomes the essential part or basis of intergenerational solidarity, while instrumental support has been reduced in importance.

In this regard, Matsunari's (1991) comments on people's attitudes toward dependence on children clearly point out the changes in necessity. For the elderly in pre-war Japan, co-residence was not only the normatively approved way of living under the *ie* ideology but also the only possible way to sustain their lives through receiving instrumental support from children. Compared with the elderly in pre-war Japan, today's elderly are much more healthy, wealthy, and well-educated. Further, because of the large generational differences produced by the drastic social changes following the world war, younger generations are more functionally, economically, socially, and psychologically independent than older generations. Today's elderly in Japan, especially the young-old, can enjoy the possibility of avoiding dependence on children. Thus, the decrease in co-residence may simply indicate the decreased frequency of the elderly having to co-reside in order to receive *fuyo* (informal support, mainly instrumental).

Of the two survey areas, Setagaya is a relatively affluent suburban area in Tokyo which has been at the forefront of social change in

Japan, whereas Yonezawa is a more traditional provincial city, a regional center for agriculture and light industry. The living arrangement of respondents showed a clear contrast between the two areas. Among the respondents who had married children and who had not lived with unmarried children, the percentage of co-residence was 40% in Setagaya, while it was 75% in Yonezawa. Although the percentage of co-residence with married daughters was only 12% both in Setagaya and Yonezawa, 91% of the respondents did not have a son in Yonezawa while 41% of them had male offspring in Setagaya. For the elderly living in Yonezawa, co-residence with married children almost exclusively means co-residence with a married son, and the lack of male offspring is likely to lead to a life without a co-residing child in the same household. The findings indicate that the traditional pattern of family life established under the *ie* ideology is present more strongly in Yonezawa than in Setagaya.

In spite of the wide differences in living arrangements, an almost identical pattern was observed for dyadic social relationships of the elderly. Both in Setagaya and Yonezawa, sources of instrumental support were almost restricted to co-resident family members, followed by children living apart, but to a lesser degree. However, even among family members living together, husbands, wives, sons, daughters, and daughters-in-law have different social relationships with the elderly. Spouses were emotionally close and well integrated in exchanges of instrumental support. Daughters and daughters-in-law living together were also well integrated in exchanges of instrumental support, but they were different in the degree of emotional closeness. Elderly parents feel emotionally close to their daughters who are either living together or apart, while they seldom feel emotionally close to daughters-in-law living together who actually provide instrumental support. Among non-kins, friends are emotionally close, but not well integrated in exchanges of instrumental support as neighbors. These findings confirm the results of Koyano, *et al.* (1994) and further explicate the differential roles of other people in the social world of the elderly.

For most relationships, the percentage of others who provided instrumental support was smaller than those to whom the elderly felt emotionally close. Emotional closeness being greater than the exchange of instrumental support seems a natural consequence of interpersonal relationships, because emotional closeness and its expression are the most common and basic rewards to be exchanged in interpersonal relationships. An unnatural pattern was found only for daughters-in-law living with their parents-in-law. Elderly parents do not feel emotionally close to their daughters-in-law, but they receive instrumental support from daughters-in-law. Further, elderly parents think their daughters-in-law are (or should be) a dependable source of long-term care though they do not feel emotionally close to their daughters-in-law. Such unnatural relationships seem to indicate the difficult situation of co-resident daughters-in-law and to explain the well-known conflict between mothers and daughters-in-law. (In Yonezawa, the same unnatural pattern was found also for co-resident daughters and sons-in-law. However, the number of respondents living together with married daughters and sons-in-law was small in Yonezawa.)

The research findings also show that co-residence enhances exchanges of instrumental support and availability of long-term care but is inversely related to emotional closeness. Further, co-residence with a married son, that is still the preferred living arrangement both in urban and provincial areas, is likely to bring harmful interactions with daughters-in-law, characterized by frequent exchanges of instrumental support without emotional closeness. Therefore, for the elderly without immediate need of instrumental support, avoiding co-residence with children might be a meaningful choice.

However, for the elderly needing instrumental support, especially long-term care, co-residence with children is still the only way to obtain necessary support. Because of insufficient social services, the lives of the disabled elderly can hardly be sustained without informal support provided by co-resident family members. Therefore, even in a suburb of Tokyo, frequency of co-residence is significantly higher for the older, disabled, and widowed elderly than for their counterparts

(Kayano, *et al.*, 1986). A large-scale survey conducted by the Metropolitan Tokyo Government (1996) reported that 91% of the disabled elderly were cared for by co-resident family members and the remaining 5% were by family members or kin living apart; 31% of principal caregivers were wives, 26% were daughters, and 22% were daughters-in-law. Such actual examples of elderly care seem to indicate that the tradition of family care is still alive even in the most urbanized, Westernized area in Japan.

At the same time, however, family care for the disabled elderly has become more and more difficult through reduced number of children and of household members, reduced percentages of the self-employed and farmers, higher geographical mobility, and increased labor force participation of women. In addition to these conditions produced by the modernization of society in general, aging of caregivers, extended duration of care, and increased financial cost of caregiving also make family care more difficult. Reflecting the difficulty of family care, people's attitudes toward elderly care have been changing rather rapidly (see, for example, Eliott & Campbell, 1993).

In 1996, the Japanese Ministry of Health and Welfare proposed establishing a new compulsory social insurance — "insurance against elderly care". Although it is too early to describe the planned system of the insurance in detail (actually, nothing has been concrete at the time of writing), it is apparent that the insurance would acknowledge the societal responsibility for elderly care formally and would guarantee a certain level of care services. As old-age pension freed adult children from financial support for their elderly parents, the insurance may possibly free the family members from the burden of long-term care. In a sense, enacting the insurance can be seen as completing the changes in family life of the elderly and elderly care begun with renouncing the *ie* ideology.

Even now, when including choices for co-residence, intergenerational relationships between elderly parents and their adult children have become more affection-based, convenience-oriented, irrelevant to the *ie* ideology, and free from the norm of filial piety than they used to be (see Naoi, *et al.*, 1984; Sakamoto, 1996). Then, if insurance reduced the importance of instrumental support further, the number of elderly avoiding co-residence with children would increase, and the frequency of co-residence would decrease further. However, it is unlikely that the traditional family life of the elderly will completely disappear within a few decades. Rather, some unique mixture of traditional Japanese and Western ways of family life may emerge gradually, inasmuch as the relatively high frequency of co-residence is still maintained without the constraint by the *ie* ideology, co-residence with a married son is preferred in spite of possible conflict between parents and daughters-in-law, and wooden floor and sofa are used without shoes. Since today's family life of the elderly is already a mixture of traditional Japanese and Western (Naoi, 1993), forthcoming ways of family life of the elderly and elderly care would be more Westernized and irrelevant to the Confucian norm of filial piety than those of today. However, this would not mean the weakening, but rather the reconstruction of intergenerational solidarity. An old thesis of family sociology known as "from institution to affection" seems to fit well the changes in intergenerational solidarity which occurred and are occurring in Japan.

Acknowledgements

An early version of this paper was presented at the 5th Asia/Oceania Regional Congress of Gerontology held in Hong Kong in 1995 and included in a special issue of the *Australian Journal on Ageing*, 15, 1996. The data used in this paper were obtained in a survey research supported by the Comprehensive Research Grants on Aging and Health (92A5101).

References

Eliot, K.S. & Campbell, R. (1993) "Changing ideas about family care for the elderly in Japan", *Journal of Cross-Cultural Gerontology*, 8: 119–135.

Hashimoto, A. (1996) *The Gift of Generations: Japanese and American Perspectives on Aging and the Social Contract*. New York: Cambridge University Press.

Koyano, W.; Hashimoto, M.; Fukawa, T.; Shibata, H. & Gunji, A. (1994) "The social support system of the Japanese elderly", *Journal of Cross-Cultural Gerontology*, 9: 323–333.

Koyano, W.; Shibata, H.; Haga, H. & Suyama, Y. (1986) "Health and living arrangement of the elderly", *Social Gerontology (Shakai Ronegaku)*, 24: 28–35 (written in Japanese with an English abstract).

Koyano, W.; Shibata, H.; Nakazato, K.; Haga, H. & Suyama, Y. (1991) "Measurement of competence: Reliability and validity of the TMIG Index of Competence", *Archives of Gerontology and Geriatrics*, 13: 103–116.

Matsunari, M. (1991) "Changes in family ideology in post-war Japan: Based on results of nation-wide public-opinion polls", *Japanese Journal of Family Sociology (Kazoku Shakaigaku Kenkyu)*, 3: 85–97 (written in Japanese with an English abstract).

Metropolitan Tokyo Government (1996) *Living Conditions of the Elderly: Report of the 1995 Basic Survey of Social Services (Koreisha no Seikatsu Jittai)*. Tokyo: Metropolitan Tokyo Government (written in Japanese).

Naoi, M. (1993) *Elderly and Family (Koreisha to Kazoku)*. Tokyo: Saiensu-sha (written in Japanese).

Naoi, M.; Okamura, K. & Hayashi, H. (1984) "Living arrangements of old people and some comments about future change", *Social Gerontology (Shakai Ronengaku)*, 21: 3–21 (written in Japanese with an English abstract).

Sakamoto, K. (1996) "Analyzing the relationship between the elderly and their children in Japan", in Minichiello, V.; Chapell, N.; Walker, A. & Kendig, H. (eds.), *Sociology of Aging: International Perspectives*. Melbourne: Thoth Solutions.

Takahashi, M. (1987) "Family consciousness among urban elderly", *Japanese Journal of Gerontology (Ronen Skakai-kagaku)*, 9: 82–95 (written in Japanese with an English abstract).

Chapter 11

The Cultural Politics of the Asian Family Care Model: Missing Language and Facts

Yow-Hwey Hu
Yang Ming University
and Yah-Jong Chou
National Taiwan University

The tremendous speed of demographic transition in the newly industrialized states of East Asia makes policy response to problems of elderly care all the more urgent. While an East Asian 'family' elderly maintenance model has emerged in the field's orthodox discourse, certain socio-cultural realities are largely absent from the research, and negative effects in policy, knowledge, and people's lives might be further amplified by the international nature of problem discourse. In this paper we challenge a quick acceptance of the 'cultural preference' argument of the model. By checking international patterns of the suicide rates of the elderly in general and suicide patterns in Taiwan in particular, the questioning of the Asian family care model has been deepened. A preliminary analysis of Chinese society on Taiwan shows that substituting undertheorized and common sense notions of family, opinion, and well-being for social science can run counter to policy aims and actually increase both suffering among the elderly and social inequality. Conversely, qualitative inquiry into the family as a relational system in daily practices focuses on the concepts of habitus, power, and gender classification to provide a basis for understanding cultural politics and social reality in the welfare of the elderly.

The East Asian Model: Cultural Preference or Cultural Myth?

It is important to emphasize the effects of rapid population aging in the newly industrialized states of East Asia on the problem of maintaining the elderly. With the movement of East Asian Newly Industrialized Countries (NICs) — first Japan, then Singapore, Hong Kong, Taiwan and Korea — across the old divides into the industrialized world, the situation dramatically changed. For example, in 1920, life expectancy in Taiwan was only 27.2, and now is over 73 years (Mirzaee 1979; Hu 1991). The proportion of people aged 65 and over is projected to grow from 4.8% in 1984 to between 12.7% and 15.6% by 2024 (Chen 1989). The decline of mortality increases the chances of people living long enough to form three-generation families (Tu, Liang and Li 1989), and the duration for such a life stage has already increased to a mean of 21.9 years for women aged 55 to 59 who lived with their parents-in-law (Hu 1994).

The "three-generation residence" and children's enormous support for the elderly in Asian countries have been viewed as a cultural asset in current international discourse on elderly care. Privatization of elder care in these nations, no longer simply inevitable, has become a choice, a policy. UN, WHO, and academic circles have begun to speak of an East Asian model of care for the elderly. For example, in a current (1990) WHO publication *Improving Health of Older People: A World*

View, Macfadyen's introduction, "Health and Social Policy Issues in Aging", states that "It is likely that Asian countries such as Singapore, the Republic of Korea, and China will parallel Japan's policies on aging, since they have comparable tradition and family support systems...." In the same book, Dr. N. Ogawa discusses the prevalence of the extended family in Japan and other Asian countries and reports that as the standard the majority of bedridden elderly are looked after at home by middle-aged women outside the labor force. He states that the "Japanese model" may be relevant to policy makers in the developing world interested in "combining the best of traditional and modern approaches in order to provide health services to the elderly" (Ogawa 1990: 628). He offers that the greater participation of this group of women in the labor force may increase economic incentives for developing alternative care, but he also declares that "the psychological and emotional well-being of the elderly sick might deteriorate more seriously in the alternative care than in the standard case" (Ogawa 1990: 643).

The practice of the three-generation family that underlies this system of elder care is in fact similar across the Asian NIC countries. For example, in Japan, 63.4% of the elderly currently live with their children (Maeda 1990: 382–386). In Hong Kong, 80% of people aged 55 and over live with their children (Census Report 1986) and about 60% of the elderly depend financially on their children (Choi 1986). Similar features are identified in Taiwan. In a current state report on the elderly in Taiwan based on an island-wide survey, 65.7% of the elderly live with their adult children, and 54.8% financially depend on them (Ministry of the Interior 1990). The prevalence of three-generation family dwelling and extensive children's support for the elderly are considered to reflect the cultural preference in elderly care among Asian societies.

The so-called Japan (or Asian) model has a powerful appeal. It promises the most humane living environment, the best care possible (because it comes from one's own blood), care consistent with indigenous values, and all this at the lowest possible cost to society. Actually, the states of these Asian countries have already developed (or borrowed from each other) policies to reinforce the 'family-care' mode; thus, elderly long-term care can be reduced to only 'medical' services and finance issues.

Social scientists engaged in this policy discourse who support the cultural preference theory often demonstrate it through attitude studies showing a preference for "living with and being supported by adult children" as an ideal for elderly care in Asian societies, in contrast to a Western ideal of "independent living and reluctance to be a burden on one's children" (Hsiao 1984: 75–76). They contend that support for familizing elder care in East Asia is not just a myth or a cynical ploy by politicians, but a fact which can be empirically specified and tested. Indeed, results from national surveys on living arrangements for the elderly and from public opinion surveys do indicate the majority of elderly in Japan and other newly industrialized Asian countries maintain the three-generation family as an ideal and as a cultural practice.

The international and local field literatures represent the model as self-evidently worthwhile and accepted where it is applied. From outside of demography and health care economics, however, we can question some of the assumptions and then focus on other potential effects of the model, notably the view that familizing costs actually means that costs are inordinately borne unnoticed by those with the least power within Taiwanese, Hong Kong, and Japanese families — the elderly themselves and women.

Against the notion that the new 'model' is just a cover for inaction on the needs for financial independence and autonomy of the elderly and needs of invisible family caregivers, it must be seen that privatization is a policy that actively constructs: Japanese and Taiwanese states, the two clearest examples, use tax, housing, and distribution policies and moral education on 'filiality' to make the family the unit of care.

Is the Asian pattern of living arrangement really a cultural preference? Is it merely a reflection of a prevailing cultural myth? Do Asian elderly enjoy greater life satisfaction or a better quality of life than their western counterparts among whom independent living is preferred and direct state finance for social security and medical care are their main concern? There is also the question of gender: Is this cultural preference versus cultural myth question closely related to which gender is being discussed? To address these questions, this paper begins with a different approach to assess the relative well-being of the caregiver and the elderly individual in different social-cultural contexts. We begin with suicide.

Clearly Better Off? Suicide as One Indicator

The idea that living within the family (or any other institution) will have a tremendous impact on the elderly is clear enough. How can we evaluate that impact across cultures? A full assessment would have to take in the physical, mental, and spiritual well-being of the elderly and their caregivers, and the interest of society in equality and efficiency. For the moment, let us, following Durkheim (1951), compare age and gender-specific suicide rates within societies and between societies with very different systems for maintaining the elderly.

The use of suicide rates as an indicator of well-being faces certain methodological limitation. The exact causal linkage between many social factors and the elders' mental well-being cannot be examined through suicide, but these data are not used for that purpose. We want to see whether the pattern in these data is consistent with the accepted view of the three-generational family's effect on well-being among the elderly.

A second methodological limitation is the possibility of reporting and selection biases in the absolute rates, biases that may vary between societies. Cultural and health service factors might also mediate the chances for successful suicides (Douglas 1967, Stengel 1966). However, within the same society and examining the same gender group, we can be more confident in the relative incidence across age groups and can draw a general picture of relative mental health conditions. Also, comparing the elders' suicide risks across the country, region, and time can tell us something far more important at the international and historical level, since reporting bias can be enormous under different sociocultural systems (e.g., Kleinman 1977). In other words, if family care in itself is the major key to the elders' well-being in these industrial societies, we expect it to have an impact on this very objective assessment of well-being, age patterns of suicide rates.

Table 1 does indeed show an association of suicide and the system of family maintenance, but exactly opposite to that predicted by the dominant view. To better understand these findings, we examine the three main columns of Table 1. First, note that there is no consistent pattern relating suicide rates of young people to the categories of East Asian and Western. At this gross level of rate comparison, no evidence stands out to suggest anything resembling an East Asian pattern of suicide.

Moving to the second major column, however, alarming differences appear: The elderly in the East Asian countries are killing themselves at rates up to five times higher than their own younger generations and eight times higher than their Western counterparts. Third, we note the sharp contrast between the experiences of older women in the two groups. Suicide rates for East Asian elderly women range from 28.4 to 39.2; rates for Western women range from 2.6 to a high of 9.2.

In the table, we compare the relative suicide rates within countries as the ratio of the elderly suicide rate to the suicide rate for the young. Once again we see a major difference between East Asia and the West, especially for women. The five Western countries show no great difference; the ratio hovers just below or just above 1, tipping slightly toward the elderly in some cases, towards the young in others. In East Asia, the least age-marked ratio stands at 2.1 in Japan. The other four countries are all above 3.

At the very least, suicide as an indicator does not support the orthodox supposition that the elderly in the East Asian system are better off than their more independent Western counterparts. Proponents of the supposed East Asian model might respond that the better life environment for the elderly in these countries is being overwhelmed

TABLE 1

Suicide Rate and Ratio by Age in Different Countries, Suicides per 100,000

	Total	Male	Female	Total	Male	Female	Total	Male	Female
Japan (1984)	20.9	30.2	11.6	45.7	54.9	39.3	2.2	1.8	3.4
Singapore (1981)	8.6	10.8	6.4	29.2	30.2	28.4	3.4	2.8	4.3
Taiwan (1984)	12.7	14.8	10.4	47.3	56.1	38.1	3.0	3.8	3.7
Hong Kong (1984)	11.2	15.0	6.4	38.1	45.3	34.6	3.4	3.0	5.4
U.S. (1984)	17.0	23.3	8.8	19.3	38.1	6.6	1.1	1.6	0.8
U.K. (1983)	13.5	20.2	6.7	15.1	28.1	9.3	1.1	1.4	1.4
Canada (1984)	16.9	26.0	7.8	10.9	27.0	7.1	0.9	1.0	0.9
France (1983)	19.6	25.1	13.9	11.9	16.6	9.7	0.6	0.7	0.7
W. Germany (1984)	20.9	30.1	13.9	22.4	59.8	2.6	1.1	1.9	0.2
Sweden (1984)	26.1	36.5	15.3	25.5	47.5	11.7	1.0	1.3	0.8
Norway (1984)	16.5	24.0	8.6	11.7	21.2	6.0	0.7	1.3	0.7

Source: Calculated from data reported in United Nations 1986 "Demographic Year Book," Tables 7 and 33. Taiwan's data is calculated from Health Statistics and Demographic Yearbook, Taiwan Area, ROC.

by a far greater force totally unrelated to the system for maintaining the elderly. First we note that this unexplained force does not affect younger people in East Asia. Second, the author's own research on suicide in Taiwan and the existing research on other East Asian countries shows no such factor.

The data suggest a stronger possibility : aspects of the East Asian model may in fact be detrimental to the well-being of the elderly.

The Asian Family System: Patriarchy

Let us recall that the basic arguments for the East Asian model revolve around the lifestyle of the elderly. In the West, the elderly are more likely to live on their own. In the East Asian newly-industrialized countries, the elderly are more likely to live with their families. This formulation is focused on residential arrangement, support, and care which are supposed to be best handled by families. The discussion of suicide impels us to ask what is happening within these families and the larger societies that could begin to account for the disturbingly negative indicator of life quality.

To specify the real differences between East and West, we consider the family not as a biological or residential unit but as a social structure, a set of relations between positions. On this basis, the so-called East Asian or three-generation family is best described not in spatial or residential terms but according to its repeated principle of relation: patriarchy.

Behind the Patrilineal System: Financial Dependence and Intergenerational Exchanges

The families of the five East Asian cases are patrilineal; the family is defined, preserved, and reproduced through the male line. Women marry out of their patrilineages and into other patrilineages. Focusing on the Taiwan case, we see that the children women produce belong conventionally, and often legally, to the patrilineage. Although women are legally entitled to inheritance, an equal devolution of property is still extremely rare. A recent survey in Taiwan indicated that only 5.3% of daughters actually received their share (Ministry of the Interior 1989). The principle of property division in terms of time and share among sons also indicates that intergenerational resource-transfer often contains formal and informal contracts that stipulate the exchange of property for care (Cohen 1976) (Table 2).

The presence or absence of a universal social security system has major consequences for the system in place. For example, in Taiwan, social security is restricted to a small segment of the elderly population, and more than half (54.8%) of the elderly have to rely on their children for living expenses. Widowed women who have the least access to social security (1.4%) and other requisites of independent living

TABLE 2

Living with Children and Financial Dependence on Children
in Taiwan: Stated Ideals and Practices of Elderly (%)

	Live with Children		Source for Living Expense	
	Ideal	Practice	Children	Social Society
In General	73.2	65.7	54.8	11.9
men	66.8	59.9	45.7	20.4
women	80.6	72.1	72.8	2.2
Widowed	87.1	78.7	78.8	4.5
male	78.2	68.1	63.8	11.8
female	90.5	83.2	84.9	1.4
Frail	–	72.7	–	–
male	–	69.6	–	–
female	–	78.1	–	–

SOURCE: Calculated from published statistics in "Report on the Living Conditions of the Elderly in Taiwan ROC", 1990, Tables 7, 8, 18, Ministry of the Interior, ROC. "Social Security" refers to pension and insurance.

depend more on children's support for living expenses (84.9%) and have the strongest preference for (90.5%), and practice of (83.2%), the three-generation residence. This leads us to question the family preference assumption further.

In the absence of strong — or in some cases any — social security systems, the categories 'son' and 'daughter' relate very differently to the senior males. Sons, particularly eldest sons, are expected to extend the family into the future and look after the parents in their old age. Regardless of affective ties or personal feelings about gender, most family heads continue to perceive that sons are likely to bring far greater monetary and status returns to investments, returns that are the basis for old age support and family preservation. Daughters, as the saying goes, are like spilled water. Once spilled out into the world, nothing comes back. They usually contribute to the family only during the period when their education is completed and before marriage. Via marriage they enter another family and direct their resources to developing a new family.

A critical consequence of differences in relation to families comes as parents age. Parents with productive property may transfer it to their sons as they age. If they do not, the transfer is usually effected after the death of the father. A woman in Taiwan, on average, can expect to live about 9 years after the death of her husband so that either form of property transfer decreases the mother's resources. Daughters as a consequence of their relation to the patrilineage are usually out of the family during their parents' old age so that while official discourse talks generally about parents residing with their children, in fact they almost always reside with their sons and daughter-in-law (Table 3).

The differences between positions in the family have another relevant effect. While orthodoxy portrays a son as taking care of his parents, the daughter-in-law provides much of the actual care. This is often a source of conflict that brings harm to all involved. Finally, position relationships change in later life and both the elderly and as a result their caregivers experience sharp discontinuities in habits, power, and space. In the following sections we develop the

TABLE 3
Three-generation Living Arrangements in Taiwan (%)

	Current Practice	Ideal in Public Opinion	
		Rural	Urban
Live with married children %	72.5	70.8	64.9
— with son/daughter-in-law	70.8	64.1	42.2
— with daughter/son-in-law	1.7	0.6	5.2
— no son/daughter preference	–	4.0	12.3

SOURCE: Ministry of Interior, 1989; Hu *et al.* 1992.

implications of each of these points for the well-being of the elderly, their kin, and the interest of equity and efficiency.

Care for the Frail and Chronically Ill: Daughter-in-law's Job

The patrilocal arrangement in Asian societies also has an enormous impact on the elders' long-term care (especially of elderly women) when they are frail and bedridden. The demanding task of caring for most bedridden elderly women in Taiwan and Japan is carried out neither by their own sons and daughters nor by the socially organized facilities/professionals. It is the daughter-in-law, the least visible member in the official discourse of the family and the most troublesome character according to popular belief, when it comes to partrilineal familial solidarity and daily encounters — who becomes the main caregiver (see Table 4).

TABLE 4
Primary Caregiver for Bedridden Elderly

	Taiwan		Japan		U.S.	
	Female	Male	Female	Male	Female	Male
Spouse	14.7	44.5	11.4	61.0	10	37
Children	29.8	31.4	27.7	10.8	34	24
Son	24.6	29.4	–	–	–	–
Daughter	5.2	2.0	–	–	–	–
Daughter-in-law	51.3	21.6	50.4	21.7	–	–
Other	3.3	2.3	7.8	5.7	35	23
Paid helper	2.6	1.9	–	–	–	–
Other acquaintance	0.5	0.4	–	–	–	–
Institutional care	0.3	0.2	–	–	21	16

SOURCES: Taiwan's data from Ministry of Interior 1989 "Survey Report on Women's Living Conditions", Tables 6–13, 6–20. Japan's data from D. Maeda (1990) "The Role of the Family in Developed Countries", Table 23.5. U.S. data from Doty (1985) "An Overview of Long-term Care", Table 3.

The invisibility of the in-laws in the Taiwanese family contributes to the non-issue of the family (the children's) burden in the policy debate that the ones who are charged with responsibility, sons and daughters, are not the primary caregivers. In practice, the apprehension of possible disruption of familial solidarity and filiality makes the burden issue even more of an unspoken topic. The problem, thus, is completely sealed into private family business and thereby becomes more the object of generational and gender bargaining inside the individual family.

Social Change and Cohort Effects:
Another Missing Reality

The demographic revolution is paralleled by and interacts with social and political transformation in Taiwan. Within a lifetime, power relations within the family have transformed a key aspect of kinship : young adult children have gained a measure of resources and autonomy. This change is evident in family formation. For the birth cohort of 1930, over 77% of married women said parents had arranged their marriages. Less than one generation later, in the cohort of 1955 only 15% of women's marriages were arranged by parents.

Another important arena where change appears is education. That education shortened the years in which a woman could contribute economically to her natal family acted earlier in the century to limit women's schooling. More than a third of women in the 1930 birth cohort had no formal schooling and only 9% had a junior high school education. Under the recent compulsory state education policy, the percentage without schooling dropped to 4% while 41% completed junior high school or more advanced education. These changes are also related to changes in Taiwan's labor market. A quarter of women in the 1930 birth cohort worked outside of the family for pay; less than a generation later, eight in 10 women were non-family wage workers.

It would be quite wrong to interpret these changes as a zero-sum shift away from the family. Much of women's work contributed to the partilineal family. Compulsory nine-year education did not give women a decisive advantage in building their own. The basic relations of the family remained in place but their content changed in ways that could affect the positions and well-being of members, particularly the daughter-in-law, mother-in-law dyad (Gallin 1986).

When the 20th century began, a young woman marrying into a patrilineage came under the control of her mother-in-law. Mothers-in-law delegated housework and oversaw its completion. The mother-in-law controlled her own time, housework management, and women's social network in the community. The daughter-in-law had virtually no autonomy and was subject to the demands of other members of her new family as well, chiefly to be compliant and to produce a son. To call it her 'new family' with the Western connotation of that phrase runs the risk of glossing over a difficult situation, since the next step into the family was production of a son to continue the patrilineage. The transition from natal to husband's family appears to have been difficult.

Interfamilial Inequality : Social Class Matters

Rapid industrialization and urbanization in Taiwan not only create social resources but also redistribute them among families. For example, the inequality of families residing in different regions has increased in this process. A current study of social factors and mortality in Taiwan (Hu, Lin and Wu 1990) indicates that women's labor force participation varies a great deal over the 365 Taiwan townships (from 5% to 90%). The proportion of people aged 15 and over who attained high school education was also reflected in the mental health indicators such as the suicide rate. In the early 1900s, there seems to have been no significant suicide rate difference between people in the rural and urban areas, and in some cases, the rate in certain cities was actually higher than the rate in neighboring areas (Wolf 1975). More recent data shows that the age standardized suicide rate by rural township not only varies a great deal (from 1.5 to 116.3 per 100,000 persons) but also is highly associated with levels of urbanization and development: the higher the level of urbanization, the lower the suicide rate.

A higher suicide risk in a less developed region applies to the elderly as well as to the economically productive population. The experience of discontinuity and the lack of alternatives can be even more severe for the elderly in rural regions in this rapid social transformation. For example, development in the urban center and nearby cities and the outmigration of the younger generation can drastically shake the social world of the rural elderly and force them into the unexpected struggle between separation and moving. Since the family is their sole source of care, rural elderly might have to move into a son/daughter-in-law's dwelling in order to receive care. They leave the world which they had known, especially the social world of people with similar dispositions, and experiences. The discontinuity in social life and physical environment, in addition to a decline in position in their family, can make them far more vulnerable and, based on my interviews, can be psychologically devastating. The condition for women can be worse if they are widowed, the property has been divided, and there is no choice but to move.

The social disadvantages of the elderly in less developed regions are reflected in their suicide risks. In Table 5, we see that both old men and women in least urbanized areas have much higher suicide rates than their urbanized counterparts. For elderly males, the relative suicide risk almost doubles (RR=1.78); for urban elderly males and elderly females, the relative risk is even larger (RR=2.4).

TABLE 5

Suicide Rates and Rate Differentials in Most Urbanized and
East Urbanized Areas in Taiwan, 1974–1985

	Suicide Rate*		Rate Differential	
	Most Urbanized (1)	Least Urbanized (2)	(2)-(1)	(2)/(1)
Male				
Young (25–44)	9.26	27.45	18.19	2.96
Old (65+)	38.63	68.40	29.77	1.78
Female				
Young (25–44)	6.98	19.54	12.56	2.80
Old (65+)	21.08	50.66	29.58	2.40

*per 100,000

Missing Language and Politics

Public Opinion : A Field of Misrecognition

In the policy arena, policymakers and experts are not unaware of the old age welfare and social services developed in the West. However, the issues have been quickly examined and discussed in terms of 'cultural' suitability while culture is simply a selected form of public opinion or practice. Results from repeated opinion surveys on the elders' wish to live with and be cared for by the 'family' and 'children' (in-laws are not mentioned) becomes a main tool to justify policy orientation. The high prevalence of the three-generation residence as ideal and as practice has thus been accepted uncritically as a cultural preference, so that family care becomes the main-policy orientation.

The main theoretical problem of the nature of public opinion is largely ignored in such policy-oriented research. Public opinion is a field of recognition and misrecognition which is constituted and imposed with the authority and necessity of a collective position adopted on data intrinsically amenable to many other structures. Bourdieu (1979) stressed the construction of a field of opinion including two parts: the explicit discourse — orthodox versus heterodox arguments — and 'doxa' — the undiscussed part which customary law governs and which remains in implicit, unformulated, and unquestionable forms.

In other words, an opinion survey carried out by using the official depoliticized language — such as family, children — in a society with a strong political philosophy that "to govern is to regulate the family" constructs as well as collects its results. Applying unquestionable moral pressure through "is the most important thing in one's life" and "filial piety is the basis of morality", and backing it up with political enforcement prevents the examination of the existing social order which has been socially produced and naturalized.

As a field of opinion, only the kind of critique which brings the undiscussed into discussion, the unformulated into formulation, can break the fit between the subjective structures — the aggregate of the 'choices' — and the objective structures. In this case, the undiscussed part is the patriarchal nature of the Chinese (or Asian) family system, the essential in-law relationship in the care-giving and care-receiving process, and the increasing resource gaps between families in different social classes and in different regions. To show how such public opinion works and, just as importantly, how its power can be questioned by unauthoritative alternative information, the authors did a survey by using two different forms of a question to elicit answers to the same question of the ideal living arrangement for the elderly. The first method is the orthodox way of inquiry — directly asking the respondent to choose between prefigured ideals; the second method is to give a morally desensitized and informative statement to the effect that "Some people say that three generations living apart but in the same neighborhood is the best arrangement as the old folks and their kids can support each other while maintaining their own space. Do you agree, or disagree?"

Table 6 summarizes the main results of such a test and showed clearly that people do respond differently to different methods of inquiry. About 70% of respondents give the official answer — the ideal happy three-generation family scene — to the standard question. However, when the question is asked indirectly with morally desensitized and informative alternatives, the overwhelming majority (about 90%) say that the alternative arrangement is the best. Also contrary to most findings and beliefs that women, the less educated, and older people are more traditional in their attitude, this study shows that when myth and moral judgment are somewhat neutralized, there are no essential attitudinal differences.

Language Which Reflexes: a Qualitative Inquiry

In order to solve the "familial support vs. elderly's dependency" puzzle and to have a better understanding of the elderly's own experience in the three-generational family situation, qualitative inquiry has been administered (Hu and Chou 1996). The study is focused on elderly

TABLE 6

What Is the Preferred Living Arrangement for the Elderly?
Two Ways of Asking and Two Ways Answering (%)

	Direct Choice Method		Indirect Response Method
	3-generation	Neighbor	Neighbor
All respondents	68.3	21.9	87.8
Region			
– rural	70.8	16.9	88.5
– urban	64.7	27.7	86.8
Gender			
– female	66.2	26.6	85.4
– male	70.5	20.9	89.3
Age			
60+	78.9	18.4	84.8
40–59	74.4	18.6	84.4
30–39	59.8	30.5	90.7
Education			
– elementary	80.0	12.3	83.5
– high school	67.2	30.8	91.0
– college+	58.7	36.7	89.4

SOURCE: Hu, Y.-H.; Chou, Y.-J. and N. Bai (1992) "Three Generation Family and Alternative: Attitudes toward Living Arrangements for Elderly in Urban and Rural Taiwan", paper presented in ASA annual meeting, Pittsburgh, Pennsylvania, USA.

women in Taiwan — the group considered the most trapped cohort in the socio-cultural transition. Information about the subjective experience and interpretations of intergenerational relationships are gathered from focused group interviews. Four groups — young-old and old-old — in the city and countryside were formed and were interviewed, and information regarding intergenerational relations were investigated in five types of specific daily activities — cooking, grandchildren-care, leisure activity, health care, and monetary transfer. These five dimensions of family relations and activities are neglected in most official talks but are essential in the elderly women's worlds. The results also provide different pictures of the elderly's life situations and welfare needs.

Table 7 is a brief summary of intergenerational relationships from elderly Taiwanese women's perspectives. In sum, there is a giant gap between their expectations and social reality in terms of children (sons and daughter-in-laws) support. All their experience and expressions reflect life-long changes inside and outside the family which create the inverse resources distribution between generations, and as a result, their hope to have three generations living together and to have children's support at old age becomes their disappointment.

Although most of the talk regarding the three-generational familial relationships was rather negative and depressing in our focused group interviews, we still detect a number of creative coping and positive talks among the elderly women. For example, many elderly women expressed intimate feelings with their daughters who managed to maintain close contact with them, even though the "married daughters are spilled water" norm is still fairly strong. Second is a new saying among elderly women that "old savings, old friends, and good old body are three major things for old people to guarantee a life with quality and dignity". In other words, some elderly people start to realize that they cannot count on their children totally, and they are looking for alternatives for their own happiness. Thirdly, many old women stressed the importance of engaging in traditional *yang-shen* activities (such as *Tai-chi* or *qigong* exercises) to maintain their physical, spiritual, and social health in their own community. The

TABLE 7

A Summary of Remarks from Old Women's Talk Regarding Changes
in Intergenerational Relationship in Five Specific Familial Encounters

Old Time Experience (when they were daughters-in-law)	Current Situation (when they became mothers-in-law)
A. Cooking	
—they had to cook for parent-in-law	— they have to cook for son's family
—parent-in-law's taste preference came first	— younger's taste came first
—food preparation was a simple task when people were poor	— youngsters are picky and wasting a lot.
B. Caring for Grandchildren	
—daughter-in-law (themselves) took the major.	—many grandmothers still take full responsibility (especially when daughter-in-law lives in and is employed outside)
—child care was rather natural and relaxing.	—child care demand more modern knowledge and full attention.
—more support from family members and neighbors.	—caregivers are more isolated socially and physically.
C. Leisure Activity	
— can enjoy many old friends' companionship	— hard to find friend when move with children to urban residence
— can chatter with old neighbors and enjoy gardening in the old farm	— now become housebound due to grandchild caring and other housework
—no TV	—do not understand the language in TV when younger generations are watching
— likes to wander around the community	—now are trapped in a big empty apartment when everyone went to work or to study

(cont'd overleaf)

TABLE 7 (continued)

D. *Monetary Transfer*	
— older generation control the whole children's earning (even children earned much less then)	— now old generation lost the control of children's earning and many have to depend on the monthly allowance from children
— older generation hold essential family property (land or house)	— most old family property is divided early or has been invested on children or had lost its value
— living expense was much cheaper then	— living expense kept increasing continuously
E. *Illness Care*	
— daughter-in-law did all the illness care	— old women have to assume the most care when their husbands were ill, but when they are ill, few daughters-in-law have the time and willingness to care for them

SOURCE: Hu, Y.H. & Chou, Y.J. (1996) *Old Women's Talk: Their voices and their rights,* Taipei:Tin-Yen (in Chinese).

revival of another traditional cultural belief and practice through the elderly's grass-root movement becomes the cultural alternatives in contrast to the medicalized health care service and the diminishing informal care from the family members, especially daughter-in-laws (Hu 1996)

Summary

The widely practised "three-generation residence" and children's enormous support for the elderly in Asian countries have been viewed as a cultural asset based on their traditions which can be mobilized and further institutionalized by policymakers for quality care of the elderly. According to this view, the Asian or Japanese model of elderly care is portrayed as the best combination of traditional and modern approaches in current international discourse. This study uses alternative facts to challenge the cultural preference view. Suicide rates and qualitative inquiries which reflect the problems of the Asian patriarchal family system were examined in this paper. Our suicide risk analysis did not support the formulation that the Asian elderly are better off when having no choice except to live with and depend completely on their sons. On the contrary, the data are consistent with the argument that Asian elderly, especially elderly women, are currently very vulnerable in their socially constructed total dependence on their children — their sons and daughters-in law. The qualitative data from old women's talks provide vivid pictures of problematic relationships regarding generation, gender, and class issues in daily life. From such alternative perspectives, the invisible but essential mother-in-law and daughter-in-law dyadic relation has undergone drastic change to the point that in many families their relative positions have not only been reversed, but more new problems are encountered by the elderly and their younger generations as well.

The three-generation family in modern Asian countries is in an important sense a powerful myth. As the myth continues to be embedded in policy and in the authorized, depoliticized, and euphemized language of family and filial morality, inequality between genders, between generations, and between social classes is naturalized in practice, and becomes the unspeakable Doha in the field of public opinion. Furthermore, the overused term — culture — is a construct and social classification (Asian versus Western), through which the world can be misrecognized, mystified, and acted upon politically in reproducing social inequality.

In order to demystify this myth, work on cultural comparison and on policy development in different social/cultural contexts needs more critical rethinking. Such thinking should first include a welfare policy at the state level which would allow elderly people (especially elderly women) at least to have the ability to make independent choices and not strengthen the economic basis of preference for sons. Other social institutions (such as education, mass media, legal forms, social service systems, and politics) which help maintain and reproduce patriarchy, dependency, and hamper the formation of lifelong intimate familial bonds (such as the mother-daughter bond), and prohibit the development of quality formal support systems (such as long-term care services in the community) should also come under serious examination.

Finally, an alternative inquiry in this study not only allows us to demystify the culture politics, but to elicit invisible cultural practices as well. For example, the revival of traditional *Yang-shen* practice seems very powerful in helping the desperate elderly hold themselves together socially, physically and spiritually. The new colloquial language of independence and autonomy has also become widely shared among some elderly groups, a change which can be considered a potentially powerful political request from the grass-root level as a quiet communitarian movement. These alternative cultural constructions are still fairly unknown, nor are they unrecognized in the policy and academic arena. To discover the local cultural wisdom and to incorporate such alternative cultural themes into future policy and academic dialogue will be the next important tasks to accomplish.

References

Bourdieu, P. (1979) *Outline of a Theory of Practice.* London: Cambridge University Press. Census and Statistics Department 1986 By-Census, Summary Results. Hong Kong: Government Press.

Chen, K. (1986) "On the Change of Household Composition in Taiwan", paper presented at the 1986 annual meeting of the American Sociological Association, New York, USA.

Chen, S.-H. and T.-Y. Wu (1986) "Characteristics of Urbanization Levels in Taiwan District", *Geographical Research* 12:287–323 (in Chinese).

Choi, H. (1983) "Cultural and Noncultural Factors as Determinants of Caregiver Burden for the Impaired Elderly in South Korea", *The Gerontologist* 33(1): 8–15.

Chou, Y. (1991) "A Study of Family Care for the Elderly", in *Chinese Family in Transition,* ed. Chaou, pp. 371–380. Hong Kong: Chinese University Press.

Cohen, M.L. (1976) *House United, House Divided: The Chinese Family in Taiwan.* New York: Columbia University Press.

Department of Health, ROC (1985) *Health Statistics.* Taipei.

Doty, P. (1985) "An Overview of Long-term Care", *Health Care Financing Review* 6(3): 69–78.

Douglas, J. (1967) *Social Meanings of Suicide.* Princeton, NJ: Princeton University Press.

Durkheim, E. (1951) *Suicide.* New York: Free Press,

Gallin, R. (1986) "Mother-in-laws and Daughters-in-law: Intergenerational Relations within the Chinese Family in Taiwan", *Journal of Cross-Cultural Gerontology* 1(1):31–49.

Hermalin, A.I.; M-C. Chang; H.-S. Lin; M.-L. Lee and M.B. Ofstedal (1990) "Patterns of Support among the Elderly in Taiwan and Their Policy Implications", presented at the Population Association of American Annual Meeting.

Hsiao, M.H.H. (1984) *A Study of Welfare for the Elderly: Analysis of Service Networks.* Taipei: Executive Yuen, Committee for Development and Evaluation (in Chinese).

Hu, Y.-H. (1990) Economic Development and Mortality Risks for Modern Disease. National Science Council Project Report NSC 79-0301-H010-01.

Hu, Y.-H. (1991) *Social Epidemiology.* Taipei: Chu-Liew (in Chinese).

Hu, Y.-H. (1992) A Study of the Social Construction of Health Care for the Elderly and Gender. NSC Project Report 81-0301-H-010-K1.

Hu, Y.-H. (1994) *Three Generation Families: Facts and Myths.* Taipei: Chu-Liew (in Chinese).

Hu, Y.-H.; Lin, Y. and S. Wu (1990) "Social Factors and Mortality in Taiwan: Analysis of Six Causes of Death in Small Areas", *Journal of Population* 13:83–106.

Hu, Y.-H.; Chou Y.-J. and N. Bai (1992) "Three Generation Family and Alternatives: Attitudes Toward Living Arrangements for the Elderly in Urban and Rural Taiwan", paper presented in ASA annual meeting, Pittsburgh, Pennsylvania, USA.

Hu, Y.-H. and Chou Y.-J. (1996) *Old Women's Talk: Their Voices and Their Rights.* Taipei, Tin-yen (in Chinese).

Hu, Y.-H. (1996) "Communitarism and The Revival of Traditional Yang-sheng Practices among Elderly in Taiwan", paper presented in Fourth Congress Physical Activity. Aging and Sports, Heidelberg, Germany, August 27–31, 1996.

Kleinman, A. (1977) "Depression, Somatization, and the New Cross-Cultural Psychiatry", *Social Science and Medicine* 11:3–10.

Kuang, H. (1991) *A Study on Living Arrangement and Housing Problems among the Elderly in Taiwan.* Taipei: Ministry of Interior.

Lee, Y.-J.; W. Parish and R. Willis (1994) "Sons, Daughters, and Inter-generational Support in Taiwan", *American Journal of Sociology* 99(4):1010–1041.

Macfadyen, D. (1990) "Introduction: Health and Social Policy Issues in Aging", in *Improving the Health of Older People: A World View*, eds. Kane, R.L.; Evans, J.G. and Macfadyen, D., pp. 616–620. New York: Oxford University Press.

Maeda, D. (1990) "The Role of the Family in Developed Countries", in *Improving the Health of Older People: A World View*, eds. Kane, R.L.; Evans, J.G. and Macfadyen, D., pp. 381–397. New York: Oxford University Press.

Ministry of Interior, ROC (1990) *Report on the Living Conditions of the Elderly in Taiwan Area, Republic of China.* Taipei.

Ministry of Interior, ROC (1989) *Report on Women's Living Conditions in Taiwan Area.* Taipei.

Mirzaee, M. (1979) "Trends and Determinants of Mortality in Taiwan — 1895–1975", PhD dissertation. University of Pennsylvania.

Ogawa, N. (1990) "Economic Factors Affecting the Health of the Elderly", in *Improving the Health of Older People: A World View*, eds. Kane, R.L.; Evans, J.G. and Macfadyen, D., pp. 627–645. New York: Oxford University Press.

Stengel, E. (1966) *Suicide and Attempted Suicide.* Baltimore: Penguin Books.

Tu, E.J.-C.; Liang and S. Li (1989) "Mortality Decline and Chinese Family Structure: Implications for Old Age Support", *Journal of Gerontology* 44(4): 157–168.

United Nations (1986) Demographic Yearbook. Geneva.

Wolf, M. (1975) "Women and Suicide in China", in *Women in Chinese Society*, eds. M. Wolf and R. Witke, pp. 111–114. Stanford: Stanford University Press.

Chapter 12

Caring for the Elderly in Singapore

Kalyani Mehta
National University of Singapore

Introduction

Care for the elderly in Singapore is shared by the family, the community, and the state. The national policy with regard to senior citizens "aims to keep every elderly person physically and mentally fit and active so that the person can retain normal living arrangements for as long as possible." The government espouses a "many helping hands" approach wherein the three pillars, i.e., the family, the community and the state, have a part to play. The family members are expected to provide immediate care, while the community and state step in to support the efforts of the family, furnish the infrastructure for financial, health and social care, and lastly, provide institutional care for the poor and destitute elderly.

Singapore is the fastest aging country in Southeast Asia. The 1990 Census of Population shows that 9% of the population has reached the aged category (60 years and above) and this will soar to 26% in the year 2030. Another significant transformation is the "aging" for the aged population. The increased longevity of the population, combined with advanced medical facilities, have led to the rapid growth of the "old old" segment of the population, i.e., those 70 years and above: "As a proportion of the population the 'old-old' will increase from 2.2% in 1990 to 7.3% in 2030, and the "young old" from 6.9% to 18.8%" (Cheung, 1992, p. 11). This phenomenon will increase both the demand for services for the frail elderly and the stress levels of family members. Life expectancy at birth for males stands at 71.9 years, and for females at 76.5 years (Shantakumar, 1994, p. 9).

The last few decades have witnessed swift and far-reaching social changes, the most prominent being a rise in women's labor force in the participation, which has modified the traditional roles of women as primary caregivers of the elderly. Presently, women comprise 52% of the labor force. While female spouses continue to play the caregiver function, daughters and daughters-in-law are rarely available to perform physical caregiving tasks during the day. These changes have implications for the capacity of the family to cope with the elderly's need for care. The other important social change is the trend towards nuclear family structure as opposed to stem or extended family structure. It must be noted that the changes are occurring at different paces in the various ethnic communities that exist. In demographic terms, the Chinese form 78% of the total resident population, Malays 14%, Indians 7% and other smaller ethnic groups 1% (1990 Census Population). Among the three communities, the Malays have the highest proportion of stem family households, i.e., three or more generations co-residing, followed by the Chinese and then Indians (*ibid.*).

This paper outlines the present systems of elderly care in Singapore and highlights two issues which bear upon the nature and extent of support for the elderly. These are living arrangements and value systems. Both issues are influenced by the cultural context in which they are encapsulated as well as the larger societal changes. The author draws on local research conducted in Singapore in the last five years to substantiate the discussion. Finally, some projections into the 21st century on the challenges facing Singaporean society regarding the aging phenomenon will be made.

Mechanisms of Elderly Care

State Mechanisms

At the macro local, the government has targeted the challenges posed by a rapidly aging population as a major area that will need to be addressed seriously. Although the destitute and aged living alone have to be given immediate attention, the Singapore government believes in maintaining a developmental and preventive thrust in its approach to the social problem. An example is the network of services which is being established for more efficient and effective care for the elderly in the west, east and central districts of Singapore (*The Straits Times*, 1/11/96, p.7). The Ministry of Health is coordinating the network with voluntary and private organizations serving the elderly in the districts. With closer working relationships between organizations serving the elderly, it is hoped that service delivery can be improved.

One of the outstanding achievements of the government is the establishment of the Central Provident Fund (CPF) which was envisaged in its early days as a compulsory savings scheme for the post-retirement years. A CPF member is entitled to withdraw a major part of his savings at the age of 55; he has to leave in his account a minimum sum and Medisave savings for later use. It has, since its inception in 1955, evolved into a social security package because the funds can be used for a variety of purposes, e.g., buying property, local tertiary education of children, and investments such as stocks and shares. The Medisave component of the CPF can be used to cover hospitalization expenses of members as well as of their elderly parents. If a parent has his/her own Medisave account, it lessens the burden on the adult child in terms of medical expenses. In a unique way, the

CPF has created a channel for the government to share its wealth with its citizens, e.g., through its CPF Top Up Scheme. The government has selectively rewarded elderly citizens and financially helped the poor through the CPF channel. While in the past only those who had worked could open a CPF account, now it is possible for a child to open an account for a parent who has never worked, such as a housewife. Thus, the scheme is reviewed and fine-tuned periodically to suit the society's needs. A visitor recently described the CPF package as generating a "stakeholder" mentality in the people while in a welfare state a "dependency" mentality is nurtured (*Sunday Review*, 14/1/96). Despite the many benefits of the CPF scheme, recently there has been rising concern as to whether the CPF savings are likely to be enough for the majority to continue living the same lifestyle after retirement. The poor, and especially widows, who may not have accumulated much savings, are identified as high risk groups. These will need a "safety net" in old age which will prevent them from falling below the poverty line. At present, there exists a Social Assistance Scheme under the Ministry of Community Development for the poor and disabled of any age group. The aged who do not have any financial support from relatives may apply for aid, but the criteria are stringent. The amount disbursed is only sufficient for basic needs. A similar "safety net" exists in government hospitals in the form of a Medifund scheme for poor patients who are unable to pay for their medical expenses. The housing policies of the Housing and Development Board (a statutory body) have been designed to encourage adult children to co-reside or to live in proximity with their elderly parents and vice versa. These schemes, e.g., the Multi-Tier Family Housing scheme, Joint Balloting Scheme (Wong and Yeh, 1985) and Grant of $50,000 for applicants to reside close to parents, are state policies aimed at encouraging families to support their elderly kin. Although there has been limited success, the schemes are constantly revised to adapt to the changing societal context.

The relatively new Congregate Housing Scheme is a joint program of the Ministry of Community Development and the Housing and Development Board. Under its recent upgrading of government flats, the single elderly living alone in selected blocks are receiving facilities which make their flat more elder-friendly at no cost to themselves, e.g., non-slip tiles in the bathroom, handle-bars and pedestal seats in the toilet and most importantly, an alarm system which alerts volunteers in a nearby voluntary organization of a crisis that the elderly may be experiencing. The alarm system also causes a bulb outside the door to light up as well as a bell to ring, which would draw the attention of neighbors to render emergency help. The single elderly living alone consist mainly of first generation immigrants who have never married or have left their families in their homeland. There are about 8,000–10,000 such elderly. There will always be a certain proportion of elderly without family support, e.g., the never married, widowed, divorced, or those who do not have positive relationships with family members. If they wish to remain in the community, these flats would enable them to do so with the reassurance that help is at hand if necessary. The other benefit of this scheme is that it links a voluntary agency with these elderly, thus emphasizing the responsibility of the community towards the vulnerable aged in their midst. In the long run such schemes engender a caring society.

In terms of tax incentives, there is an aged dependency relief of S$4,500 for a child supporting a dependent elderly parent who has no income, and a relief of S$1,500 for a non-co-residing child providing parental care. As the cost of living (including medical costs) in Singapore soars, the relief will require revision.

Finally, mention must be made of a bill that has been passed by Parliament called 'The Maintenance of Parents' Act (1995). It allows elderly parents to sue their irresponsible child/children in a tribunal court for financial support. One condition attached is that the elderly person should have been responsible in the past in looking after his/ her children. Although the problem of abandoned elderly parents is negligible at this point, such an Act is deemed to have preventive value. To what extent it will be utilized by elderly in the future remains to be seen, since it is common for Asians not to "display" their family problems in public.

Community Mechanisms

Community-based services for the elderly range from institutional care to care provided to the elderly in his own home. There are approximately 25 Nursing Homes for the aged, 16 Community Homes for the Aged (for the mobile and less frail elderly), 12 Rehabilitation and Day Care Centers, three hospice institutions and two community hospitals (Directory of Social Services, 1995, p. 437). The Community hospitals cater to patients who need long-term care under medical supervision. Three day care centers specialize in looking after dementia patients. Counseling is provided by professional social workers at Family Service Centers and staff of the Singapore Action Group of Elders (SAGE). Ten Centers provide social and recreational facilities to the elderly in the neighborhood. Apart from all these, there are about 350 Senior Citizens' Clubs across the island which are operated by various organizations to meet the socioemotional needs of the healthy, normal elderly. These Clubs organize tours, exercise classes, e.g., tai chi, qigong, gateball and badminton, dancing classes (both eastern and western), free health screening, and chess competitions.

A separate category of services consist of those delivered to the doorstep of the elderly. These include mobile medical clinics, domiciliary nursing care, meal delivery, home help service, e.g., household chores, escort service, e.g., accompanying the elderly to the clinic or hospital. A nominal rate is charged for the poor, but a sliding scale is used for those who are better off. This category of services is still not available island-wide. In future, as the population of elderly increases, especially the frail, these services will need to be extended island-wide and designed to cater to the specific needs of the major ethnic groups in Singapore, e.g., diet and language preferences.

Other services are available for the caregivers of the elderly. These include support groups based at hospitals or voluntary agencies, e.g., family service centers. These 25 family service centers distributed in various parts of the island serve as multi-purpose one-stop helping agencies. They are run by different voluntary bodies and partially funded by the Ministry of Community Development. There are plans to increase these to 35 by the end of the century. Respite care to relieve the primary caregiver temporarily is offered by a few Homes for the Aged as well as by community hospitals. Lastly, talks and workshops are organized to improve the coping and physical caring skills of family caregivers. The Tsao Foundation, a non-profit organization, has taken an active role in this arena, which will require much attention in the 21st century as the dependency ratio increases and families experience rising stress levels.

Although the range of community services is increasing rapidly, it is fragmented (Ng, G.T., 1991, p. 139) and lacks proper planning. As a result, duplication of services and gaps and inefficiency in delivery often result. Some efforts are being made by the National Council of Social Services to address this issue but progress is slow.

Other Societal Mechanisms

In schools, family values emphasizing filial responsibility and concern for family members are stressed by teachers as part of the curriculum. Community service projects are conducted in Homes for the Aged, as well as in "old" housing estates, e.g., painting the homes of the elderly and repairing electrical appliances. Rehabilitative programs for juvenile offenders also include voluntary work, which has enhancement value for the giver of help as well as the care receiver. At the national level, annually the Senior Citizens' week held during the third week of November increases awareness as well as involvement of the public in the problems faced by the aged.

The mass media effectively distributes the message of caring for the aged in the community. Television, radio and newspaper articles address this issue in many ways, sometimes by highlighting the deeds of samaritans and sometimes by sanctioning uncaring actions by Singaporeans. An aspect that must be kept in mind in reaching out to the elderly of the present generation is their limited literacy skills. Their lack of knowledge of many of the available services has emerged in the research (Mehta, 1994; Report of the National Survey of Senior

Citizens, 1995). Hence, more creative and ethnic-sensitive ways of reaching these poorly educated populations are required. Greater use of radio media and visual presentations such as roadshows are suggested so that public education can be made more effective.

Family Mechanisms

The living arrangements of the elderly provide the physical and social context within which relationships are played out, in most cases familial relationships. The context also shapes considerably the availability and accessibility of support, be it financial, instrumental, social or emotional. However, living arrangement cannot tell us the *degree* of availability of this support nor does it inform us of the *quality* of care received. The Survey of Aged Living in the Community (1986) indicated that about 85% of aged Singaporean lived with their children. These aged could be living with unmarried children, i.e., in a nuclear family household or with married children, i.e., in a stem family household. The remaining 15% included those elderly who were living with spouse only, non-relatives, or living alone. Only about 2% of the elderly in the survey lived alone (Chen and Cheung, 1988, p. 35). In an earlier survey, it was reported that institutionalized elderly comprised less than 2% of the total population (National Survey of Senior Citizens, 1983).

Findings from an international project, "The Comparative Study of the Elderly in Four Asian Countries", revealed interesting insights regarding living arrangements in old age (Mehta *et al.*, 1995). Focus group discussions with the elderly and adult children showed that institutionalization was viewed by both generations as the last resort. The preferred choices of the different ethnic groups studied, i.e., the Chinese, Malays and Indians (from the three major ethnic communities) varied in terms of which child they wished to live with. Although almost all elderly wished to live with their children in old age, there was a gender preference after all the children were married. The Chinese and Indians preferred to live with one of the sons, usually the eldest, while the Malay elderly preferred to live with a daughter.

The study noted that these preferences were gradually becoming flexible, depending on the actual circumstances, e.g., whether there was a caregiver available during the day. The findings lend support to Mason (1991) who believed that the preferred living arrangements of the elderly were influenced by ethnocultural norms and family systems. However, practical exigencies did influence the actual living arrangements in Singapore.

Another set of qualitative data consisted of multiple in-depth interviews with 45 non-institutionalized elderly aged 70 years and above. This research, which was conducted between June 1991 and May 1992, highlighted the major psycho-social concerns of "old-old" Singaporeans and their ethnic manifestations. A consistent finding in both sets of data was the automatic link between living arrangements and care from the perceptions of the elderly. Often, a question such as,

"Who do you live with?" received the reply,

"My son/daughter takes care of me."

This conceptual linkage in the minds of the elderly was supported by the data evidence, which indicated that it was the co-resident children, children-in-law, spouse (if physically fit) and grandchildren who provided the greater amount and range of support to the elderly. Non-co-resident children, children-in-law and other family members such as siblings, nieces and nephews contributed their share in terms of financial and emotional support (often via the telephone) and transport facilities but these contributions were limited in scope. However, those kin who lived in proximity were more likely to render assistance to the elderly than those living at a distance. An intervening variable was the nature of the relationship between the two parties.

Table 1 elaborates on the care providers for the elderly in relation to their sex, age and marital status. Relatively more females provided care to their spouses than males; the majority of widowed and the "old-old" were taken care of by their sons/daughters-in-law, followed by the daughters/sons-in-law. The earlier discussion of gender preferences for co-residence by the different ethnic groups explains the gender-based profiles.

TABLE 1

Care Provider for the Elderly when Ill/Need Care
by Sex, Age and Marital status

Care Provider	Sex		Age Group			Matirial Status		Total
	Male	Female	60–69	70–79	80+	Widowed	Married	
Self	11.0	15.1	14.0	12.9	8.3	15.7	10.1	13.2
Spouse	47.9	9.2	32.5	22.8	6.4	0.2	47.9	27.3
Son/Daughter-in-law	16.9	38.8	23.6	33.9	43.9	43.9	18.6	28.6
Daughter/Son-in-law	8.3	19.6	13.2	15.8	15.9	21.6	9.0	14.3
Grandchildren	0.5	3.4	0.4	2.2	14.0	4.4	0.5	2.1
Others	2.3	3.2	2.9	2.4	3.8	2.7	1.7	2.7
No Need	13.1	10.7	13.5	10.0	7.6	11.5	12.1	11.8

SOURCE: Survey of the Aged Living in the Community, 1986 cited in Chen, A.J. & Cheung, P.L., 1988:42.

Table 2 summarizes the type of support that is likely to be provided by each family member. While spouses, sons, and daughters rate high on almost all the major caregiving functions, friends and neighbors are valuable resources for the elderly too. The table illustrates the interdependent roles and functions that family members carry out in caring for the elder members. It is also to be expected that these would change over the life cycle of the family unit. The interface of life development stages of each member and the life cycle of the family unit constitutes the backdrop for understanding the dynamic interplay of caring duties which are shared and constantly changing in a typical family. To illustrate, the focus group data revealed that life transitions such as widowhood lead to a redefinition of caregiving roles and even living arrangements at times.

An important principle that explained the level of integration of the elderly in the family arena, and also the level of satisfaction with life stage was *reciprocity*. The elderly who felt that they were able to contribute in some way to the family, either in tangible or intangible forms, i.e., giving advice, consolation at times of crisis, felt a greater sense of satisfaction in old age. This supports the Equity theory which posits that an imbalance in relationships results in dissatisfaction and distress regardless of whether the imbalance is too great or too small. In an equitable relationship, both parties perceive the interaction to be mutually satisfactory, i.e., neither party feels over-benefited or under-benefited (Roberto and Scott, 1986). Those aged who felt that they were giving a great deal but receiving little in return were experiencing despair. The reciprocal exchanges were not necessarily confined to the present-deferred reciprocity, i.e., across the lifecourse, and generalized reciprocity, i.e., across generations, was often cited in the interviews as integral to the family life cycle (Antonucci and Jackson, 1989). The principle of reciprocity highlights a dynamic aspect of familial exchanges within the structure of living arrangements.

An interesting dimension of the findings was the strong emphasis placed by the elderly on their role as transmitters of cultural heritage. The elderly from all three ethnic groups stressed that the seniors in a

TABLE 2

Types of Help Received by Types of Helper (Percentage)

Helped Received	Spouse	Son	Daughter	Daughter-in-law	Friend	Neighbor	Others
Daily Tasks	17.4	28.2	25.4	16.4	1.4	1.9	9.4
Emotional Support	30.3	24.2	23.6	5.5	9.1	1.2	6.1
Financial Help	4.9	67.8	21.9	0.6	0.6	—	4.4
Emergency Help	11.0	45.0	21.5	7.0	1.5	6.5	7.5

SOURCE: Cheung, P.L. *et al.* (1991): 335.

household had the responsibility of teaching their children and grandchildren about their customs, traditions, festivals, and religious knowledge. The extent to which they actually managed to carry out this responsibility out depended greatly on the willingness of the children/grandchildren to learn, availability in terms of time and distance, and the facility of a common language. Relatively speaking, the Malays and Indians found it easier to carry out this function than the Chinese elders. Some of the reasons given by the latter were lack of interest on the part of the grandchildren, and lack of a common language. The passing down of cultural heritage encompasses the transmitting of cultural values to younger generations. Two values common across the cultures were respect for elders and filial piety (caring for one's parents).

During the focus group discussions with the elderly and adult children, the question, "Do you think the elderly in Singapore are well-cared for?" led to a lively discussion as to the definition of care. The following quotes illustrate,

> We should actually try to understand the word 'care' and what it means. You can give your parents money; is that care?...Let us look at our generation. Our parents have always made it a point that when they grow old it's our duty to look after them. I think among the Indians, some do it grudgingly, some do it because they think they should do it. I've seen that to many people giving money is care. I don't think so...
>
> *(Adult Childrens' Indian Group)*

> I think, on the other hand, you can be poor but if you have love in the family, I think all will be happy because the old people will know they can't expect much money but in the house they are together. Whatever you eat, we eat. All are treated well and there is love in the family.
>
> *(Elder Chinese Group)*

Material comfort without social and emotional support was seen as meaningless by both generations. Living with family members gave the elderly the reassurance that they would be taken care of in case of a health crisis. In an emergency, if there was no one at home, an elderly person reiterated that a neighbor would be more useful than a relative who lives far away. However, due to the changing urban environment, lifestyles had changed:

> In the past, when they stayed in villages there were neighbors to help look after the elderly. The circumstances were different. But now, when we live in government housing flats, the circumstances are different. In the past the neighbors were so near and would help if needed, but now each family is concerned about its own business so they don't bother about others. Lifestyles are changing.
>
> *(Adult Childrens' Chinese Group)*

With changing lifestyles, a slow but identifiable change in value systems of the younger generations had evolved:

> I could give them a lot of things, a lot of material things, but I know for myself that many times I do not spend as much time as I would like to with them because of work or social obligations.
>
> *(Adult Childrens' Indian Group)*

Analysis of the focus group transcripts showed that the consensus was that respect towards elders was eroding as compared to the past. In two groups it was perceived to be the same, and in only one group was it seen as being higher than in the past. The elderly noted a growing trend towards materialism, which meant that the middle generations had a serious dilemma in terms of which area to prioritize — family or job. In addition, adult participants voiced their conflicting obligations between giving attention to their own growing children and to their aging parents. The strain on the "sandwich" generation is universal; it is compounded, however, within an urban environment like Singapore with a comparatively high cost of living.

The practice of moral values is tempered by a very crucial variable, the relational factor. Relationships between family members are built over many years. Whereas in the past adult children practised filial duty "blindly", the data indicated that at present it is not so. Filial obligations seem to have been linked to the earlier history of parent-child relationship. A close parent-child bond was, invariably, a strong predictor of care and support in old age and vice versa. This also helps to explain the position of half of the groups that smaller family size, due to lowered fertility rates, would not make a great difference in future patterns of care for the elderly. As one of the participants stated, it takes only one child to look after the parents. So long as that child has a close bond with the parents, old age care was assured, to some extent.

The focus group discussions offered some insights into the strains of co-residence and caregiving to aged parents. It was one thing to desire to care for one's elderly parents but the actual experience of caregiving could be traumatizing. This was especially true for low income families whose economic resources were so limited that they had no access to commercial services, e.g., paid domestic help. A project being conducted by the author on Support Group for Family Caregivers of the Elderly has indicated the anxiety and stress that caregivers undergo. In general, the only child and the single child who carry the sole responsibility of caring for frail or impaired elderly are especially vulnerable.

The three major sources of strains of co-residence which emerged from the focus group data (Mehta *et al.*, 1995) were:

1. intergenerational conflict
2. in-law relationship problems and
3. strain of caregiving

The first and second strains were generally centered on differences regarding lifestyle, such as spending patterns; diet preferences such as younger generations preferring non-traditional dishes while the elderly preferred traditional dishes; communication difficulties and differences over upbringing of grandchildren. The strain of caregiving included physical exhaustion, emotional burnout, and competing demands on time for the caregiver who often held a job and had to care for growing children.

Reflection on the dynamics of interpersonal relationships within caregiver families, especially those with multigenerational households, draws attention to an important yet often glossed over point. This is the absolute need for human values, such as concern for another individual, to be practised by both older and younger generations towards each other. The author has noticed that in the Singaporean setting, sometimes children were filial but elderly parents were not appreciative and wanted to exercise control over their children's lives. This behavior pattern can be interpreted that elderly were not willing to relinquish their parental roles and functions. In addition, they may be taking their "children" for granted without recognizing the needs of the children/children-in-law for appreciation and independence. The author believes that this type of scenario is more common among conservative families where there is a gap in the educational levels between the older and middle generations. At this point in Singapore's history, the aged population is predominantly lower educated, i.e., below secondary educational level (Shantakumar, 1994, p. 48) and many of them are foreign-born, which creates a "cultural lag" in the interaction between generations. The elderly were probably brought up (in their childhood) in extended families, where their elders continued to exercise control over their adult children; on the other hand, their children were brought up in the fast modernizing urban Singapore environment where individualism and independence are highly valued qualities.

There were also difficulties faced by the middle generations in straddling their responsibilities in the "private" and "public" spheres. Within the ethnic cultures, reciprocity and inter-dependence were valued in the family and community context. However, competitiveness and survival were the qualities promoted in the public, especially economic, arenas. These apparently discrepant values in economic and social contexts have spillover effects in the family sphere, requiring maturity and dexterity in adapting from one context to the next. Herein lies the root of family friction that gives rise to heartaches and misunderstandings. Generally, 72% of Singaporean elderly reported in a recent WHO survey that they have high levels of satisfaction with their lives (*The Straits Times*, 11/8/93). These statistics have to be viewed together with other indicators such as the rising numbers of calls made by the elderly to the Singapore Action Group of Elders Hotline regarding their problems (*ibid.*) and the relatively high rate of elderly suicide in Singapore (*The Straits Times*, 26/10/94). Among the various age groups, the aged were identified as having the highest suicide rate.

On a constructive note, the qualitative data included suggestions by participants about some ways in which relations between generations could be improved, thereby leading to better family care of the elderly:

1. Socialization of children with emphasis on transmitting values such as filial care and respect for elders. An effective method was role modeling of these values through behavior and attitudes by the middle generation to provide social learning for children. Such living examples made a greater impact on growing children than mere teaching by instruction.
2. Religious education in general was underscored as an important avenue for the teaching of human values which, if instilled in the early years of life, had a deeper influence on the individual. The Indian and Malay ethnic groups stressed this path more than the Chinese groups.
3. If parents invested time and effort in building close affective ties and understanding through regular communication with their children, they engendered greater chances of care in old age. Although extraneous factors also influenced the actual circum-

stances, e.g., attitude of children-in-law, participants felt that a close parent-child bond did contribute positively towards care in old age.

Interestingly, elderly participants offered explanations such as "fate" and "luck" to anecdotes of the elderly who had sacrificed for their children, yet whose very children had turned their backs on them in old age. These anecdotes indicated that there is no guarantee, despite efforts by parents, of family care in old age. The three factors discussed above enhanced the possibilities of family care in old age, but they did not guarantee it.

Conclusion

This paper has described the present paradigm of elderly care in Singapore, indicating the functions played by the family, community, and state in this overall design. Two issues which have bearing upon the nature and extent of support for the elderly have been underscored, namely, living arrangements and value systems. In analyzing the present state of affairs, the author notes that there are areas that still need to be addressed, e.g., raising of the maximum age of insurance coverage which presently stands at 70 for most private medical insurance policies (the government has set an example of increasing the upper age limit to 75 years in July 1996 for its Medishield Scheme); continuing education programs for the elderly which are almost non-existent; elder-friendly facilities at places of relaxation, e.g., parks, shopping malls. Many of these do not have ramps, and shopping malls often do not have sufficient seating arrangements. The Mass Rapid Transport System is not yet elder-friendly and taxis may sometimes be beyond the budget of many elders. There is an urgent need to look into devising an integrated master plan of services that are island-wide, ethnic-sensitive, and address the whole range of needs for the elderly. The continuity of family care for the elderly into the future is highly dependent on a comprehensive, affordable range of community-based services for the elderly in Singapore.

References

Antonucci, T.C. & Jackson, J.S. (1989) "Successful Aging and Life Course Reciprocity", in A. Warnes (ed.) *Human Aging and Later Life.* London: Hodder and Stoughton: 83–95.

Census of Population (1990) *Release 1,* Department of Statistics. Singapore: Singapore National Printers.

Chen, A.J. & Cheung, P.L. (1988) *The Elderly in Singapore,* Singapore Country Report, Phase 3 Asean Population Project: Socio-Economic Consequences of the Aging of the Population. Singapore: Ministry of Health.

Cheung, P.L.; Ngiam, T.L.; Vasoo, S. & Chan, Y.Y. (1991) "Social Support Networks for the Elderly in a High-Rise Public Housing Estate in Singapore", in H.L. Sheppard (ed.) *Social Services and Aging Policies in the U.S. and Asia.* Florida: International Exchange Center on Gerontology: 305–341.

Cheung, P.L. (1992) *Population Aging in Singapore,* Paper presented at the World Health Organization-Ministry of Health Joint Workshop on Healthy Aging, Singapore.

Directory of Social Services (1995) Singapore: National Council of Social Service.

"Elderly in Singapore lead healthy, fulfilling lives due to family care" (1993, October 11th) *The Straits Times*: 3.

Mason, K.O. (1991) "Family Change and Support of the Elderly in Asia", *Population Aging in Asia.* Asian Population Studies Series No. 108: 96–106.

Mehta, K. (1994) *The Dynamics of Adjustment of the Very Old in Singapore.* Unpublished Ph.D. Thesis. Department of Social Work and Psychology, National University of Singapore.

Mehta, K.; Osman, M. & Lee, A.E.Y. (1995) "Living Arrangements of the Elderly in Singapore: Cultural Norms in Transition", *Journal of Cross-Cultural Gerontology* 10 (1&2): 113–143.

"Network to treat elderly in west, east and central Singapore" (1996, November 1st), *The Straits Times*: 7.

Ng, G.T. (1991) "Service Directions for Voluntary Welfare Organizations Serving the Elderly", in M.T. Yap (ed.) *Social Services: The Next Lap,* Institute of Policy Studies. Singapore: Times Academic Press.

Report on the National Survey of Senior Citizens (1983) Singapore: Ministry of Social Affairs.

Report on the National Survey of Senior Citizens (1995) Singapore: Ministry of Community Development.

Roberto, K.S. & Scott, J.P. (1986) "Equity Considerations in the Friendships of Older Adults", *Journal of Gerontology* 41(2): 241–247.

Shantakumar, G. (1994). *The Aged Population of Singapore.* Monograph No. 1. Singapore: Singapore National Printers.

"Suicide rate of elderly Chinese men here among the world's highest" (1994, October 26th), *The Straits Times*: 6.

"Will Britain become a nation of coolies?" (14th January 1996), *Sunday Review*: 6.

Wong, A. & Yeh, S.H.K. (1985) *Housing a Nation: 25 Years of Public Housing in Singapore.* Singapore: Housing and Development Board.

Yap, M.T. (1991) *Social Services: The Next Lap.* Institute of Policy Studies. Singapore: Times Academic Press.

Chapter 13

Living Arrangements and Elderly Care: The Case of Hong Kong

Rance P.L. Lee, Jik-Joen Lee
The Chinese University of Hong Kong
Elena S. H. Yu
San Diego State University
Shong-Gong Sun
Beijing Medical University
and William T. Liu
East Asian Institute, National University of Singapore

Introduction

Hong Kong had been a British Colony for more than one and a half centuries. The British had provided a legal-administrative framework under which the Chinese lived and worked (Chan and Lee, 1995). The Census has shown that 98 per cent of the Territory's total population are ethnically Chinese. In 1991, nearly one-half of Hong Kong's residents were immigrants from the Chinese Mainland, and two-thirds of the remaining were Hong Kong-born offspring of immigrants from the mainland. Although expatriates from other countries account for the remaining 2 per cent of the population, a majority of expatriates are from overseas Chinese communities in Southeast Asia: Singapore, Malaysia, Thailand, Philippines, Vietnam, Cambodia, and Burma. It cannot be overstated that Hong Kong has fairly homogeneous cultural values that can be described as "Chinese". Beliefs with respect to filial piety and honoring one's ancestors still play a significant role in shaping and regulating local Chinese social life and familial behavior.

For centuries the most desirable living arrangement for the Chinese has been the multi-generational household. Joint families have been described by anthropologists among overseas Chinese communities that interstitched commercial, financial, and market networks, further strengthening the value of multigenerational households and joint families as described by Freedman (1966, 1979). Inspite of the ideal norm of lineal extension under the same roof, historically, however, poverty, short life expectancies, natural calamities, sporadic epidemics, and forced migrations because of war and famine, have prevented most families from forming stable multi-generational households (Hsu, 1947) in premodern China. Only local elites and rich households could attain the ideal cultural norms. The multi-generational household has been the old and convenient way to care for the elderly.

It has been argued that industrialization and Westernization have had an enormous impact on the family constellation over the last few decades (Wong, 1972; 1975; 1979). The assumption was that once neo-local residence takes hold in Hong Kong society, intergenerational cohesion will gradually and irreversibly decrease over time; adult children will place their own parental role as having a higher priority than their filial obligations to their parents. On the other hand, opponents of changing values as a result of the modernization of Hong Kong argued that living patterns may take a number of varied forms, ranging from neo-local residence among the younger generation to living with either the husband's or the wife's parents, or having any one or both sets of parents living with the younger couple in the home of the young couple. It is difficult in any case to expect that the elderly parent would be left alone. Although the most likely form of residence pattern is the elderly sharing a household with one adult child and his/her young family, there are other alternatives. Residential pattern undoubtedly can greatly impact the way older parents are being cared for (Lee, 1991: 138).

Sharing a residence is not necessarily the preferred way to take care of one's parent *willingly* on the part of the adult child and without feeling some degree of sacrifice. When the cost of real estate is among the highest in the world, sharing residence may be economically motivated. We have no way of telling if the common practice of sharing a residence with an elderly parent indeed reflects a collectively committed value or is a temporary pragmatic measure until residential units become more affordable, or huge sums of money for elderly housing are injected into the economy. However, the government does provide public housing, and, more recently the introduction of an affordable housing purchase scheme for the "sandwich class" (household income is above "poverty" — which is not financially eligible for governmental housing — and at the same time cannot afford to purchase private residential units). Such housing policy has, at least in part, eliminated the utilitarian motive. It is plausible that the extensive co-residential patterns may greatly influence, or in themselves reflect adult children's attitudes towards filial care-obligations. We are still unsure about the precise nexus between co-residence and willingness to care for elderly parents in Hong Kong.

This paper attempts to identify the attitudes of older community residents in Hong Kong toward parental care at old age by offspring, toward residential patterns, and toward the family relations of elderly people, though not all these questions are answered directly.

The Study

A Hong Kong territory-wide random sample of 2,203 elderly Chinese aged 65 and over was selected and interviewed in 1991. The study reported that an overwhelming majority of elderly community residents preferred and were in fact living with their adult children at the time of the study. The largest category of "living with adult children" reported staying with one adult child only, a type of co-residence of lineally related relatives known as the *three-generation stem family*. Other adult children tended to move out at various stages of the family cycle and form their own nuclear units. As expected, sons were more likely than daughters to be regarded by elderly parents as the *primary* source of help in the event of crisis, including sickness. For most elderly people, adult children were also the primary source of subsistence-income. Support from adult children was especially important for widows and divorcees or for those not living with husbands.

In short, data clearly suggested that in Hong Kong, the family is still by far the most important institution to care for the elderly, a fact which is both surprising and expected. It is surprising because Hong Kong had been a British colony for nearly 150 years, with an unusually high non-native and mobile population, and after three decades of rapid industrialization and an expanded export port, measurable intergenerational relations have remained stronger than expected. This has happened although many experts have predicted a weakening of such ties because of Westernization and industrialization, two of the strongest agents underlying trends toward global nuclearization of the family. These predictions have been made for nearly three decades by experts, yet the anticipated change has not yet taken place. On the other hand, that Hong Kong's family remains the chief elderly care institution is also expected because of the lack of government policy on elderly care in terms of adequate social security and facilities of community care. Others argue that the traditional Chinese cultural value of filial piety was interpreted as the basis of a centripetal family by Canadian sociologist Salaff (1981). These are perhaps the most commonly quoted reasons for the slow pace of family value change in Hong Kong. Family care for the elderly up until now has been free of serious problems of any kind. However, with a global trend of expanded life expectancy, Hong Kong is said to anticipate a growing proportion of adults in mid-life eligible for "sandwich generation" status, who will face the prospects of having to take care of both their offspring and their aged parents at the same time.

The Traditional and Changing Family Values in Hong Kong

Traditionally, the Chinese family was patrilineal. The oldest male was the head of the family, even if he was very old and was economically inactive. He and his elderly wife lived with their offspring and were cared for by their adult children and daughters-in-law. For decades, the Hong Kong Government appeared to take this for granted, providing few public services for the elderly in society. The situation in recent years has improved but only to a limited extent, since the Government maintains a policy of encouraging care for the elderly by family members within a family context (Hong Kong Government, 1994). The question is this: Can elderly persons count on the support of their own families, especially their adult children?

The status of the elderly and the actual family pattern in Hong Kong today appear to increasingly deviate from the traditional ideal. A multitude of social-economic and demographic forces have increased the size of the elderly population in society and have also led to probable decline of the status of the elderly along with a reduction in family size.

The percentage of population aged 65 and over has increased significantly over the last few decades. According to the Population Census, it increased from 4.5 per cent in 1971 to 6.6 per cent in 1981, and to 8.7 per cent in 1991. Prolonged life-span is one of the contributing factors. The life expectancy at birth was 68 years for men and 75 years for women in 1971, increasing to 72 for men and 78 for women in 1981, and to 75 for men and 81 for women in 1991. These trends naturally have implications for the care of people in later life. For many generations, the elderly Chinese expected to be taken care of by their own families, especially their adult children. As the elderly population has increased in size and has achieved a longer life-span, the issue of whether or not a family can still care for its elderly members deserves systematic investigation. There are reasons to believe that the rapid industrialization and urbanization of Hong Kong over the last two to three decades may have weakened the caregiving function of the family.

Most modern housing facilities in Hong Kong are limited in space and designed primarily for small families. The small nuclear family, rather than the large extended family, has in fact emerged as the predominant form of household in Hong Kong (Wong, 1975; Lee, 1991). According to the 1991 Census, 61.6 per cent of the 1,582,215 domestic households were nuclear families, 10.7 per cent stem families, 6.6 per cent extended families, 14.8 per cent single person households, and 6.3 per cent others. Moreover, since the early 1970s, Hong Kong has been undergoing a marked decline in fertility. The crude birth rate was 19.7 per thousand in 1971, 16.8 per thousand in 1981 and 12.0 per thousand in 1991. Age-specific fertility rates over the period have also declined sharply (Hong Kong Census and Statistics Department, 1992). As a result, household size has been reduced from 4.5 in 1971 to 3.9 in 1981 and to 3.4 in 1991 (Lee, 1993). The ability of small families to care for the elderly is questionable.

The changing status of women might also have affected care for the elderly. Women are now given equal rights to education and to participation in social and economic affairs. In particular, there are nearly as many job opportunities for women as there are for men. As a result, the status of women has been rising. Women today have become more independent than women of previous times both socially and financially (Wong, 1981; Lee, 1995). Many of them may not be willing to stay home and serve elderly parents. No less importantly, the standard of living in Hong Kong has been greatly improved in recent decades. Most adults, both men and women, are busy making money to cope with inflation and to meet their ever-increasing desire for consumption. There is little time for them to take care of their elderly parents at home. These and other changes in the family and society, at least in theory, appear to have adversely affected caregiving for the elderly by the family in Hong Kong.

Nevertheless, it seems that the long-standing Confucian concept of filial piety, a dominant force in the care for the elderly in the past, is still widely shared by Chinese people in Hong Kong (Wan, 1992). Adult children are expected to live with their parents and to take care of them until death. However, as explained earlier, prolonged life expectancy and the changing family pattern may have made it increasingly difficult for adult children to take care of their parents at home these days. The extent to which the elderly are still living with and being cared for by their adult children is a significant research area to be explored. In this paper, we shall examine, from the perspective of the elderly themselves, their preferred and actual living arrangements and the care they are given.

Research Procedures

The Sample Design: In April 1991, the Census and Statistics Department of Hong Kong carried out its decennial census enumeration. The Department agreed to incorporate our proposed health survey on the elderly as the Second Phase of the Department's General Household Survey. The targeted sample size from all districts in the Territory was used to estimate how many monthly *replicates* (about 4,500 quarters per month) would be needed to obtain a total of 2,500 households in the entire population that contained at least one person aged 65 and older. The total elderly population 65 years of age and over was about 8.6 per cent for the entire Territory. It was estimated that to obtain 2,500 households, a total of 22,500 households had to be screened. The minimum replicates needed would be five monthly listings.

The usual General Household Survey (GHS) covered the land-based civilian non-institutional population in Hong Kong. By definition, the following categories of people were excluded in the survey: (1) hotel transients and inmates of institutions; (2) military personnel and dependents; and (3) persons living on board ships and boats. In addition, the census defined its sample frame as one in which sampling units were drawn as a computerized frame of quarters maintained by the Department, which was divided into two parts: (1) addresses of individual quarters in permanent buildings; and (2) only temporary quarters in area segments, known in other countries as squatters and unregulated. Each of these area segments was a cluster of 8 to 15 temporary structures delineated by easily identifiable boundaries.

Sampling units in the frame were first sorted in order of District Board, type of living quarter (i.e., public or private housing), Tertiary Planning Unit, Street Block, plot, and building number. Replicates of about 500 quarters each were then chosen, with the living quarters in each replicate selected at systematic intervals after a random start. The GHS adopted an overlapping sample design such that about half of the living quarters sampled for each month were enumerated once every three months previously, while the other half was newly selected from the general population not previously in the sample. Hence, about half of the sampled living quarters in any quarterly round of the survey was the same as in the preceding quarterly round. The procedure was described as follows:

Eligible households for the health survey were those addresses at which lived at least one person aged 65 and above from the overlapping samples of the GHS conducted for the months of December 1990 to July 1991. Assignment sheets include information available from the GHS core questionnaire: (1) address; (2) month of last visit by the Census and Statistics Department of Hong Kong for conducting the GHS; (3) name of the head of the household; (4) telephone number, if any; (5) name and sex of a member 65 or older randomly selected from the household for the interview. Household letters were then sent to the sampled households by the Census and Statistics Department on its stationery before interviewers made their visits. Unlike the usual GHS, however, the voluntary nature of this survey was emphasized and was described in the letter. It was repeated orally at the time of the visit. The overall completion rate was 77.9

per cent, resulting in a total sample of 2203 cases. The field work was conducted in an face-to-face interview; interviewers asked questions that were well articulated in Chinese.

It should be explained that since elderly respondents were an at-risk population with respect to dementia, an instrument was employed to assess the cognitive functioning of each selected elderly. The instrument was a Chinese version of the Mini-Mental State Examination (MMSE) devised by Folstein, Folstein and McHugh (1975). It was found that a total of 225 elderly scored below 21 points of the maximally possible 30 points in the MMSE score. These elderly were not required to continue the interview. Hence, 225 out of the 2203 respondents were not asked to provide information on some of the questions dealt with in the present paper, such as their preference in living arrangements and their views on care given by others.

In looking at sample characteristics, Table 1 shows that among the 2203 elderly Chinese under study, there were more women (56.3%) than men (43.7%). Moreover, the older the age groups, the greater proportion of women (Chi-square = 90.543, df = 4, p < 0.001). These findings reflect the general pattern that women tend to live longer than men.

Most respondents — about 68.2 per cent — were aged below 74. These people were generally regarded as the young-old. A total of 27.6 per cent could be regarded as the middle-old (aged 75–84), and the remaining 4.2 per cent as the old-old (85 and over). The average age was 72.3 years, with a standard deviation of 6.0. As regards literacy and educational standard, those who reported no education, kindergarten, or less than three years of informal "si-shu" education, are classified as illiterate or semi-literate persons. From Table 1, the overall illiterate or semi-literate rate was as high as 43.6 per cent. Those who had received primary education (including those who had 3 or more years of informal "si-shu" education) added another 42.4 per cent, revealing that a total of 86 per cent of the old people in Hong Kong born before 1926 had virtually no or little formal education. Further analysis revealed that women were generally less educated than men (Chi-square = 427.565, df = 2, p < 0.001), and

TABLE 1
Selected Characteristics by Age
(Number of respondents in parenthesis)

| | Age Groups | | | | | |
	65–69	70–74	75–79	80–84	85 +	Total
	%	%	%	%	%	%
Gender	(893)	(610)	(375)	(233)	(92)	(2203)
Male	54.2	42.5	33.9	32.6	18.5	43.7
Female	45.8	57.5	66.1	67.4	81.5	56.3
Age						(2203)
65–69	—	—	—	—	—	40.5
70–74	—	—	—	—	—	27.7
75–79	—	—	—	—	—	17.0
80–84	—	—	—	—	—	10.6
85 and over	—	—	—	—	—	4.2
Education	(892)	(602)	(373)	(232)	(89)	(2188)
Illiterate and Semi-literate	34.9	41.9	52.0	59.5	65.2	43.6
Primary	50.0	41.7	33.8	34.5	28.1	42.4
Secondary +	15.1	16.4	14.2	6.0	6.7	14.0
Missing	[1]	[8]	[2]	[1]	[3]	[15]
Marital Status	(891)	(608)	(374)	(231)	(91)	(2195)
Married	57.7	41.0	31.0	23.4	15.4	43.1
Separated / Divorced	6.8	8.2	8.3	6.9	3.3	7.3
Widowed	33.4	47.2	56.4	66.2	79.1	46.5
Never married	2.0	3.6	4.3	3.5	2.2	3.0
Missing	[2]	[2]	[1]	[2]	[1]	[8]
Children	(892)	(608)	(374)	(233)	(90)	(2197)
None	5.9	8.9	9.9	10.3	8.9	8.0
1	11.3	11.5	14.4	21.9	30.0	13.8
2	12.1	16.0	17.1	21.0	14.4	15.1
3	12.3	13.2	13.4	10.7	20.0	12.9
4	13.9	15.1	12.3	10.7	11.1	13.5
5 or more	44.4	35.4	32.9	25.3	15.6	36.7
Mean number of children	4.08	3.63	3.53	2.98	2.69	3.69
Missing	[1]	[2]	[1]	—	[2]	[6]

that the older the respondents, the less educated they were (Chi-square = 88.747, df = 8, p < 0.001).

Table 1 also shows that 43.1 per cent were married and were living with spouse. The separated (including married but not living with spouse) or divorced rate was low, 7.3 per cent only. The highest separated or divorced rate occurred among those aged between 70 and 79, while the lowest rate was among those aged 85 and over. The proportion of widowhood also increased with age (from 33.4% to 79.1%). The overall percentage for those never married was extremely low, 3.0 per cent only. It is noted that the age differences in marital status were statistically significant (Chi-square = 184.554, df = 12, p < 0.001), and so were the gender differences (Chi-square = 518.628, df = 3, p < 0.001). Women were most likely to be widowed (66.9%), followed by being married (23.6%), whereas men were most likely to be married (68.3%), followed by being widowed (20.4%).

Table 1 also shows that only 8 per cent had no living children. One-way ANOVA confirms that the number of living children was inversely associated with age (F = 15.39; df = 4; p < 0.001). In other words, the older the respondents, the smaller the number of living children they had. Also, women tended to have fewer living children than did men (Chi-square = 76.508, df = 5, p < 0.001). Sample statistics are very nearly identical with the population statistics as reported in the 1991 Census (Hong Kong Government, 1994).

Findings

The myth that elderly community residents really do not wish to live with their adult children was our first concern. Therefore, we asked who would be their first choice with whom to share the same household. The last column of Table 2 shows that when the respondents were asked what living arrangement they preferred most, about one-half said children, followed by one-quarter preferring their spouses and only 13 per cent choosing to live alone. The remaining small proportion named children-in-law and other relatives or friends.

Only one out of one hundred said they preferred living in a home for the elderly. The number of elderly who preferred to live alone exceeded the number who preferred a home for the elderly in a ratio of ten to one.

There were significant differences between men and women with respect to the preference in living arrangement (Chi-square = 196.536, df = 7, p < 0.001). A closer look at the data revealed that the major difference occurred between living with a spouse or living with adult children and their families. Women clearly preferred children (59.6%) to spouse (13.4%), while men were about evenly divided between children (39.1%) and spouse (40.6%). Table 2 shows that such a gender difference was generally held among respondents of all age-categories.

Compared to preferences indicated by the subjects for the record, what is the actual pattern of their living arrangement ? Was their wish granted?

Of the 2203 elderly in the sample, 43.1 per cent reported living with a spouse at the time of the interview. The percentage of

TABLE 2

Preferred Living Arrangement by Age and Gender

Preferred Arrangement	M			F			
	65–69	70–74	75+	65–69	70–74	75+	Total
	%	%	%	%	%	%	%
Alone	10.7	11.7	15.8	12.9	16.7	12.9	13.1
Spouse	43.0	41.3	34.2	19.3	12.9	7.8	25.9
Children	40.0	37.1	39.3	59.1	59.5	60.2	50.2
Children-in-law	2.4	2.9	3.1	4.0	3.2	5.1	3.5
Other relatives	1.1	2.5	2.6	1.3	2.6	6.2	2.6
Friends	1.3	1.7	1.5	0.5	1.6	2.2	1.4
Elderly home	0.2	0.8	1.5	1.1	1.6	3.0	1.3
Others	1.3	2.1	2.0	1.8	1.9	2.7	1.9
(N)	(467)	(240)	(196)	(379)	(311)	(372)	(1965)

respondents living with spouse declined from 57.1 per cent among those aged 65–69 to 40.8 per cent among those aged 70–74, and 26.7 per cent for the cohort age 75 and over. Since wives tend to live longer than their husbands, female respondents (23.6%) were also found to be less likely to live with their spouses by a large margin than male respondents (68.3%).

The great majority (92.0%) of the respondents in the study who also had living children at the time of the interview were far more likely to live with their adult children than with a spouse. From the first sub-table of Table 3, a total of 77.4 per cent of those with living children actually stayed with one or more children in the same house. In this regard, there was little difference between those living with spouse and those not doing so. It can also be seen from the sub-table that most respondents lived with one child only (52.3%), followed by sharing with two (15.1%). As to whether or not living with spouse would make a difference, those who lived with spouses were more likely to live with two or more children (a total of 36.7%) than were those who did not live with spouse (15.2%). Here age may be a factor, since younger couples may still have unmarried adult children living with their aged parents, whereas older cohort elderly may be over-represented by widows with children already married and living away from them. It is shown in Table 1 that those not living with spouse (including separated, divorced, widowed, and never married) were likely to be older and to have fewer living children.

As reported earlier in this paper, most respondents showed a preference for living with a spouse; but more than with spouse, they preferred to be with their adult children. The actual living situations appear to be congruent with the arrangements preferred by the elderly. Further analysis shows that among those who indicated the strongest preference for living with spouse (*n* = 509), an overwhelming majority (94.1%) were actually living with their spouses. Consistency in response patterns was found for both male and female subjects and for all age cohorts. Also, among those who wanted most to live with their own children (*n* = 986), a very great majority (89.4%) were actually living with their children in the same house. Again, the same

TABLE 3
Number of Children Living with the Elderly by Whether or Not the
Elderly was Living with Spouse, Stratified by Whether the Elderly had
any Living Children

STRATUM 1. Elderly with Living Children[a]

(A) Living with Children in the Same House

Number of Children Living in Same House	Living with Spouse		
	Yes	No	Total
	%	%	%
None	23.7	21.8	22.6
1	39.7	63.0	52.3
2	21.3	9.9	15.1
3	8.9	3.5	5.9
4	4.2	1.0	2.5
5+	2.3	0.8	1.5
(N)	(925)	(1093)	(2018)

(B) Not Living with Children in the Same House[b]

Number of Children Living in Same District	Living with Spouse		
	Yes	No	Total
	%	%	%
None	65.8	75.0	70.5
1	16.4	17.8	17.1
2	11.9	4.2	7.9
3	2.7	1.3	2.0
4	2.7	1.3	2.0
5+	0.5	0.4	0.4
(N)	(219)	(236)	(455)

TABLE 3 (continued)

STRATUM 2. Elderly without Living Children[c]

Living with Spouse	N	%
Yes	21	12.2
No	151	87.8
Total	172	100.0

NOTES : [a] The total number of elderly with any living children was 2021. Three of the 2021 had missing information on whether living together with spouse (*n*=1), or whether living together with children (*n*=2).

[b] These were 457 elderly with children but not living with them in the same house. Of these, 2 had missing information on whether the children was living in the same district.

[c] 176 elderly did not have any living children. Of these, 4 had missing information on whether living with spouse.

pattern applied to all age cohorts and for both sexes of respondents. Though responses may be influenced by the current living arrangement, in the absence of evidence contrary to available statistics, these findings suggest that most of the elderly Chinese in Hong Kong were able to do what they prefer, that is, live with their spouses and adult children when financially and physically able to do so.

In spite of the consistency between preferred living arrangement and the actual living pattern, however, not all the elderly had the opportunity to share the same residence with their children. One-fifth (457 out of 2203) of the respondents said they had living children but were not sharing the same house with them at the time of the interview. It seems that the second best arrangement is to find a place near where their children lived. The second part of Table 3 shows that nearly 30 per cent of these elderly had one or more children living in the same district. Those who lived with their spouses were more likely to have one or more children living in the same district (34.2%) than those not living with a spouse (25%). This may be the best indication that crowding was the main reason for not sharing a residence between the two generations of primary kin.

Sharing the same residence can be the most natural assumption of care in case of need. Nonetheless, given a direct question on the relationship between caregiving and the type of social ties, we asked the elderly respondents to tell us the different types of care needed according to possible different caregivers. These needs were primary sources of help in case of emergency, the possibility of depending on children for old age, and major sources of income.

In case of crisis or sickness, who could be counted on to help the elderly as they viewed the possible sources of such help? For the sake of clarity, the elderly Chinese in the study were asked to name one person who came to mind. Table 4 shows that 26.3 per cent named their spouses, while 35 per cent said their sons and 17.1 per cent mentioned their daughters. The response pattern is consistent with the culturally preferred caregiving in that sons are accorded filial responsibilities over daughters, and children over one's spouse. Similarly, the elderly were more likely to trust their children (a total of 52.1 per cent including both sons and daughters) than their spouses to help in the case of an emergency. Sons were also more likely than daughters to be regarded as the primary source of help.

The statement can be misleading because Table 3 did not differentiate between respondents with spouses and those without in Table 4. Also, these two groups of subjects were separately shown. Once the absence of spouse is treated separately from the presence of spouse, a different, even opposite conclusion was evident. Those who were staying with a spouse were more likely to rely on spouse (57.4%), next on sons (26%) and on daughters (9.5%). Those not living with a spouse did not have any choice; they had to depend on the next preferred primary family members: their sons (42.5%) and daughters (23.3%). In either case, the elderly were more likely to name *their sons rather than their daughters* as the most helpful persons in case of emergency, a pattern significantly different from findings reported

TABLE 4

Person to Help in Case of Emergency by Whether or
Not Living with Spouse
(N = 1978)[a]

Helper	Total Responding	Reporting the Specified Helper	Living with Spouse			
			Yes		No	
	N	%	n	%	n	%
Spouse	1963[b,d]	26.3	510	57.4	7	0.7
Sons	1963[b,d]	35.0	231	26.0	457	42.5
Daughters	1963[b,d]	17.1	84	9.5	251	23.3
Children-in-law	1963[b,d]	3.7	17	1.9	56	5.2
Sibling	1963[b,d]	1.5	4	0.5	26	2.4
Friends	1963[b,d]	2.4	6	0.7	41	3.8
Neighbours	1963[b,d]	2.2	5	0.6	38	3.5
Other relatives	1963[b,d]	3.9	4	0.5	72	6.7
Others	1963[b,d]	3.9	15	1.7	62	5.8
No one can help	1964[c,d]	5.2	31	3.5	72	6.7

NOTES : [a] By design, 225 persons were not asked this question because of the MMSE score below 21.

[b] 14 cases had missing information on "Who can help?".

[c] 13 cases had missing information on "Who can help?"

[d] 1 case had missing information on marital status.

in Europe and North America, where unmarried and middle-aged daughters were overwhelmingly mentioned as primary caregiver to the extent that elderly care in the family has become a gender issue in welfare policy debate (Brody, 1981; 1984; 1986).

A strategically important question has to do with the realistic assessment of whether or not the elderly can expect care from their children. This question was asked only to those who had living children at the time of the interview. Table 5 shows that seven out of ten respondents (72%) gave an affirmative answer to this question; a quarter were not sure, and only 3.8 per cent gave negative answers.

TABLE 5

Possible Dependency on Children for Old Age by
Whether or Not Living with Spouse[a]

Children Dependable	Living with Spouse		Total
	Yes	No	
	%	%	%
Yes	69.3	74.6	72.0
Not sure	27.6	21.0	24.2
No	3.1	4.5	3.8
(N)	(860)	(916)	(1776)

NOTE : [a] This question was asked only of elderly with living children (N=2021). However, by design, 236 persons out of 2021 elderly were not asked this question either because they had MMSE score below 21, or refused to answer. 9 cases have missing information.

There were differences between those living with spouse and those who were not (Chi-square = 11.766, df = 2, p < 0.005). Those who did not have a spouse were more likely to say they could depend upon their children for old age (74.6%) than were those who were living with a spouse (69.3%). The absence of a spouse tests critically the sense of filial responsibility of adult children in elderly care. To put it in a different perspective, the sense of caring responsibilities became most critical on the part of adult children when the elderly assumed the added status of widowhood.

In addition to care as a form of assistance when the elderly becomes disabled, chronically ill, and/or facing crisis, one issue is economic dependency. In Hong Kong, mythically known for having been influenced by Western values and its industrial economy, and for a high proportion of nuclear households over other types of dwellings, what was the cash-assistance liability of adult children regarding their aged parents?

TABLE 6

Sources of Income by Whether or Not Living with Spouse

Sources of Income	Total Responding	Reporting the Specified Source		Living with Spouse			
				Yes		No	
	N	n	%	n	%	n	%
Children	2194	1348	61.4	558	59.0	790	63.3
Relatives	2192	58	2.6	22	2.3	36	2.9
Wages	2194	252	11.5	152	16.1	100	8.0
Savings/Interests	2194	134	6.1	57	6.0	77	6.2
Retire Benefits	2194	72	3.3	39	4.1	33	2.6
Investment	2192	71	3.2	46	4.9	25	2.0
Public Assistance	2194	96	4.4	20	2.1	76	6.1
Old Age Allowance	2194	182	8.3	52	5.5	130	10.4
Disability Allowance	2194	29	1.3	10	1.1	19	1.5
Others	2193	35	1.6	21	2.2	14	1.1

Though not asked directly, one question in the interview schedule had to do with sources of subsistence income. In Table 6, the majority of respondents (61.4%) reported economic dependency exclusively and/or primarily upon their children. In other words, income from other sources such as savings, cash income from part-time work, rental receipts, welfare checks, etc. existed for only one-third of the sample population.

However, those living with spouses were more likely than those spouseless elderly to be economically self-sufficient, whereas the latter were more likely than the former to live on public welfare. Specifically, among those living with spouses, a total of 31.1 per cent relied on their own wages and salaries, savings and interests, retirement benefits or investment profits, whereas only a total of 18.8 per cent of those not living with spouse were self-sufficient. On the other hand, among those living with a spouse, about 8.7 per cent were living on public assistance, old age allowance or disability allowance, but among those not living with spouse, a total of 18 per cent were dependent on public welfare, old age allowance or disability allowance. The Elderly not living with spouse were generally older than those living with spouse. They were less likely to be economically self-sufficient and were thus more likely to depend on other sources of financial support, including the government.

Summary and Discussion

The present study of living arrangements and care for the elderly was based on a random sample survey of 2203 elderly Chinese aged 65 and over in Hong Kong in 1991. The findings indicate that most elderly people prefer living with their spouses and particularly with their children. More importantly, a great majority were able to achieve what they preferred. The survey revealed that while about half of the elderly people under study were living with a spouse at the time of the interview, over 90 per cent of them had living children, and nearly four-fifths of this group of elderly were actually living with their offspring in the same house. Among the remaining one-fifth, about one-third had one or more children living in the same district. In Hong Kong nowadays, therefore, actual living arrangements are largely consistent with the preference of the elderly population. Most of them preferred and were actually living with their adult children.

Living with children under the same roof has been a cultural ideal shared by the Chinese people over many centuries. The Confucian concept of filial piety exerts great demands on the Chinese to live with and to care for their aging parents. It is generally taken as a right of the elderly to live with their adult children and to be taken care of by them. The present study confirms that such a tradition is still widely shared by the people in Hong Kong. In fact, elderly Chinese in Hong Kong and elsewhere seldom live alone. According to the 1991 Population Census in Hong Kong, only one-tenth of those aged 60 and over lived alone. Other studies showed somewhere below 6 or 7 per cent. In general, probably less than 10 per cent of all the elderly community residents in urban China reported residing in a household alone (Pan, 1991; The Chinese Academy of Social Science, 1985; Chan, *et al.* 1994; Hu, *et al.* 1991).

It is a general consensus in Hong Kong that adults in mid-life are generally under pressure to keep their aging parents at home. It is considered "bad and shameful" if elderly parents live alone or by themselves, and it is even more shameful if they are sent to live in a home for the elderly.

The present study reveals that most elderly in Hong Kong stay with only one adult child. This is also the case in Singapore (Mehta, Osman and Lee, 1995). It seems that there exists a typical pattern of family life in contemporary Chinese society. When the children grow up and get married, they leave the parental home and form their own small families. But, one of them stays and takes care of the aging parents, which is the basis of a large number of stem families enumerated in the Census.

The housing situation in Hong Kong is a factor in intergenerational sharing of residence. Hong Kong's housing, second only to Tokyo, constituted the second most expensive real estate market in Asia. Beginning in 1994, the government gave priority to families with elderly parents applying for public housing. This is considered a major force in expanding the proportion stem families in the Territory, and the formation of family lives in Hong Kong. Government housing constitutes about 40 per cent of all housing in Hong Kong.

It should be added that another force encourages married children to live with their elderly parents. The rising rate of women's participation in the labor force makes it necessary for many families to find someone to do the household work. An important advantage of living with elderly parents is that unless they are too old or too weak to work, they are probably the most reliable persons to help with child care, cooking, laundry and many other household duties. There is a popular saying in Hong Kong: "Having an elderly at home is like possessing a treasury."

The present study shows that about one-fifth of the elderly population did not have the opportunity of living with their children.

Nevertheless, many of them have children living in the same district. They can easily get access to their offspring for practical assistance or companionship. It is obvious that Confucian values of filial piety keep the adult children living near their aging parents. It can also be, as explained before, due to the practical consideration of enabling the elderly parents to come and help with child care and other household responsibilities.

As reported earlier, the present study shows that the elderly Chinese in Hong Kong most live with family members including their spouses and particularly their adult children. The question is are they being cared for within a family context? The answer is positive. Findings from the present study suggest that most elderly persons trust that their spouses and particularly their children would come to help in case of trouble or illness and that they could depend on their children during their old age. More important, most elderly people are actually dependent upon their adult children as the primary source of income. Other relatives, friends, neighbors, or public welfare services are seldom regarded by the elderly Chinese as major sources of help or income. Further analysis shows that those living with a spouse are more likely to turn to their spouses rather than to children for help in case of trouble or illness, while those not living with spouse seem to have little choice but to rely primarily on their adult children for practical, emotional and financial support.

Adult children, therefore, constitute the most important source of support for most elderly Chinese in Hong Kong, especially for those who are so old that they can hardly rely on themselves and who have no spouse to live with. It should be noted that, as indicated by our survey data, sons are more likely than daughters to be considered by the elderly Chinese as the most reliable source of support. This is the case regardless of whether or not the elderly live with their spouses. This illustrates that the patrilineal family tradition continues to exist in the modern society of Hong Kong. Such is the case in other Chinese societies as well (Lee, Parish and Willis, 1994; Mehta, Osman and Lee, 1995). Family properties are usually transferred from elderly parents to sons rather than to daughters. Sons rather than daughters are strongly obligated to take care of their aging parents. Traditionally, daughters are "married out". After marriage, a daughter belongs to the husband's family and lives in his place. She is expected to take care of her parents-in-law rather than her natural parents. Accordingly, elderly Chinese consider it appropriate and natural to rely on their adult sons for the care they need and consider it improper and even shameful to ask their "married out" daughters to return home and help.

The traditional pattern of care for the elderly by sons rather than by daughters appears to persist in the modern society of Hong Kong. A closer look at our survey data, however, reveals that some changes have taken place. While 35 per cent of elderly respondents regarded their sons as primary caregivers, as many as 17.1 per cent considered their daughters as the most helpful persons in case of trouble or illness (see Table 4). In Hong Kong today, quite a number of elderly Chinese have, in fact, turned to their daughters for the support they need.

Daughters are supposed to be married out, but the emotional ties the daughters have been building with their own parents over many years do not disappear (Lee, Parish and Willis, 1994). Often, married daughters are emotionally attached to their own parents more than to their parents-in-law. It is also easier for aging parents to get along with their own daughters than with daughters-in-law. Of no less importance is that as Hong Kong is a compact society with a well-developed system of transportation and telephone communication, elderly people can easily get access to their adult daughters even if they do not live together. The data in Table 4 clearly suggest that daughters are becoming the expected helpers of aging parents in modern times, and that children-in-law are seldom counted on by the elderly as the primary sources of support.

As we have argued, most elderly Chinese in Hong Kong are able to achieve what they want, i.e., living with their spouses and, more importantly, living with their adult children and being cared for by them. Despite rapid modernization and industrialization, the traditional value of filial piety appears to persist in society, allowing the elderly to be cared for in a family context. Very few elderly would entertain the idea of staying in a home for the elderly, nor would they like the idea of relying on public welfare. In Hong Kong today, family is still the most important institution to care for the elderly. However, the persistence of this traditional practice in contemporary society may create tension in family life.

Adults who in mid-life increasingly face the challenge of caring for their aging parents are being turned into the so-called "sandwich generation" (Machines, 1995, Chapter 14). On the one hand, they need to nurture and support their young children and, on the other hand, they are expected to live with and to look after their aging parents. Since life-expectancy is increasing, the sandwich generation would have a longer and longer period for taking care of their elderly parents. To care for parents beyond the age of seventy or eighty is, in many ways, no less demanding than raising young children. In recent years, an increasing number of middle-class or wealthier families have employed maids from the Philippines to help take care of the young and/or the elderly at home, but there are many families which cannot afford to do so. Even among families who have hired Filipino maids, language and cultural differences may create difficulties in the care for the elderly. The role and the problems of Filipino maids as caregivers for the elderly Chinese in a family context deserves systematic research by social scientists in the years ahead.

Up to now, we have presented and discussed findings from the total sample of elderly respondents concerning their living arrangements and the care they were given by others. Most of them preferred and were actually living with their spouses and particularly their children. They were also cared for by their spouses and especially children. There were, however, elderly people who were "lonely" or "helpless" at the time of the interview. From the last sub-table of Table 3, about 7 per cent of the total sample, i.e., a total of 151 respondents indicated that they had no children nor were they living with their spouses. These were lonely elderly without close family members to live with. Moreover, as Table 4 has shown, about 5 per cent, i.e., a total of 103 respondents, believed that no one would help them in case of trouble or illness. These were helpless elderly who had no person to count on. The social and demographic characteristics of these two groups of elderly, i.e., the lonely and the helpless, deserve our attention.

TABLE 7
Comparison of Selected Characteristics of Elderly Reporting
(1) no one to help in case of emergency and
(2) not living with spouse and no living children,
with the total sample

| | (1) | | (2) |
	No one to help *n*=103	Not living with spouse, no children *n*=151	Total sample *n*=2203
Gender			
% Female	56.3	73.5	56.3
Age			
% >75 yrs	41.7	43.7	32.0
Education			
% Illiterate/Semi-literate	40.8	53.6	43.6
Marital status			
% Widowed	48.5	49.0	46.5
% Married with spouse	30.1	—	43.1
% Never married	11.7	43.0	3.0
Children			
% No living children	31.1	—	8.0
Perceived health			
% Poor/very poor	25.3	22.5	16.4
Major income			
% Children	33.0	—	61.4
% Relatives	5.8	12.6	2.6
% Wages	16.5	16.6	11.5
% Savings/Interests	4.9	15.2	6.1
% Investment	0.0	4.0	1.2
% Old age allowance	9.7	23.2	8.3
% Public assistance	17.5	23.2	4.4
% Other	4.9	3.3	1.6

Table 7 compares each of the two groups of disadvantaged elderly with the total sample in selected characteristics. Compared with the total sample, both the helpless and the lonely elderly were more likely to be female, older than 75 years, never married or widowed, and without living children. As regards their major sources of income, they were also more likely than the total sample to rely on public welfare or their own wages and salaries, rather than upon their adult children. It is noted that both the helpless and the lonely elderly were more likely than the total sample to suffer from poor health.

There are lonely or helpless elderly in every society, and Hong Kong is no exception. Based on our survey data in Hong Kong in 1991, roughly 7 per cent of the elderly population aged 65 and over are lonely people while 5 per cent are helpless. These lonely or helpless elderly are not the focus of the present study. However, their experiences and their sufferings very much deserve the close attention of policymakers and social science researchers. Hong Kong is becoming an affluent society. It should not ignore the welfare of those who have made contributions in the past but are now in a helpless or lonely situation.

References

Chan, Chen-Zhang, *et al.* (1994). "A Survey on the Health Status of the Elderly in Guangzhou", *Hong Kong Journal of Gerontology* 8(2), 17–25 (in Chinese).

Chan, Hoiman and Rance P.L. Lee (1995). "Hong Kong Families: At the Crossroads of Modernism and Traditionalism", *Journal of Comparative Family Studies* XXVI(1): 83–89.

Folstein, M.F., S.E. Folstein and P.R. McHugh (1975). "Mini-Mental State: A Practical Method for Grading the Cognitive State of Patients for the Clinicians", *Journal of Psychiatric Research* 12: 189–198.

Hong Kong Census and Statistics (1992). "Past and Future Trends of Fertility in Hong Kong", *Hong Kong Monthly Digest of Statistics — May.* Hong Kong: Government Printer.

Hong Kong Government (1994). *Report of the Working Group on Care for the Elderly.* Hong Kong: Government Printer.

Hu, R.Q.; J.J. Lee; I. Chi; R.Y. Wang and N.Z. Ye (1991). "A Comparative Study of the Elderly's Life Patterns between Nine Metropolitan Cities in Mainland China and Hong Kong", *Hong Kong Journal of Gerontology* 5(1): 8–15.

Lee, Jik-Jeon (1993). "Types of Publicly Financed Residential Facilities for the Elderly: The Housing Authority's Housing Plans", *Hong Kong Journal of Gerontology* 7: 28–40 (in Chinese).

Lee, M.K. (1991). "Organization and Change of Families in Hong Kong", pp. 161–170 in Chien Chiao, *et al.* (eds.), *Chinese Family and Its Change.* The Chinese University of Hong Kong (in Chinese).

Lee, M.K. (1995). "The Family Way", pp. 1–19 in Lau Siu-kai, *et al.* (eds.), *Indicators of Social Development: Hong Kong 1993.* Hong Kong Institute of Asia-Pacific Studies, The Chinese University of Hong Kong.

Lee, Rance P.L. and Cheung Yuet-Wah (1995). "Health and Health Care", pp. 59–112 in Lau Siu-kai, *et al.* (eds.), *Indicators of Social Development: Hong Kong 1993.* Hong Kong Institute of Asia-Pacific Studies, The Chinese University of Hong Kong.

Lee, Yean-Ju.; William L. Parish and Robert J. Willis (1994). "Sons, Daughters, and Intergenerational Support in Taiwan", *American Journal of Sociology* 99(4): 1010–1041.

Macionis, John J. (1995). *Sociology.* 5th edition. Englewood Cliffs, N.J.: Prentice-Hall.

Mehta, Kalyani; Mohd. Maliki Osman and Alexander Lee E.Y. (1995). "Living Arrangements of the Elderly in Singapore: Cultural Norms in Transition", *Journal of Cross-Cultural Gerontology* 10: 113–143.

Wan, Po-san (1992). "Subjective Quality of Life", pp. 173–204 in Lau Siu-kai, *et al.* (eds.) *Indicators of Social Development: Hong Kong 1990.* Hong Kong Institute of Asia-Pacific Studies, The Chinese University of Hong Kong.

Wong, F.M. (1975). "Industrialization and Family Structure in Hong Kong", *Journal of Marriage and the Family* 37: 958–1000.

Wong, F.M. (1981). "Effect of the Employment of Mothers on Marital Role and Power Differentiation in Hong Kong", pp. 217–233 in Ambrose Y.C.King and Rance P.L. Lee (eds.), *Social Life and Development in Hong Kong*. Hong Kong: The Chinese University Press.

Yang,C.K. (1974). "The Chinese Family: The Young and the Old", pp. 430–445 in R.L. Coser (ed.), *The Family: Its Structure and Functions,* 2nd edition. London: Macmillan.

Chapter 14

Children and Children-in-law as Primary Caregivers: Issues and Perspectives

Odalia M.H. Wong
Hong Kong Baptist University

Introduction

An aging population in any society tends to exert increasing pressure on caregiving resources. Institutional elderly care has not been able to keep pace with the demand, and one can expect the bulk of caregiving to fall on informal caregivers who have other responsibilities such as employment, family, and children. The increasing demand for informal care has many social ramifications that are related to the gender issues such as household division of labor, potential role conflicts and caregiving stress, among others.

Previous studies have shown that women have taken up a disproportionate share of informal caregiving for the elderly, in much the same way that they have primary responsibility for housework and child care, even accounting for the fact that many of these women caregivers also participate in the labor market (Dwyer and Seccombe, 1991). Furthermore, this phenomenon was found to be particularly apparent in a Chinese society like Hong Kong (Ngan, 1990). For these reasons, rising demand for elderly care would likely have the strongest impact on women; especially those who need to juggle competing roles.

Informal caregiving usually takes place in the home, and in Hong Kong the informal caregiver often shares the same household with the elderly under care. But while the literature usually focuses on the conflicts between caregiving and other activities that take place in the household, it is important not to overlook the potential complimentarities either, such as when the elderly under care helps out with baby-sitting or other household chores. In fact, an important thesis of this paper is that informal care can introduce subtle but important changes in the organization of household activities, by redeploying household resources and reorganizing the household division of labor to exploit complimentarities and minimize conflicts. Furthermore, whether sufficient resources are available for caregiving and whether such resources are managed in an effective manner often determine whether role conflicts and caregiver's stress are minimized — more generally, whether the caregiving task can be considered as being handled successfully or not.

Another interesting gender dimension of caregiving which warrants further research is that of the daughters-in-law as primary caregivers. Daughters-in-law tend to view caregiving and the associated problems in a very different light from caregivers who are children of the elderly under care. As daughters-in-law are often involved in caregiving primarily to help their spouses, it is useful to conceptualize and analyze this phenomenon as a gender division of labor and specialization.

Although informal caregiving has been found to be primarily a woman's task, the literature is lacking for its disproportionately scant study of the male caregiver. For not only is the case of the male caregiver of significance *per se*, it is also indispensable in gaining a full understanding of the gender dimension of caregiving, especially concerning the access to resources for caregiving and caregiver's stress. The survey used in the present study is fortunate in that half of our respondents were male caregivers, and a substantial portion of the female caregivers were helping their spouse by caring for their in-laws. This has allowed us to explore the important aspects of gender differences in caregiving, as well as the increasingly important issue of daughters-in-law as caregivers.

Methodology

This paper studies elderly care from the perspective of the children and children-in-law serving as caregivers. The present analysis is based on an original, in-depth interview of a small sample of ten informal caregivers. Although the small sample used in this paper cannot claim to be representative of the general population, there are certain advantages in conducting in-depth interviews with a small group versus the use of a general survey of a larger group. The use of a small sample allows us to ask much more detailed and open-ended questions to explore more subtle issues that may not be readily captured by tightly structured questions used typically in larger samples. Specifically, it allows us to delve much more deeply into complex issues where the respondent may feel ambivalent, or even hesitant to address, because these issues may carry certain social stigma. One example from our study is the potential conflict between caregiving and work. Caregivers who hold jobs may at times feel stigmatized because of the perception that their caregiving obligation could cut into their job commitment. Therefore, when asked a simple question as to whether they feel that caregiving has created conflicts with their job, some respondents may answer rather mechanically in the negative because they are habitually eager to dispel such perceptions. But, in a more in-depth discussion, the same respondents may become more amenable to address the conflicts that are involved. More generally, we believe that the advantages of the use of a more detailed interview with a smaller sample are apparent in the results of this study, where some of the findings have remained heretofore under-explored in the literature.

Because we do not claim that the small sample used in this study is representative of the general population, in the presentation of the results and the analysis to follow we will be brief on the detailed profile and characteristics of our sample. We will be equally brief in reporting the results of our study which simply confirmed previous findings by other researchers. Instead, we will focus our discussion on the more novel and original findings.

Several criteria were used for the selection of respondents, who were primary, informal caregivers for parents and parents-in-law. First, they had elderly parents or in-laws aged 60 or over who suffered from physical/cognitive impairment or poor health, or were unable to care for themselves without assistance from others over a period of time. Secondly, they provided the greatest amount of unpaid assistance to the care receiver in terms of physical, psychological, or financial support. Thirdly, the elderly being cared for and the other family members also agreed that the interviewee in question was indeed the primary caregiver. Snowball sampling was used in the interview, where a combination of open-ended and closed-ended questions were used to allow for greater flexibility for the respondents to freely delve into issues that may not be captured by the use of standard questions.

Contents of the Interviews

The interview questions can be categorized into six primary areas:

1. *Primary caregiver's characteristics*: Respondents were asked about their age, sex, marital status, number of children, education achievement, income, relationship with the elder; and whether they were living with them.

2. *Elderly parents' dependency*: Respondents were asked to rate the care receivers' current health status and to report on their marital status, age, physical and cognitive problems, and degree of financial

dependence. Respondents were also asked whether the elderly under their care were capable of performing routine activities of living without assistance.

3. *Perceived reasons for caregiving*: The information collected in this area is important in analyzing the problems and conflicts that confront the caregivers. Respondents were asked open-ended questions as to the circumstances that had led them to become the primary caregivers for their parents. Information on the circumstances concerning the respondents' siblings was also collected.

4. *Present helping behavior*: Respondents were asked detailed questions about the type and intensity of care that they rendered, in six different areas: help for daily chore, help for personal care, cognitive aid, psychological or emotional support, living arrangement for the elderly, and financial assistance. It should be noted that our interview relied on behavioral reports rather than the respondent's perceptions of the aid rendered. The use of behavioral reports allowed us to pinpoint the type and amount of aid rendered in a more objective and quantitative manner.

5. *Filial obligation*: Filial obligation is seen as a strong motive for informal caregiving in the literature (Lee, Netzer, and Coward, 1994; Piercy, 1998; Stein Wemmrus, Ward, Gaines, Freeberg, and Jewell, 1998). In accordance with Lee, *et al.* (1994), filial obligation can find expression in the following six statements: (a) Adult children have the duty to take care of their elderly parents and to help them deal with the aging process, (b) Adult children should be willing to sacrifice their personal and family's time, money, energy, and other interests in order to help and support their elderly parents, (c) Adult children should be able to help their parents when they are sick and in need of care, (d) Adult children have the duty to not only care for parents physically and materially, but should also express concern and love for them, respect their dignity and establish closer contact and understanding, (e) Married children should try to live close to their parents, and where that is not

possible they should maintain close and regular contact, (f) Adult children caring for their parents should do so without complaint or expectation of any return. Respondents were asked whether they agree or disagree with the above statements, with four possible response options. Respondents who tended to strongly agree with the statements were classified as having a sense of higher filial obligation, etc.

6. *Problems faced by caregiver*: Respondents were asked whether they were facing difficulties with their caregiving role, and to elaborate on them. The interview focused on four aspects of potential problems: financial, physical, psychological, and role conflicts. The interview made use of role theory in focusing on four sets of variables in analyzing problems faced by caregivers: role strain variables, role demand overload variables, role conflict variables, and coping resources variables.

Findings and Analysis

We begin our analysis by describing the key characteristics of the caregivers and their caregiving activities. Table 1 shows the detailed profile of the caregivers in our study, while Table 2 shows the profile of the elderly under care. Here, we will focus our attention on some of the more salient characteristics of the caregivers in our sample. (1) The caregivers were evenly divided between males and females. (2) We have a large number of caregivers whose relationship to the care receiver was that of daughter-in-law. (3), Almost all of the respondents lived with the elderly under their care. (4) Seven of the ten respondents were married with the rest being never-married. Of the married respondents, most of them had young children under the age of twelve. (5) All of the respondents were active participants in the labor market at the time of the interview. (6) Most of the respondents had been providing elderly care for a long period of time, with the mean years of service being eleven years. Finally, all the respondents were caring for their parents or parents-in-law.

TABLE 1
Demographic Characteristics of Primary Caregivers (N=10)

Characteristics of Caregivers	N	%
Age	10	33.6
Sex		
Female	5	50.0
Male	5	50.0
Relationship with their elderly parents		
Son	5	50.0
Daughter	1	10.0
Daughter-in-law	4	40.0
Marital Status		
Single	3	30.0
Married	7	70.0
Age of children		
Birth to 2 years	3	30.0
3 to 7 years	4	40.0
8 to 12 years	4	40.0
13 to 20 years	3	30.0
Education		
Primary School	1	10.0
F.3	1	10.0
F.5	6	60.0
University	1	10.0
Master	1	10.0
Employment status		
Currently employed	10	100.0
Income (Per month)		
$10000 or below	7	70.0
$10000 – $15000	1	10.0
$16000 – $20000	1	10.0
$21000 or above	1	10.0

(cont'd overleaf)

TABLE 1 (continued)

Characteristics of Caregivers	N	%
Living arrangement		
Living with parents	9	90.0
Not living with parents	1	10.0
Total Household Income		
$10000 or below	2	20.0
$11000 – $20000	3	30.0
$21000 – $30000	2	20.0
$31000 – $40000	0	0
$41000 – $50000	1	10.0
$51000 – $60000	0	0
$61000 or above	1	10.0
Unknown	1	10.0
Numbers of siblings		
1 – 2	3	30.0
3 – 4	3	30.0
5 – 6	1	10.0
7 – 8	2	20.0
No siblings	1	10.0
Perceived Health Status		
Excellent	0	0
Good	2	20.0
Fair	8	80.0
Poor	0	0
Duration of caregiving		
1 – 5 years	3	30.0
6 – 10 years	2	20.0
11 – 15 years	3	30.0
16 – 20 years	2	20.0

TABLE 2
Demographic Characteristics of Respondents Elderly Parents (N=12)

Characteristics of Frail Elderly Parents	N	%
Age		
Young old (60–74)	9	75.0
Old old (74+)	3	25.0
Sex		
Female	10	83.3
Male	2	16.7
Marital Status		
Married and with living spouse	4	33.3
Widowed	8	66.7
Health Status		
Excellent	0	0
Good	5	41.6
Fair	4	33.3
Poor	3	25.0
Major Illness		
Stroke	3	25.0
Problems with vision	3	25.0
High blood abnormalities	3	25.0
Others	3	25.0
Cognitive Impairment		
Severe	0	0
Moderate	6	50.0
Mild or no impairment	6	50.0
Financial Dependence		
Mainly on primary caregivers	10	83.3
On primary caregiver and other family members	2	16.7
Mainly on government assistance	0	0
Needs for assistance		
Daily living and Personal care with aids	1	8.3
Walking with aids	0	0
No needs on above assistance	11	91.7

Daughters-in-law as Caregivers

As noted above a large proportion of the respondents in our sample were related to the elderly under care as daughters-in-law. While this proportion is large in our sample perhaps it is not exceptional. After all, as Piercy (1998) has discussed, when adult children provide assistance to their parents, daughters and daughters-in-law usually assume the role of the primary caregiver, and sons and sons-in-law provide supplemental help to their spouses or sisters. Stone, Cafferata and Sangl (1987) reported that sons who provided care were more likely than daughters to receive assistance. In a similar vein, Horowitz (1985) has found that sons who provided care were more likely to receive assistance from their wives than daughters could expect from their husbands. Therefore, for daughters-in-law to become the primary caregiver can be viewed as an extension of this phenomenon. Indeed, an interesting (but not surprising) contrast is that there were no sons-in-law serving as primary caregivers in our sample.

Indeed, the daughters-in-law in our sample all reported that they were involved in caregiving primarily to help their husbands who, in turn, seemed to have to bear the caregiving role by default. All of the daughters-in-law reported that their husband was either the youngest or only child in the family, or being the only child residing locally in Hong Kong. The fact that the daughters-in-law reported that they were involved in caregiving primarily to help their husbands is interesting in that it shows that the caregivers in this case did not feel a direct affinity or obligation to the elderly under care in the first place.

Indeed, the attitude expressed by the daughters-in-law as caregivers was very different from that of sons or daughters such as the perceived reasons for caregiving. As Table 3 shows, whereas all the sons and daughters in our study cited filial obligation as an important reason for caregiving, *none* of the daughters-in-law did. This result is striking because filial obligation is often seen as the *raison d'être* for caregiving among sons and daughters (Hamon, 1992; Spitze and Logan, 1990; Stein *et al.*, 1998). The daughters-in-law were also much less likely to cite affectional bond with the elderly under care as a reason for caregiving. The view expressed by Cindy is rather illustrative: "I take up the caregiving role as my husband requires me to. I actually do not think that I have a duty to take care of my husband's parents".

Furthermore, the daughters-in-law often expressed the view that their task or duty had largely been discharged as long as proper *physical* or *financial* care was provided. Similarly, daughters-in-law in our sample typically felt less obligated to provide companionship or emotional support to the elderly under care. For example, the daughters-in-law did not feel obligated to confide in their in-laws or to listen to them patiently. As one respondent, Mrs. Ho, said, "I admit that I provide less psychological aid (compared to physical aid) to my parents-in-law. This is because I think that I do not have any duty to do so. I am not their daughter. I am only responsible for looking after their daily living and personal care. I pass the job of providing psychological aid to my husband because they are after all his parents, and his parents would appreciate their son to give psychological support to them".

In sharp contrast, the sons or daughters in our survey felt much more direct emotional attachment to the parents whom they were

TABLE 3

Relationships between Primary Caregivers Family
Status and Their Perceived Reasons of Caregiving

Caregivers Perceived reasons of Caregiving	Son (N=5)		Daughter (N=1)		Daughter-in-law (N=4)	
	N	%	N	%	N	%
Good affectional bond	5	100	1	100	2	50.0
Filial obligation	5	100	1	100	0	0
No one is willing to care	1	20.0	1	100	1	25.0
Family structure and position	1	20.0	0	0	1	25.0
Time available and Higher income	1	20.0	0	0	2	50.0
Caregiving is woman's work	0	0	0	0	1	25.0

caring for. Also, sons and daughters were much more likely to view caregiving as a repayment to their parents, and they tended to emphasize reciprocity regarding the care that they had previously received from their parents. Naturally, this type of reciprocity is typically absent in an in-law relationship.

Another aspect of the role of daughter-in-law as caregiver that has transpired in our interview is that daughters-in-law typically suffer less stress from their caregiving role. Our results suggest one explanation for this phenomenon. The incidence of caregiver's stress is directly related to elderly impairment. Previous studies on caregiver stress have distinguished between two types of elderly impairment: physical impairment and cognitive-behavioral problems. These two kinds of impairment have a differential impact in causing stress on the part of the caregivers. Indeed, the study by Starrels, Ingersoll-Dayton, Dowler and Neal (1997) have found that employed children (sons or daughters) who rendered care to parents suffering from cognitive-behavioral disorders reported higher levels of strain than did employed children who rendered care to physically impaired parents. One reason for this is that given that caregivers usually share a close emotional bondage with their parents, they find the deterioration in cognitive abilities of their parents particularly difficult to handle. As Cantor (1983) has reported, the closer the emotional bond between the child and parent, the more stressful the caregiving role. Now, if such emotional bondage is not as strong to begin with, as appears to be the case for daughters-in-law, then one should find daughters-in-law in general being less stressed out as well.

It should be stressed that none of the results here suggests that daughters-in-law may be less effective as caregivers compared to sons or daughters. Daughters-in-law are more likely to look at their caregiving task as a duty to be discharged effectively without a lot of emotional burden common among caregivers who are sons or daughters. By being less emotionally attached to the elderly individuals under care to begin with, daughters-in-law perhaps share something in common with professional caregivers. It is entirely possible for them to discharge their caregiving tasks effectively without the emotional attachment exhibited by caregivers who are sons or daughters.

Sons as Caregivers and Gender Differences in Caregiving

The issue of sons serving as primary caregivers remains a controversial one. The literature has a long tradition of treating the male caregiver as the exception rather than the rule to begin with. Horowitz (1985) reported that sons often became caregivers because there was no one else available. In their literature review, Spitze and Logan (1990) have found that daughters are more likely than sons to be in contact with and provide assistance to their parents in old age. Ngan (1990) noted that in a Chinese society such as Hong Kong, there is an even greater tendency for the task of caregiving to fall on women. However, Horowitz's findings were challenged by Chang and White-Means (1991), who have found no difference between males and females in terms of the motivations for giving care. Specifically, Chang and White-Means found no evidence that males take up caregiving only because no one else is available.

Our sample strongly sides with the finding by Horowitz (1985). To begin with, we saw previously that the daughters-in-law in our sample were involved in serving as caregiver primarily to help their husbands, all of whom became responsible for the caring of their parents because no one else was available. As for the cases where the primary caregivers were married men, all reported either having received assistance from their wives, or that the elderly under their care were in sufficiently good health as to not require a lot of assistance. As for the two single male primary caregivers in our study, there were no female siblings to take up the caregiving task. In sum, in our in-depth study of men involved in caregiving, among the married men the primary caregiving responsibility was either not too substantial to begin with, or passed on to the wife where it became substantial, while in the cases of the single male caregivers no female siblings were available. Hence, our study confirms that there is strong gender specialization in the caring of the elderly.

This is not to suggest that men are not motivated to become primary caregivers for their parents. Indeed, most of the male caregivers in our sample expressed strong commitments to their role, and they often cited filial obligation as a prime motivation. The sentiment expressed by Mr. Cheung is illustrative: "I have developed an intimate relationship with my mother since childhood. So, I think I want to help and protect my mother throughout my life". Such sentiment was echoed by Mr. Chan, who said, "Due to my affectional bond with my mother, I want to care for her and live with her. In other words, I want to stay with her most of the time".

It is also interesting to compare the results of our survey with those in the literature regarding the issue of gender differences in caregiving tasks. In our study, the women were much more likely to provide help with daily living and personal care compared to the men (Table 4). This is significant because help with daily living and personal care tend to be time-consuming and labor intensive, and often accounts for the bulk of the physical care rendered. Our results are generally consistent with the mainstream observation found in the literature. For example, Chang and White-Means (1991) found a difference between males and females in terms of the type of tasks performed.

TABLE 4

Relationships between Primary Caregivers Gender
and Their Most Frequent Caregiving Activities

Types of Help	Son (N=5)		Daughter and Daughter-in-law* (N=5)	
	N	%	N	%
Help for Daily Living	1	20.0	4	75
Help for Personal Care	1	20.0	4	75
Cognitive Aid	5	100	5	100
Psychological Aid	2	40.0	1**	10.0
Living Arrangement	5	100	5	100
Financial Aid	5	100	5	100

NOTES: * one is a daughter and four are daughters-in-law.
      ** the one who provided psychological aid is a daughter, not daughter-in-law.

One possible reason for the greater involvement of women in rendering help for daily living and personal care is that these activities fall into the realm of traditional housework where women have been institutionalized to take up in the first place (Abel, 1991). Indeed, our study confirms that gender specialization in caregiving may follow patterns similar to the gender specialization in the household division of labor between couples (Stephens and Christianson, 1986; Stoller, 1990). Furthermore, the gender specialization in caregiving tasks could also have a differential impact on the male and female caregivers. In a survey of the literature, Abel (1991) reported that "sons are more likely to assist parents with routine household maintenance and repairs, while daughters are far more likely to help with indoor household chores and personal health care". In other words, "sons take responsibility for tasks they can perform whenever they choose. Daughters, however, often assume responsibilities that keep them on call twenty-four hours a day."

Another observation from our study that points to the gender division of labor is that the married sons did not provide any help with daily living and personal care to their elderly parents, while daughters and daughters-in-law readily did. At the same time, single sons also provided more care in this area than married sons. (See Table 5.)

Previous studies have found that male caregivers as a whole tend to suffer from less stress than female caregivers. One reason that has been put forward is that male caregivers receive more reciprocal assistance from the elderly under care because the latter are particularly appreciative of the male caregivers (Starrels *et al.*, 1997). It should be noted that this observation itself actually suggests that men tend to spend less time on caregiving to begin with, so that when men are involved in caregiving they are seen to be making the extra effort and therefore doubly appreciated. Another reason that male caregivers may feel less stressed than women caregivers is alluded to above — that men tend to receive more help from their spouses. More generally, one has reasons to suspect that the real reason why male caregivers tend to be under less stress for their caregiving activity is that they

Odalia M.H. Wong

TABLE 5
Relationships among Primary Caregivers' Marital
Status and Family Status and Their Most Frequent Care-
giving Activities

	Single (N=3)				Married (N=7)			
Types of Help								
	Son (N=2)		Daughter (N=1)		Son (N=3)		Daughter-in-law (N=4)	
	N	%	N	%	N	%	N	%
Help for Daily Living	1	50	1	100	0	0	3	75
Help for Personal Care	1	50	1	100	0	0	2	50
Cognitive Aid	2	100	1	100	3	100	4	100
Psychological Aid	1	50	1	100	1	33.3	0	0
Living Arrangement	2	100	1	100	3	100	4	100
Financial Aid	2	100	1	100	3	100	4	100

tend to have more resources at their disposal (such as financial) and receive more support for their caregiving activity. Seen in this light, support from the spouse is just one aspect of the kind of resources that male caregivers in general have more ready access to.

Interestingly, the three married male caregivers in our survey did not seem to feel particularly stressed by their caregiving activity, while the two single men felt stressed. In the cases of the married men in our study, the reasons why they appeared to be not under a lot of stress were a combination of the fact that the elderly under care was in relatively good shape, that they were not financially burdened, and that they enjoyed sufficient resources or support for their caregiving activity, including hired help or help from the spouse.

As for the two single men in our sample who served as primary caregivers, they both expressed feeling abandoned and having to deal with the caregiving task on their own, and they were resentful. These caregivers also expressed an exceptional sense of filial obligation to the parent under their care.

In fact, among the female caregivers we also observed that women who received relatively more support and resources found their caregiving task less stressful. For example, Mrs. Yau in our study seemed to be really well adjusted to her caregiving role. Many factors were involved, but they all pointed to Mrs. Yau having more resources at her disposal or receiving adequate support for her caregiving task. Thus, Mrs. Yau found her job stable and not too demanding. She was financially quite well off, as she and her husband enjoyed good joint income. Also, her in-laws under her care owned property and received regular rental income, and the brothers of her husband also chipped in financially. Her in-laws were in good physical shape and did not need too much care. Furthermore, Mrs. Yau's husband was supportive with the house work and caregiving tasks, while her mother-in-law helped to care for her father-in-law and her children too. All in all, the whole family seems to cooperate very well together and conflicts appear to be minimized.

In contrast, Ms. Tse had much less access to resources and received less support. Ms. Tse was single and the oldest child. She lived with three younger brothers and their mother. The younger brothers were all in school or unemployed. Ms Tse reported that she was heavily burdened in caring for the whole family financially. At the same time she was responsible to do housework and care for her elderly mother. Ms. Tse reported that she felt heavily burdened, was constantly worried about the future (including job security and the livelihood of her family), and expressed resentment of her situation, particularly the lack of support from her brothers.

Among the female caregivers in our study, Mrs. Yau was among the least stressed, and her success seems to be due to the support that she received. In contrast, Ms. Tse, who was single, felt a lot of stress because she received little support. The result here corresponds with the result for male caregivers very well.

To summarize, we found that caregivers who received relatively more support or resources had suffered from relatively less stress, regardless of the sex of the caregivers. Hence, we conclude that male caregivers appear to suffer less from stress than female caregivers because male caregivers as a whole receive relatively more support and resources for their caregiving activity.

Problems of Caregiving and Role Conflicts

Our results above show that caregivers are likely to feel more stressed when they receive little support for their tasks. Nevertheless, stress appears to be a common ailment among caregivers even under the best circumstances (Litvin, 1995; Starrels *et al.*, 1997). Indeed, the majority of the respondents in our study encountered various problems in caregiving. These problems involved four aspects: financial strain, physical deterioration, negative emotional response, and role conflict.

Most of the respondents in our study felt burdened by the extra financial commitment involved in caregiving. Many felt pressured by the fact that they were responsible for the very livelihood of the elderly under their care. This is all too understandable, as some respondents reported that they were spending half or more of their income on the elderly under their care. The need for extra money has also compelled some of the respondents to remain employed or work longer hours for extra pay despite the fact that they already felt over-extended by their multiple responsibilities. Even among the respondents who were financially better off, however, nearly all of them expressed concern about the medical expenses of the elderly under their care.

While not all the respondents reported that they felt physically fatigued from caregiving, most readily admitted that caregiving required time and energy, especially in the area of helping with daily living and personal care. Not coincidentally, the respondents who felt the most physically drained usually attributed their fatigue to juggling their responsibilities between caregiving and employment.

Negative emotional response was common among the respondents, who reported experiences of anxiety, helplessness, guilt, and even depression. Often respondents were troubled by feelings of guilt because they felt that their own caregiving efforts were insufficient, while feelings of anxiety seemed to be greatest when the elderly fell sick. Importantly, and as we have seen above, the respondents who expressed the strongest negative emotional response tended to be those who were resentful of their situation, particularly when they felt that their siblings and other relatives had not chipped in sufficiently to share the responsibility, thus leaving them holding the bag.

In the literature, it is well recognized that an important source of caregiver's stress is role conflicts, and our study readily confirms this view. All the interviewees in our study have had to deal with a combination of major roles, since all of them held jobs. In addition, most of them were married with young children under their care. As Lang and Brody (1983) have reported in a study of daughters as caregivers, being married and being employed could operate as competing demands to caregiving. Not surprisingly, most of the interviewees in our study reported that they found caregiving stressful in creating excess demands on their energy, time, and commitment, and brought about worries and anxiety about the elderly's well being. They also readily pointed to the conflicts between caregiving and their other roles in life. The different types of conflicts identified in our study include conflicts with work, marriage life, caring for children, as well as social and personal life. Our study also points to the fact that the extent of the problems and conflicts faced by caregivers is a function of the resources they have available. In general, caregivers who have more time available, more support from family members, more reciprocal help from the elderly under their care, higher income, and less multiple responsibilities were likely to experience less problems with caregiving.

However, while many studies, including ours, have readily identified the conflicts between caregiving and other responsibilities, it is actually possible for caregiving and other responsibilities to be complimentary of one another as well. A good example in our study is that of Jenny. Jenny had a baby daughter and lived with her mother-in-law for whom Jenny served as the primary caregiver. Jenny's mother-in-law was in relatively good physical health, and not only did she not require a lot of physical assistance from Jenny, she was actually in a position to care for Jenny's daughter as well. In this case, the household division of labor can work to the benefit of everyone because there is actually complimentarity rather than conflict between elderly care and the caregiver's child-rearing responsibility. Actually, Jenny's case is just a more interesting example among many of how the presence of an elderly in the household does not necessarily have to be a burden. In fact, most of the interviewees in our survey reported that the elderly under care had provided help with some household work. The point is that when researchers looked at the multiple responsibilities that caregivers are faced with, too often they have focused solely on the conflicts involved and overlooked the possible complimentarities. Indeed, it is important to keep in mind that, when family members start to assume the task of caregiving for elderly relatives, that could well transform the household division of labor in many important ways, creating many complimentarities and conflicts in the process, and it is equally important to study the complimentarities and the conflicts.

A finding from our study which we reported in the previous section also illustrates this point well. We found that single caregivers in our study were under more stress compared to the married caregivers, despite the fact that single caregivers had the advantage of dealing with at least one less important source of potential conflict — that between caregiving and marriage. Similarly, Suitor and Pillemer (1994) also found that relatively few adult children or children-in-law reported that caregiving had a detrimental effect on their marital relationship. This shows that caregiving and marriage can involve complimentarities as well as conflicts.

Nonetheless, while sometimes it is easy to overlook the complimentarities in caregiving, similarly sometimes the conflicts that may arise from caregiving may go unreported or underreported. Here, Mrs. Ho presents a very interesting case concerning the potential conflicts between caregiving and work. When asked whether she felt that caring for her in-laws had come into conflict with her part-time job, Mrs. Ho's initial answer was negative. However, when asked about the details of the physical care that she had to render to her in-law, Mrs. Ho responded that she had to take time to call her in-laws to check on them, and that on several occasions she had to take time off from work to take her in-laws for doctor visits. Clearly, then, Mrs. Ho's caregiving had at times come into conflict with her work, despite her initial assertion to the contrary. A plausible reason for Mrs. Ho's contradictory assessment is that caregiving could well be stigmatized in the work place, and that employees who have the added responsibility of caring for the elderly may be seen as having to take time away from their jobs and thereby compromising their job commitment. Hence Mrs. Ho could well be subconsciously trying to downplay the impact of caregiving on her employment.

Summary and Conclusions

This paper has examined some of the problems of caregiving from a caregiver's perspective using in-depth interviews of ten caregivers. While the small sample used in our study cannot claim to be representative, we believe that there are important advantages in conducting in-depth interviews which is often not practical when working with large samples. By making use of open-ended questions and engaging the interviewees in in-depth discussions, it becomes possible to uncover the true feelings of respondents on certain issues that may carry certain stigma and where the respondents may feel ambivalent or reluctant to discuss. Another reward to the use of more flexible, open-ended questions is that it more readily opens one up to results that may be quite different from the priors of the researcher. A specific example is that we were able to identify role complimentarity in caregiving where we expected to find role conflicts and vice-versa.

A highlight of our findings concerns the role of daughters-in-law as caregivers. Specifically, we found that the primary reason for daughters-in-law to involve in caregiving was to help their husbands, rather than out of filial obligation or affectional bonds which were the most common reasons cited by caregivers who were sons or daughters. Partly for this reason, daughters-in-law often expressed the view that they felt that their caregiving duties were properly discharged as long as they provided adequate physical care or financial support, and that they were under little obligation to provide emotional support to the care receiver. By the same token, the daughters-in-law also generally felt less emotional bondage to the elderly under care. For this reason, they were likely to find their caregiving experience less stressful as well. It bears emphasizing that the fact that daughters-in-law may be relatively less emotionally attached to their caregiving tasks in no way suggests whether daughters-in-law make for "better" or "worse" caregivers compared to sons and daughters.

As for the male caregivers in our study, among the married men the primary caregiving responsibility was either not substantial to begin with (usually because the elderly in question were in good health), or it was passed to the spouse (daughter-in-law) where it became substantial, while in the cases of the single male caregivers it is notable that no female siblings were available. These results suggest that caregiving remains very much a woman's task. Indeed, strong gender differences were also found in the types of caregiving tasks that male and female caregivers were engaged in, and that the pattern of gender specialization in caregiving tended to follow the gender division of labor in housework.

Also, on the issue of whether men tend to suffer less from caregiver's stress compared to women, we found that the key to caregiver's stress is the amount of resources and support received by the caregiver rather than gender. Specifically, the more caregiving resources and support that the caregiver enjoys, the less stress the caregiver is likely to experience. On the other hand, there are reasons to suspect that men as a whole tend to enjoy more resources and support compared to women, which may explain why the literature has reported a lower incidence of caregiver stress among men. In other words, while we do not refute the contention that women caregivers generally suffer from more stress, we argue that this phenomenon is due primarily to the fact that women as a whole receive less resources and support for their caregiving tasks.

We also found that, even under the best circumstances, caregivers have reported a variety of problems with caregiving, including financial strain, physical strain, negative emotional response, and role conflicts. Our results suggest that caregiving and employment present a very important source of role conflict, and that this source of conflict may be under-reported. This is due to the stigma that may be attached to employees who have the added responsibility of caregiving, leading them to consciously or subconsciously deny or downplay the existence of such conflicts. On the other hand, our results suggest that the incidence of conflicts between caregiving and marriage and children may be much lower. The reason is that caregiving within the family is one part of the household division of labor which could create complimentarities as well as conflicts. Indeed, our study suggests that future research should focus as much on the potential complimentarities between caregiving and other household activities as the potential conflicts.

Indeed, the use of in-depth interviews has revealed the diversity in the experience of the caregivers, and it shows how every situation is unique. One lesson from our study is that it shows that there is no single magic formula to make caregiving work. For example: sometimes having both elderly and children around could create conflict, while under different circumstances it could create complimentarities, such as having the caregiver caring for the elderly, while the elderly helps caring for the young children. In this situation having both elderly and young children around could actually create a more efficient division of labor within the household which makes everybody better off.

All in all, our study suggests that the key to addressing the problems of caregiving and alleviating caregiver's stress is more and better utilization of resources for the caregiver. The most ready source for such resources and support is within the family. Where such resources and support are absent or inadequate within the family, community or social support is necessary to help fill the void.

References

Abel, Emily K. (1991) *Who Cares for the Elderly?: Public Policy and the Experiences of Adult Daughters*. Philadelphia: Temple University Press, U.S.A.

Chang, C.F. & White-Means, S.I. (1991) "The Men Who Care: An Analysis of Male Primary Caregivers Who Care for Frail Elderly at Home", *Journal of Applied Gerontology*, 10(3): 343–358.

Chow, W.S. (1987) "Factors Influencing the Support of the Elderly by their Families", *Hong Kong Journal of Gerontology*, 1(1): 4–9.

Chow, N.W.S. (1987) "Caregiving in Developing East and Southeast Asia Countries", *The Hong Kong Journal of Social Work*, 21(1): 1–8.

Chow, N.W.S. (1996) "The Chinese Society and Family Policy in Hong Kong", in Sussman, Marvin B. & Hanks, R.S., eds., *Intercultural Variation in Family Research and Theory*. The Harworth Press.

Dwyer, J.W. & Seccombe, K. (1991) "Elder Care as Family Labor", *Journal of Family Issues*, 12(2): 229–247.

Finley, N.J. (1989) "Theories of Family Labor as Applied to Gender Differences in Caregiving for Elderly Parents", *Journal of Marriage and the Family*, 51: 79–86.

Hamon, R.R. (1992) "Filial Role Enactment by Adult Children", *Family Relations*, 41: 91–96.

Horowitz, A. (1985) "Sons and Daughters as Caregivers to Older Parents: Differences in Role Performance and Consequences", *The Gerontologist*, 25: 612–617.

Lang, A.M. & Brody, E.M. (1983). "Characteristics of Middle-aged Daughters and Help to Their Elderly Mothers", *Journal of Marriage and the Family*, 45: 193–201.

Lawton, M.P.; Moss, M. & Duhamel, L.M. (1995) "The Quality of Daily Life Among Elderly Care Receivers", *The Journal of Applied Gerontology*, 14(2): 150–171.

Lee, G.R.; Netzer, J.K. & Coward, R.T. (1994) "Filial Responsibility Expectations and Patterns of Intergenerational Assistance", *Journal of Marriage and Family*, 56: 559–565.

Leung, A.K.P. (1996) "Aging in Transition: Meeting the Challenges of an Aging Population into the Next Century", *Hong Kong Journal of Gerontology*, 10(2): 3–5.

Litvin, S.J.; Albert, S.M.; Brody, E.M. & Hoffman, C. (1995) "Marital Status, Competing Demands, and Role Priorities of Parent-Caring Daughters", *Journal of Applied Gerontology*, 14(4): 372–390.

Mancini, J.A. & Blieszner, R. (1989) "Aging Parents and Adult Children: Research Themes in Intergenerational Relations", *Journal of Marriage and the Family*, 51: 275–290.

Ngan, R. (1990) "The Availability of Informal Support Networks to the Chinese Elderly in Hong Kong and Its Implications for Practice", *Hong Kong Journal of Gerontology*, 4(2): 19–25.

Ngan, R.; Leung, E.; Kwan, A.; Yeung, D. & Chong, A. (1997) "Long Term Care Needs, Patterns and Impact of the Elderly in Hong Kong", *Hong Kong Journal of Gerontology*, 11(2): 22–27.

Piercy, K.W. (1998) "Theorizing About Family Caregiving: The Role of Responsibility", *Journal of Marriage and the Family*, 60: 109–118.

Spitze, G. & Logan, J. (1990) "Sons, Daughters, and Intergenerational Social Support", *Journal of Marriage and the Family*, 52: 420–430.

Starrels, M.E.; Ingersoll-Dayton, B.; Dowler, D.W. & Neal, M.B. (1997) "The Stress of Caring for a Parent: Effects of the Elder's Impairment on an Employed, Adult Child", *Journal of Marriage and the Family*, 59: 860–872.

Stein, C.H.; Wemmrus, V.A.; Ward, M.; Gaines, M.; Freeberg, A.L. & Jewell, T.C. (1998) "Because They're My Parents: An Intergenerational Study of Felt Obligation and Parental Caregiving", *Journal of Marriage and the Family*, 60: 611–622.

Stephens, S.A. & Christianson, J.B. (1986) *Informal Care of the Elderly*. Lexington, Massachusetts: Lexington Books, U.S.A.

Stoller, E.P. (1990) "Males as Helpers: The Role of Sons, Relatives, and Friends", *The Gerontologist*, 30(2): 228–235.

Stone, R.I.; Cafferata, L. & Sangl, J. (1987) "Caregivers of the Frail Elderly: A National Profile", *The Gerontologist*, 27(5): 616–626.

Suitor, J.J. & Pillemer, K. (1994) "Family Caregiving and Marital Satisfaction: Findings from a 1-Year Panel Study of Women Caring for Parents with Dementia", *Journal of Marriage and the Family*, 56: 681–690.

Tam, T.S. (1981) "A Report of the Problems of the Elderly in Hong Kong", *The Hong Kong Journal of Social Work*, 15(2): 20–32.

Chapter 15

Caregiving Survey in Guangzhou: A Preliminary Report

Elena S.H. Yu
San Diego State University
Lai Shilong and Wen Zehuai
Guangzhou University of Chinese Traditional Medicine
and William T. Liu
East Asian Institute, National University of Singapore

Introduction

Based on a sample of 5,055 persons 55 years and older, the Shanghai Study screened for senile dementia and Alzheimer's disease. The results have been published (Katzman *et al.* 1988; Yu *et al.,* 1989 and 1992; Levy *et al.,* 1988, 1989; Zhang *et al.,* 1990; Liu *et al.,* 1992). In that survey we also conducted a substudy of caregiving burden between caregivers who took care of Alzheimer disease victims and those who took care of physically dependent victims.

Over the past two decades, there have been a number of publications on caregiving and caregiving burden. For example, Zarit *et al.* (1980) in their study of caregivers of demented elderly, found that the caregiver's felt burden was affected by the presence or absence of social support. Poulshock Walker and Deimling (1984) noted that studies needed to consider not only the impact of the objective impairment on the caregiver but caregivers' subjective interpretations of impairment as well, which was also the basis of the Montgomery and Borgatta's work (see Chapter one in this volume). In a previous paper, Montgomery *et al.* (1985) pointed out that impairment should be distinguished in terms of the different ways it affects caregivers; for instance, disruptive behaviour from, say, cognitive deficits.

Position in the family and types of ties with the patients should also be differentiated in terms of burden felt. For example, Elaine Brody (1981) stressed the special heavy burden felt by an unmarried middle-aged daughter, whereas Shanas (1979 and 1980) emphasized that the adult offspring, rather than other family ties of the elderly are particularly important in providing caregiving. Johnson and Catalano (1981 and 1983) reminded us that the family status of the elder is important as a variable in determining subjective burden. They found that impairment affects a childless married elder differently than a childless unmarried one. The explanation they gave was that impairment led childless married elder to withdraw from other social ties, and increases the intensity of spousal relations. On the other hand, childless unmarried elder adapt to the impairment situation by means of extended, long-term kinship ties and friendships. The nature of social ties often dictates the way people use different strategies in the caregiving relationships. Wentowski (1981) reported that an elder without kins often incorporated non-kins as if they were adapted kin members. In short, as argued by Gurbrium (1995), the subjective nature of care-burden can be explained by a number of cultural and familial factors. In the Hong and Liu chapter (this volume) the authors point out that caregiving is essentially a special type of social relationship, and needs to be studied by incorporating theories of social psychology, with the understanding that caregiving relationship is a unique dyadic relationship.

The Guangzhou Caregiving Study

In August 1994, a team of multi-national investigators from the United States and Mainland China launched the Guangzhou Aging and Alzheimer's Disease Research Project. A two-stage sampling procedure was used to obtain estimates of the prevalence of dementia and Alzheimer's Disease among persons 75 years and older living in Liwan District of Guangzhou City in Guangdong Province, China.

The first stage of sample design is a case-finding survey in which 3,825 persons were screened for symptoms of possible cognitive impairment using our Chinese translation of Folstein *et al.*'s Mini-Mental Status Examination Instrument (CMMSE, see Yu *et al.*, 1989). The second stage is a case-identification survey in which all those persons scoring at or below a pre-defined education-dependent cut-off score of 20/21 CMMSE score for persons with elementary or lower level of education, and 24/25 for those who had higher than elementary level of education were considered to be "MMSSE-Positive".

At the second interview, a standardized battery of neuro-psychological tests, and psychiatric as well as physical examinations were performed by a team of experts in Neurology, Neuropsychology, and Clinical Psychiatry. An additional group of controls called the "MMSE-Negative", representing 6.25% of those who scored above the education-dependent cut-off scores, were also randomly sampled for inclusion in the second stage survey. The sampling fraction was chosen to allow for anticipated non-response in the second stage of study.

All elderly interviewed in Phase 1 whose MMSE score was 20 or less were interviewed with Caregiver Survey Instrument. Those elderly whose MMSE score was in the 21–30 range were first administered a set of filtering questions. These questions are: a score of 2 (needed help), or 3 (simply cannot do the task alone) on any of the following 8 ADL items: transferring, climbing stairs, walking near home, eating, dressing, bathing, toileting, and maintenance. All persons who either needed help or simply could not do any of the above ADL items were interviewed. Next, we targeted for interviews the caregivers of a random sub-sample of the remaining subject of elders whose MMSE score were in the 21–30 range and who had no difficulty at all, or were able to perform the ADL without help despite minor difficulties.

Some Findings

Preliminary findings that are germane to the central theme of this publication are reported in this chapter under three headings. The first heading, namely caregiving in Chinese communities, focuses on questions pertaining to the kind of social relationships, in contrast to previous studies conducted in the West. The second heading deals with co-residence pattern of elders and their families in Guangzhou. The third heading has to do with the re-formulation of the care-burden scale through factor-analytic process. While additional work will follow the factor analysis operation to link burden with types of social relations, this report provides the reader with a new insight into the multi-dimensional nature of burden as reported.

1. The Relational Ties between the Caregiver and the Elder

A substantial percentage (34.5%) of the caregivers are male, and 65.4% are female. The caregiver's ages range from 10 to 86 years old, with a mean age of 54.5 years (s.d.=17.3) and a median of 57.0 years with 42 years for the first quartile; 68 years for the third quartile. Some 74.1% of the caregivers are married and living with their spouses. In terms of educational attainment, some 16.5% of the caregivers are illiterate, 8.3% are semi-literate. In other words, about one-quarter of the caregivers is functionally illiterate. A little over 24% has elementary education, about 2% has vocational training, 22.7% has junior high school education, and 19.8% has senior high school education. About 6.6% has gone to college or has postgraduate education.

About 43.5% of the caregivers in the sample are retired from work, 35% has another paying employment in addition to caregiving. About

15% are housewives, unemployed but not seeking jobs. Only 6.8% identify themselves as full-time caregivers with no other jobs.

We were sensitive to previous studies which pointed out that most caregivers are middle-aged women, normally an unmarried daughter. Guangzhou data shows that about a third (30.3%) of the caregivers are the elder's spouse. But 18.7% are sons and 17.7% are daughters. Daughters-in-law constitute only 12.7%. Note that sons and their spouses are separately enumerated. In this case we carefully distinguished sons from daughters-in-law with regard to the actual work performed as caregivers. In addition, when other relatives are indicated, 1.1% is the sons-in-law. Thus caregiving is neither the exclusive responsibility of daughters, nor of daughters-in-law. Non-kin caregivers constitute only 6% of the sample. *Compared to reports in previous studies based on investigations made in Euro-American communities, the gender issue in caregiving in Guangzhou, as it was pointed in the Shanghai study, deserves attention.*

In view of previous studies that reported that caregiving burden fell on a single, perhaps primary, caregiver, the Guangzhou data shows that many members of the family pitch in to help in most cases and there is no pre-defined division of labour. Only 98 of 381 caregivers who had shared responsibilities also reported that they took turns to care for the elder. Slightly more than one-third of the caregivers (35% of 844) responded that they cared for the elder on a 24-hour basis.

2. Living Arrangement of the Elder in Guangzhou

Some 94.1% of the caregivers were living with the elder, and 2% did not share the elder's residence, but lived in the same multi-storey building as the elder (such as upstairs, downstairs, next door, or across the hallway). Only 3.9% lived away from the same building where the elder resided. In 63.2% of the cases, the caregiver and the elder had lived together during their entire life course even before the caregiving relationships were formed. Among those who did not live together in their entire lives, all came to share residence with the elder when caregiving began. The median length of co-residence is 15 years (mean years 21 years, with range between one month to 64 years). The data showed that caregivers and the elder most likely share residence. Given the long years of caregiving, it is important for us to point out that *not* all elders given care were functionally dependent, thus caregiving is conceptualized in China on the basis of age attainment, regardless of health conditions and dependency (ADL) status. In our interviews, we were often told by younger members of the family, as well as spouses (if age differential is sufficiently large) that "older" people need, as well as are entitled to, help; such as doing housework, running errands and work involving physical labour.

The difference in the cognitive mapping of the caregiving concept is an important discovery, in spite of the fact that in our research instrument the word caregiving was clearly defined for our respondents, namely, rendering assistance when the elder is incapable of doing such chores either partially or completely. The way our respondents in Guangzhou understood the concept was that caregiving is like having a second person as a backup in doing daily tasks that are group centered.[1] When the incumbent of the role is older, requiring extra strength or needing compensatory efforts, the younger person in the family comes to assist, thus entering the normal (clinical) caregiving role later is a seamless transition. *This is a new way to conceptualize "caregiving" as an on-going social process in family relationship that may deserve attention.*

Caregiver's Attitudes Towards the Elder

The Guangzhou Caregiving Study is an attempt to assess the caregiver's attitude towards caregiving. It appears that at the time of our survey, many Chinese caregivers adhered closely to the traditional cultural values of respecting and caring for elder members in the family, held a positive attitude towards caregiving, and had high self-esteem for being able to provide caregiving to the elder.

For example, 55.1% of the 844 respondents said that they frequently or sometimes thought that if were not for their role in caregiving, the elder would not have been so healthy, or done so well. Some 44% of the caregivers reported that they sometimes or frequently felt that family members were grateful for their role as caregivers, i.e., a positive sense of self-respect. About 84.1% reported that they sometimes or frequently thought that no matter how tiring the task of caregiving is; they should still care for their elderly parents. Similarly, 84% reported that they were sometimes or frequently satisfied with the care they have provided for their elder. Some 66.2% frequently or sometimes felt that the elder was very nice towards them and did not make excessive demand. About 65.4% of the caregivers reported frequently or sometimes thinking that they would be willing to live at a lower level of material comfort just to take care of their elder. Some 57.1% felt frequently or sometimes that caring for the elder allowed them to pay back or reciprocate all that he/she had done for the caregiver in the past. Another 26.9% reported thinking frequently or sometimes that they could not thank the elder enough for everything the elder had done and for being so nice. Some 19.5% said they frequently or sometimes thought that, if possible, they would rather do other types of work instead of being with the elder all day long. Only 6.5% reported feeling frequently or sometimes that it was really worth their time and effort to do what they were doing just to take care of the elder.

The data indicate that most of the caregivers in Guangzhou are satisfied with caregiving and are willing to do it.

3. The Dimensions of Caregiving Burden

Based on the Montgomery and Borgatta Scale of Caregiving Burden, we added several new items to assess Chinese caregiver burden in the Guangzhou study. Those items were conceived first in Chinese, discussed with indigenous collaborators, and pre-tested by interviewers with another non-overlapping community sample. After data were collected, these new items were then translated into English. The intention was to avoid injecting "Western" style of expression and thinking pattern into a scale intended to capture Chinese caregiver's sense of burden, if any, in caregiving. Through the principal axis factor analysis with oblimin rotation, we found that the 10 items formed a scale with only two factors. These factors explained 42.41% of the variance in caregiver's burden in the Chinese context, with the first factor explaining 37.849% and the second factor explaining an additional 4.517% of the variance. The 10-item scale produced a Cronbach Alpha of .8504 (standardized item alpha = .8519), indicating very high internal consistency. These items and the frequency distribution of response patterns, together with their inter-item correlations, internal consistency reliability analysis, and results of principal-axis factor analysis with oblimin rotation are shown as follows.

Percentage Distribution for the 10-Item Chinese Caregiver Burden Scale (N=844)

	Never	Rarely	Sometimes	Frequently
Taking care of the elderly is an extremely tiring job such that I frequently feel exhausted or worn out.	42.2	18.8	22.6	16.4
Caring for the elderly has adversely affect your health.	66.2	18.7	10.2	4.9
It is unfair that family members shove the responsibility of caring for the elderly to me alone.	83.5	10.1	3.9	2.5
Caring for the elderly has disrupted your daily routines and activities.	58.8	20.5	15.2	5.6
Taking care of the elderly has affected your relationship with friends because it prevents friends from coming to visit you.	71.4	16.4	8.2	4.0
Taking care of the elderly has given me additional psychological burden.	48.9	18.2	21.4	11.4
Taking care of the elderly has made me a worrisome and anxious person.	61.6	16.1	12.8	9.5
Taking care of the elderly has forced me and my family to give up some material comfort.	55.0	21.0	16.4	7.7
You feel it is really not worth your time and effort to do what you are doing so that the elderly is assured of his/her psychological well-being.	80.5	13.0	3.7	2.8
You feel ambivalent about your relationship with the elderly.	78.8	10.5	6.6	4.0

Inter-Item Correlation Matrix for the 10-Item Chinese Caregiver Burden Scale (N=844)

	Tiring	Health	Unfair	Routines	Friends	Burden	Worries	Economic	Time	Ambivalent
Tiring	1.0000									
Health	.5035	1.0000								
Unfair	.2669	.3493	1.0000							
Routines	.4721	.5240	.3896	1.0000						
Friends	.3394	.3777	.3275	.4596	1.0000					
Burden	.5426	.4758	.3023	.4797	.4541	1.0000				
Worries	.4545	.4867	.3247	.4018	.3532	.6187	1.0000			
Economic	.3207	.3550	.2607	.3597	.3382	.3671	.3252	1.0000		
Worth	.2945	.3402	.4274	.3440	.3822	.3575	.2286	.2815	1.0000	
Ambivalent	.1938	.2445	.2766	.2970	.2420	.2896	.3199	.2128	.3736	1.0000

Item-Total Statistics for the 10-Item Chinese Caregiver Burden Scale (N=844)

	Scale Mean if Item Deleted	Scale Variance if Item Deleted	Corrected Item-Total Correlation	Squared Multiple Correlation	Alpha if Item Deleted
Time	4.9834	26.6901	.5863	.4044	.8346
Health	5.5782	28.3865	.6215	.4124	.8305
Unfair	5.8614	31.0140	.4747	.2776	.8435
Routines	5.4396	27.7271	.6420	.4492	.8280
Friends	5.6671	29.3327	.5552	.3487	.8365
Burden	5.1623	26.1812	.6818	.5251	.8234
Worries	5.4135	27.2559	.6171	.4432	.8302
Economic	5.3472	28.9078	.4697	.2250	.8445
Worth	5.8258	30.6019	.5112	.3224	.8410
Ambivalent	5.7559	30.0530	.3920	.2037	.8409

Reliability coefficients for 10 items: Cronbach alpha=.8504; standardized item alpha=.8519.
Statistics for scale: mean =6.1149;variance=34.8468;s.d.=5.9031
Inter-item correlations:mean=.3652;variance=.0083;minimum=.1938;
maximum=.6187;range=.4249.

The preceding table shows that each of the 10 items made a unique contribution to explain the scale variance. If any one item were deleted from the scale, Cronbach alpha would decrease rather than increase. Thus,there is no redundancy in the scale items. We have achieved maximum parsimony with these 10 items, each tapping a slightly different aspect of caregiving burden. Results of the factor analysis by means of principle-axis factoring follow.

Pattern Matrix

	Factor 1	Factor 2
Taking care of the elderly is an extremely tiring job such that I frequently feel exhausted or worn out.	.792	-.137
Caring for the elderly has adversely affect your health.	.614	9.171E–02
It is unfair that family members shove the responsibility of caring for the elderly to me alone.	5.427E–02	.564
Caring for the elderly has disrupted your daily routines and activities.	.529	.217
Taking care of the elderly has affected your relationship with friends because it prevents friends from coming to visit you.	.359	.302
Taking care of the elderly has given me additional psychological burden.	.815	-4.91E–02
Taking care of the elderly has made me a a worrisome and anxious person.	.633	6.310E–02
Taking care of the elderly has forced me and my family to give up some material comfort.	.374	.170
You feel it is really not worth your time and effort to do what you are doing so that the elderly is assured of his/her psychological well-being.	-3.77E–02	.727
You feel ambivalent about your relationship with the elderly.	4.241E–02	.465

Extraction Method: Principal Axis Factoring.
Rotation Method: Oblimin with Kaiser Normalization.
a. Rotation converged in 6 iterations.

Communalities

	Initial	Extraction
Time	.404	.497
Health	.412	.463
Unfair	.278	.363
Routines	.449	.486
Friends	.349	.370
Burden	.525	.611
Worries	.443	.459
Economic	.225	.256
Worth	.322	.256
Ambivalent	.204	.245

Extraction Method: Principal Axis Factoring.

Factor Correlation Matrix

Factor	1	2
1	1.000	.688
2	.688	1.000

Re-arranging the 10 items by the magnitude of factor loadings, we gain a greater appreciation of the non-redundant components that make up each of the two factors which form a remarkably reliable scale. (See table that follows.) For Factor 1, the item "Taking care of the elderly has given me additional psychological burden" has the highest factor loadings, followed by "Taking care of the elderly is an extremely tiring job such that I frequently feel exhausted or worn out". The item with the third highest factor loading is "Taking care of the elderly has made me a worrisome and anxious person". That these three items deal with psychological or mental anxiety is consistent with our intuitive understanding of the concept of caregiving burden. The next few items by size of factor loadings reflect the many aspects of caregiving burden. They are: adverse effect on caregiver's health, disruption of caregiver's daily routines and activities, caregiver's giving up some material comfort, negative effect on caregiver's social relationship with friends as a result of being home-bound with the elderly. Thus, Factor 1 captures the essence of caregiving burden. The 7-item subscale has a Cronbach alpha of .8382 (standardized item alpha = .8399).

Scale Item Arranged by Size of Factor Loadings (N = 844)

Items	Factor 1	Factor 2
Psychological burden	.815	
Extremely tiring	.792	
Become worrisome and anxious	.633	
Adversely affect health	.614	
Disrupt daily routines	.529	
Give up material comfort	.374	
Affect relationships with friends	.359	
Not worth your time and effort		.727
Unfair to shove responsibility to you		.564
Feel ambivalent about relationship with elderly		.465

For Factor 2, the highest factor loading is found for the item that expresses the unworthiness of caring for an elderly (.727), followed by resentment against family members for shoving the caregiving responsibility to the caregiver alone (.564), and ambivalence towards the elderly (.465). Thus, Factor 2 amplifies the construct of caregiving burden by adding a sense of futility and resentment. There is a high correlation between Factors 1 and 2 (r = .688), which suggests that Factor 2 is an integral component of the caregiving burden. The Cronbach alpha for the 3-item subscale is .6203 (standardized item alpha = .6271). Considering the limited number of items, such an internal-consistency is remarkably impressive.

Conclusion

Our Guangzhou data have provided some answers to questions about cross-cultural research on caregiving that are based on empirical evidence. We would like to recapitulate the results of our study, their significance, and implications for future research.

First, within the constellations of family relationships when the elder is being cared for by members of the family, it is not always easy to pinpoint any specific individual as the sole caregiver. It seems that, at least in Guangzhou, family care is literally a group task. Family members often take different parts of a task in order to care for their older relatives either serially or in rotation as appropriate to their specific gender and age roles. The sandwiched-in-the-middle female caregiver concept that has been so widely accepted and quoted based on studies conducted in the West, does not always fit the caregiving milieu in China. Like family decision making, it is essentially a collective activity based on interactions that evolved into a familial norm on caregiving. We found that normally the spouse, by virtue of seniority and long-term close companionship with the person being cared for, tends to assume more responsibilities than the children. When the elder is spouseless, there is no evidence that the daughter is necessarily the primary caregiver. In fact, in East Asia's patriarchal and patrilineal family system, sons tend to assume a lot of responsibilities both because men are stronger and because of the non-symmetric loading of filial obligations.

Second, the caregiving relations is a component of a dyad relations within the family that undergoes progressive adjustment as one member gets older and the younger members reach the peak age of carrying the caregiving responsibilities. When the elder needs to put up more effort to do certain things, younger members tend to pay special attention to the perceived need for help even on such matters as making a special trip to the post office. The offering of help in such a context is not necessarily because of functional dependency. Rather, it is based on the younger family member's perception that the elder should be helped, by virtue of respect for their aged status.

The family is constantly in the process of adjusting the way the division of labor is assigned or assumed, based on age and other occupations members of the family may have. Thus, the beginning of "caregiving" to functionally dependent elders and the end of helping the older member of the family after dysfunction is a seamless transition. Under these circumstances, a new conceptual paradigm on caregiving in East Asian societies seems warranted. We have just begun the inquiry. Research that goes beneath the surface of the caregiving relationships as defined in studies of American families is very much needed.

Third, we have gained from Borgatta, Borgatta, and Montgomery's pioneer efforts to measure the various dimensions of caregiving burden. As we moved into measuring caregiving burden cross-culturally, we need to re-examine the original instrument by adding more culture-appropriate items to the scale. Additional psychometric exercise becomes desirable. This work needs to go forward by applying the scale we have developed to different samples.

Note

1 Schneider (19xx) made a similar point in his study of Chinese hospitals, see his excellent report from the viewpoint of a Western medical anthropologist.

References

Brody, E. (1981) "Women in the Middle and Family Help to Older People", *The Gerontologist,* 21: 471–480.

Gubrum, J. F. (1995) "Taking Stock", *Qualitative Health Research,* 5: 267–269.

Johnson, C.L. and D.J. Catalano (1981) "Childless Elderly and Their Family Support", *The Gerontologist,* 20: 610–618.

Johnson, C.L. and D.J. Catalano (1983) "A Longitudinal Study of Family Support to Impaired Elderly", *The Gerontologist,* 23: 231–240.

Katzman, R., Zhang, M.Y. *et al.* (1988) "A Chinese Version of the Mini-Mental State Examination: Impact of Illiteracy in a Shanghai Dementia Survey", *Journal of Clinical Epidemiology,* 41: 971–978.

Levy, P.; E.S.Y. Yu; W.T. Liu *et al.* (1989) "Sample Design of the Shanghai Elderly Survey: A Variation of Single Stage Cluster Sampling", *International Journal of Epidemiology,* 17: 931–933.

Liu, W.T. and E.S.H. Yu (1992) "The Functional Significance of Education in Senile Dementia and Alzheimer's Disease", *Shanghai Archives of Psychiatry,* 2: 59–64.

Montgomery, R.; D.E. Stull and E.F. Borgatta (1985) "Measurement and Analysis of Burden", *Research on Aging,* 7(1): 137–152.

Poulshock, S.; A. Walker and G. T. Deimling (1984) "Family Caring for Elders in Residence: Issues in the Measurement of Burden", *Journal of Gerontology,* 39: 230–239.

Shanas, E. (1979) "The Family as a Social Support System in Old Age", *The Gerontologist,* 19: 169–174.

Shanas, E. (1980) "Old People and Their Families: The New Pioneers", *Journal of Marriage and the Family,* 42: 9–15.

Wentoski, G.J. (1981) "Reciprocity and the Coping Strategies of Older People: Cultural Dimensions of Network Building", *The Gerontologist,* 21: 600–609.

Yu, E.S.H.; William T. Liu *et al.* (1989) "Cognitive Impairment Among Elderly Adults in Shanghai, China", *Journal of Gerontology: Social Sciences,* 44: S97–S106.

Yu, E.S.H.; William T. Liu *et al.* (1992) "Caregivers of Cognitively Impaired and Disabled in Shanghai, China", in S.H. Zarit, L. Pearlin and K.W. Schaie (eds.), *Caregiving Systems: Informal and Formal Helpers,* Lawrence Erlbraum Associates, Inc.

Zhang, M.Y. *et al.* (1990) "The Prevalence of Dementia and Alzheimer's Disease in Shanghai, China", *Annuals of Neurology,* 27: 428–437.

Zarit, S.H.; K.E. Reever and J. Bach-Peterson (1980) "Relatives of Impaired Elderly: Correlates of Feelings of Burden", *The Gerontologist,* 20: 649–655.

Chapter 16

Middle-aged Women's Supporting Behavior to Elderly Parents: The Comparison of Parents-in-law and Own Parents

Byung-Eun Cho
Korea National University of Education

The present study examines the supporting behavior of 293 middle-aged women toward their parents-in-law compared with those of 259 middle-aged women toward their own parents, and the effect of demographic variables, familism, and responsibility on supporting behaviors toward both parents-in-law and parents. The respondents were 552 married women in their thirties, forties, and fifties.

Married women perceived relatively high levels of familism and filial responsibility and a moderate level of supporting behavior toward their in-laws and parents. Married women reported similar levels of filial responsibility of support towards parents-in-law and their own parents. However, a significant difference was found in the amounts of supporting behavior between parents-in-law and their own parents.

Living arrangements, the level of filial responsibility, and education level proved to be significant predictors of the supporting behavior toward parents-in-law, explaining 46% of the total variance. On the other hand, filial responsibility, living patterns, and the income level of the parents were powerful in predicting supporting behavior toward their own parents, accounting for 23% of the total explained variance. A path analysis model indicated that while educational level and living arrangement influenced directly supporting behavior toward parents-in-law, living arrangement, income level of parents and familism were directly associated with supporting behavior for parents of their own. Therefore, supporting behavior of middle-aged women was significantly mediated by familism and filial responsibility for support toward both parents-in-law and their own parents.

The family, especially adult children, has been both the primary context of social integration for the aged and the major provider of economic support and physical assistance to the elderly. Reciprocal support relationships and the exchange of services have characterized intergenerational relationships. These ties were reinforced by a societal value and normative system that governed children's obligations (Choi, 1970). Traditionally in the context of Confucianism the two-valued system has been dominant (Choi, 1971; Cowgill, 1980). The primacy of family values over individual values and the ethics of filial piety have been essential norms governing relationships of adult children with elderly parents. The family was depicted as the core of the social structure. Individual members were expected to sacrifice for the family and to avoid bringing shame on the family name. Familism is the value system that strongly assigns first priority to the family (Cowgill, 1980; Ock, 1990). Individual interest was to be subordinated to family interest, and the family was favored and emphasized over other groups. Familism was another important norm. The norm of filial piety imposed heavy obligations upon the children for the care of elderly parents. The family was depicted as the core of the social structure, and the honor of the family was crucial. Solidarity between parents and children, particularly the father-son dyad, is emphasized, and cultural expectations for filial performance are differentiated by gender.

Major responsibility has been imposed upon the eldest son. Daughters are not involved in the support of the aged (Choi, 1970).

Most adult children have had a strong sense of responsibility to provide care for their aging parents. Such responsibilities have been accepted without doubt. However, rapid industrialization and urbanization have resulted in a dramatic increase in nuclear families. With the change from a traditional extended family based on consanguineous values to one based upon bonds of conjugality, consanguineous solidarity has been undermined and much of the obligation to support aged parents has been weakened (Adam, 1970; Cowgill & Holmes, 1972; Cowgill, 1980). Although joint living is still prevalent, the trend towards separate living arrangements is increasing. The proportion of co-residence with eldest son is decreasing whereas elderly parents living with other sons is increasing (Koh, 1979; Park, 1984). Pooling economic resources and a sense of obligation are the major motivations in joint living arrangements (Choi, 1980; 1985). Since residence patterns have shifted in the direction of a nuclear family, daughters are not constrained to have as much contact and to be involved in activities supporting their own parents.

In addition to changes in living arrangement, legal changes may alter the role of children in supporting parents. Under the amended family law in 1979, all children, including daughters, are obliged to support their parents. Furthermore, all children regardless of gender and birth order equally inherit their parents' properties. A current inheritance doctrine, which was revised in 1991, no longer favors the eldest son exclusively regarding the inheritance of the parents' resources. Other sons and daughters are entitled to receive a fair share.

The rapid increase in labor force participation by women also poses significant questions as to a potential reduction or reallocation of filial care. The issue of parent care becomes increasingly pertinent in the context of these continuing societal and legal trends.

Women have been identified as primary caregivers in numerous studies (Lee, 1990). In a national survey, 80% of primary caregivers were women, and 60% of these were daughters-in-law of the dependent person who was receiving care.

These social and legal forces would influence the attitudes of obligation of married women to support their parents-in-law and own parents. To study these attitudes is important, since the meaning of aging and the behavior of children toward the elderly cannot be accurately assessed without paying attention to the value systems within which these items are embedded (Bengtson, Dowd & Inkels, 1975; Choi, 1970; Lee, 1980; Mancini, 1984).

Persistence of attitudes of filial responsibility among adult children has been indicated by studies of family support systems for aging parents (Choi, 1970; Kim, 1982; Park, 1984). Many studies (Park, 1984; Sung, 1995) report that adult children still manifest a strong sense of filial responsibility. Previous research also suggests considerable interaction between elder persons and their families (Kim, 1984; Yoon, 1985). The research indicated that children frequently give help, exchange services, and visit with older family members.

In the examination of filial responsibility, many studies examined the variation in individual attitudes or the structural constraints that shaped these attitudes. Many authors have referred to general expectations of filial responsibility without having to note the relation to individual supporting behavior. The popular image is that supporting behavior simply emerges from obligation of the children. Less attention has been paid to the relationship of attitudes of filial obligation toward aging parents to the supporting behavior of children. Research is lacking, furthermore, which compares married women's supporting behavior toward in-law parents and own parents with regard to protection and care.

The goal of this study is to determine how the roles of married women as daughters-in-law and daughters have changed and how norms regarding familism and filial responsibility affect middle-aged women's supporting behavior. The present study further explores this line of research by focusing on differences in norms and actual supporting behavior of married women toward parents-in-law and parents.

Method

Hypothetical Causal Model

A causal model of supporting behavior of middle-aged women toward parents-in-law was investigated in comparison with data from middle-aged women's support of parents. In this model, filial responsibility and parent dependency are central variables considered responsible for much supported behavior to parents. Two separate aspects of norms are considered in the model: familism and filial responsibility. Parent dependency reflected in health, income, and marital status has frequently been advanced in exploring adult children's interaction with and help to elderly parents (Bengtson & Treas, 1987; Cicirelli, 1983; Choi, 1990; Sussman, 1985).

Because many elderly parents had great need for help, it was expected that familism, filial responsibility, and perception of parental dependency can be regarded as causally prior to supporting behaviors. Other things being equal, middle-aged women who have stronger familism and filial responsibility would support more than those whose familism and filial responsibility are weaker. Demographic variables of age, educational level, occupational level, and religion among middle-aged women were also considered for inclusion in the model. These variables are considered as some social background factors which create opportunity or limit the supporting behavior of adult children.

Poor health and income may increase the motivations and amount of help due to the parent's greater dependency. Marital status may also influence the extent of dependency and create a realignment of a person's role in relationships (Lopata, 1979; Morgan, 1983; Mancini, 1984). Supporting behavior toward parents may be substantially increased when the parent is widowed. Parent dependency will also lead to increased filial responsibility and supporting behavior as parents become older and more dependent. We might expect the sense of obligation of adult children to parents and willingness to help parents to be affected as dependency increases. Therefore, parental dependency was hypothesized to have both a direct effect on supporting behavior and an indirect effect through its effect on familism and filial obligation.

Sample

Data were obtained from a questionnaire survey conducted in 1994 in metropolitan Seoul. The sample was collected through a block sample procedure of residents in the southern part of Seoul and consisted of 552 married women. Each middle-aged woman in the sample had at least a living elderly parent over 60 years of age and a living elderly parent-in-law. Two hundred and fifty-nine (259) middle-aged women responded regarding their relationships with parents-in-law, and 293 women responded as those with own parents. The middle-aged married women who participated in the study were mostly of middle-class status.

Measures

The self-administered questionnaire included items on respondents' characteristics regarding demography, norms, and supporting behavior. The questionnaire was pilot-tested with 30 women and slightly modified prior to its use in the study.

Background variables — education, age, and socioeconomic status of both parent and adult child — were used as background variables. Since associations between background variables and norms have been found in previous studies (Ock, 1990; Kim, 1984), these variables were included as independent variables. Self-reported health and economic status of parent were measured on a 4-point scale: excellent=4, good=3, fair=2, and poor=1. The marital status of parent was coded as a binary variable (married=1, widowed=0).

In addition, the respondent's age, income, and educational level were used in an attempt to control for possible cohort differences (given the age range of 35–59) and socioeconomic status differences in the sample. Age was measured in years. The level of income was measured in categories of 300,000 won (one U.S. dollar is equivalent to 800 won) increments, from 1 indicating 300,000–600,000 monthly to 9 indicated above as 2,000,000 won monthly. The level of education was also measured in categories from 1 to 6, with 6 indicating having a college diploma. The number of children was coded in a straightforward manner; reported numbers ranged from 0 to 5 for sons and 0 to 5 for daughters.

For the regression analyses, co-residence with a parent was coded as a binary variable on the basis of a parent living in the same household, with a parent living in the same household coded 0 and no parent living in the same household 1. The religion and marital status of parent was also tested as a binary variable.

Familism. Familism refers to norms of collectivism held by the adult children. This measure assesses children's attitudes of general obligation toward extended family excluding their parent or in-law-parents. To what extent are children expected to contact and to provide support to their relatives? The norms of familism are defined as a global concept operant throughout the entire kin system (Choi, 1980).

Familism was measured by a composite scale of 20 Likert items. This measure was non-specific. Respondents were not asked to think of a particular relationship with an elderly parent but rather to think of general attitudes they would have if they had responsibility for any of their kindred. Coefficient alpha for the measure was .79.

Filial responsibility. An adaptation of the Filial Expectancy Scale (Seelbach, 1978) and Filial Piety Scale (Sung, 1991) was used to provide a measure of the obligation that married women felt toward their parents-in-law and parents. The filial behavior included in the scale was providing financial support to parents, living close to parents, taking care of parents when they are sick, visiting parents weekly, and feeling responsible for parents. Each of the nine items on the scale was rated by subjects on a five-point scale to indicate the extent of their agreement with the item. The total filial responsibility score was obtained by summing the nine item scores. Scores ranged from 5–45, with a high score indicating greater filial responsibility. Internal consistency reliability for the scale was .83, computed for the subjects of the study.

Supporting behavior. The measure of supporting behavior developed from items adapted from Chang (1990) and Cicirelli (1983) was designed to tap supporting behavior to meet parental needs. Respondents were asked to consider the specific relationship with their elderly parents. A composite score of these items for each type of parent was developed. The middle-aged married women were asked to indicate the amount of help presently given to the parents and parents-in-law on a five-point scale ranging from "none" to "all or almost all" for each of twelve service areas: homemaking, housing, income, allowance home maintenance, personal care, home health care, transportation, emotional support, personal advice, social and recreational activities. A principal components factor analysis of the twelve items scores indicated the presence of a single general factor; therefore, the item scores were summed to yield a total score which could range from 12 to 60; the coefficient of reliability was .84.

Results

Respondents ranged in age from 30–59, with a mean age of 41.6 years. They had a median education level of high school graduate and an average annual income of approximately 1,400,000 won. In general, the respondents rated their health as good, with a mean of 2.75 on a 4-point scale. They had a mean of 2 children. Regarding the birth order of daughters, 39% were the eldest, 32% were the second, 9% were the only child, and 20% were either third, fourth or fifth. 84% were not employed. A majority of the respondents (80.6%) were not living with parents in the same household. Those living with parents had done so with their parents-in-law for an average of 15 years. About half of the respondents' parents are married and the rest (55%) are not married. About half of the respondents (49.5%) rated the economic status of parents as poor, and 74% of the women perceived the health of parents as fairly good.

Looking at the individual item means in familism, the middle-aged women agreed most strongly with the item concerning maintaining contact with relatives (M=4.64). The next highest was the mean for feeling responsible for siblings (M=4.21), followed by younger siblings having respect and feeling close to older siblings. The lowest item is practice of ancestor worship up to great, great-grandfather (M=2.32) followed by raising a son under any circumstances (M=2.40) and child's marrying a person whom the parent chose (M=2.47).

Examination of the items on filial responsibility indicates that middle-aged married women support filial responsibility on all nine norms. For both parents and parents-in-law, keeping contact with elderly parents (M=4.35, M=4.30) and having major responsibilities for care of elderly parents rather than relying on a paid helper or societal programs received the most support (M=4.32, M=4.40). The norms that produced the weakest support of middle-aged women toward parents-in-law and parents were those which stated that married children should provide financial support for their parents (M=3.02, M=3.37) and those indicated that children should live nearby after marriage (M=3.44, M=3.21). Thus married women tended to have contact with parents and were less likely to expect to provide financial support for them. Table 1 shows the means, standard deviation, and t-tests of married, middle-aged women for filial responsibility score and supporting behavior toward parent-in-law and own parents. Rather than presenting the entire differences for each filial norm and behavior, the data for the total score are shown. Middle-aged women generally had high levels of filial responsibilities to aging parents; this was true toward both parents-in-law and their own parents. Their responses on filial responsibility were very similar. However, considerable difference exists among respondents in actual supporting behavior toward parents-in-law and parents.

The intercorrelations of variables for parents-in-law and parents are presented in Table 2 and Table 3 respectively. As expected, supporting behavior toward parents-in-law shows a positive association with filial responsibility, and the income of parent and rather strong negative relationship with education, co-residence, and marital status of parent.

For parents of their own, women's supporting behavior is negatively correlated with education, co-residence and marital status of parent and positively correlated with filial responsibility, and income level of parent.

An inverse association exists between age and endorsement of the familism and filial responsibility, such that the support for familism and filial norms decreases with young age. Age differences in familism and filial responsibility were found for both parents-in-law and parents.

Multiple regression analysis was used to determine partial regression coefficients for predictors of the hypothesized path model. Only those linkages with partial regression coefficients significant at the .05 level were retained in the model. Also, any path coefficient smaller than .10 was regarded as negligible and that linkage deleted. Regression coefficients for the reduced model are presented. The regression analyses for respondents who have their own parents are shown in Table 4. The beta coefficients and their significance levels indicated that, for one's own parents, responsibility has a strong association with supporting behavior after controlling for other variables. The greater the obligation for the mother, the greater the supporting behavior.

TABLE 1

Means and Standard Deviation for Filial Responsibility and Supporting Behavior of Middle-Aged Women toward Parents-in-law and Parents

	Parents-in-law (N=259)	Parents (N=293)	t-value
Filial Responsibility	3.11 (0.68)	3.69 (0.73)	0.58
Supporting Behavior	3.26 (0.52)	2.80 (0.61)	6.54***

*** P<.001

TABLE 2

Intercorrelation for Variables for Parents-in-law in the Path Model
(N=259)

Variables	1	2	3	4	5	6	7	8	9
1. supporting behavior									
2. filial responsibility	0.39								
3. familism	0.33#	0.45#							
4. religion	0.02	0.15	0.15*						
5. educational level	−0.40#	−0.37#	−0.31#	0.02					
6. living arrangement	−0.53#	−0.23#	−0.18*	0.15*	0.17*				
7. marital status of parent	−0.14	−0.11	−0.05	0.09	0.21#	0.19**			
8. health status of parent	−0.10	0.08	0.10	0.08	0.18**	0.13	0.18**		
9. economic status of parent	0.28#	0.16*	0.00	0.02	−0.35#	−0.23#	−0.40#	−0.34#	

*p<.05 **p<.01 #p<.001

TABLE 3

Intercorrelation for Variables for Parents in the Path Model
(N=293)

Variables	1	2	3	4	5	6	7	8	9
1. supporting behavior									
2. filial responsibility	0.30#								
3. familism	0.37#	0.34#							
4. religion	0.04	0.03	0.21#						
5. educational level	0.18**	−0.36#	−0.28#	0.07					
6. living arrangement	−0.33#	−0.07	−0.02*	0.05	0.01				
7. marital status of parent	−0.13*	−0.05	−0.00	0.07	0.17**	0.18**			
8. health status of parent	0.05	−0.00	0.12**	−0.03	0.08	−0.20#	0.07		
9. economic status of parent	0.24#	0.13*	0.03	−0.07	−0.41#	−0.18#−	0.44#	−0.15*	

*p< =. 05   **p< = .01 #p< = .001

TABLE 4

Multiple Regression of Demographic Variables, Familism and Filial Responsibility on Supporting Behavior toward Parents-in-law
(N=259)

Dependent Variables	Familism		Filial Responsibility		Supporting Behaviour	
Independent Variables	b	β	b	β	b	β
Religion	0.19	0.16**	–	–	–	–
Educational Level	–0.43	–0.31**	–0.04	–0.21#	–0.04	–0.21#
Living Arrangement	–0.19	–0.17**	–0.16	–0.11*	–0.70	–0.42
Marital Status of Parent	–	–	–	–	–	–
Health Status of Parent	0.08	0.16*	–	–	–	–
Economic Status of Parent	–	–	–	–	–	–
Familism	–	–	0.66	0.47#	–	–
Filial Responsibility	–	–	–	–	0.33	0.32#
R2		.16		.36		.46

*p<=.05   **p<=.01   #p<=.001

TABLE 5

Multiple Regression of Demographic Variables, Familism and Filial Responsibility on Supporting Behavior toward Parents
(N=293)

Dependent Variables	Familism		Filial Responsibility		Supporting Behaviour	
Independent Variables	b	β	b	β	b	β
Religion	0.25	0.23**	–	–	–	–
Educational Level	–0.04	–0.31**	–0.05	–0.29#	–	–
Living Arrangement	–	–	–	–	–0.58	–0.33#
Marital Status of Parent	–	–	–	–	–	–
Health Status of Parent	0.08	0.15*	–	–	–	–
Economic Status of Parent	–	–	–	–	0.07	0.15*
Familism	–	–	0.36	0.26#	–	–
Filial Responsibility	–	–	–	–	0.28	0.30#
R2		.10		.19		.23

Discussion

The findings of this study suggest that in general familism and filial responsibility norms are strongly supported. Most filial norms were endorsed by a majority of the respondents. Filial responsibility, then, was of major importance to the respondents. This finding may signify a reliance on children rather than on their institutions to help in support and care of the aged in the absence of society support.

The present research found normative support for certain health, financial and visiting norms, but not for residence sharing. Middle-aged women tended to support contact, mutual aid, and emotional support but not residence sharing and residential proximity. The lack of support for residence sharing may be partially a result of strong desires for independence and autonomy from aging parents on the part of middle-aged children. These desires may affect the willingness and expectation for support to provide service to the aged parents. Contrary to research on actual residence behavior, from the perspective of aging parents, the present findings demonstrate that a majority of adult daughters feel that children do not prefer to live with their parents and parents-in-law. Rather, they wish to provide mutual aid if the parents' financial and health situation deteriorates.

In the past, women have borne and have been socialized as having major responsibility for the social, psychological and physical needs of elderly parents-in-law. For both daughters-in-law and daughters, norms had a significant effect on supporting behavior. Respondents who had less sense of responsibility were likely to provide less support to elderly parents. Filial responsibility had a significant effect on supporting behavior toward both parents and parents-in-law. Middle-aged women exhibited supporting behavior toward parents-in-law rather than toward their own parents. This is an expected finding because the kin status of parents had been considered an important variable in predicting extended family ties. These data suggested that higher supporting behavior toward parents-in-law did not result from different filial expectations and norms. Attitudes of familism and filial obligation are products of the social and structural world in which a person lives. Norms of filial obligation toward parents-in-law held by daughters-in-law may be very costly; abandoning the norms may seem costly to daughters-in-law.

The variable of major comparison and interest in this study, the kin status of parents, was found to be associated with support for filial responsibility and supporting behavior, showing stronger supporting behavior toward parents-in-law than toward one's own parents. This pattern is the same as was predicted. This study may have measured actual supporting behavior and adherence to norms as well. There may in fact be a stronger response bias toward giving socially acceptable answers among daughters-in-law than among daughters.

The finding that no differences exist between parents-in-law and parents regarding filial responsibility is particularly interesting in light of the differences in actual supporting behavior. Only changes in attitudes toward supporting their own parents seem to occur among middle-aged daughters, allowing them to feel they should support their own parents.

The findings of this study suggest that the older one is, the more likely that one would support filial responsibility norm and actual supporting behavior. The oldest cohort endorsed filial responsibility to a greater extent than the younger ones. This may be the result of older persons being socialized in a different way than persons of younger cohorts.

Co-residency emerged as having the most significant effect on supporting behavior toward parents-in-law and own parents. The prospect of support from an adult is mainly a function of the location of children's residences. The dominance of co-residency is chiefly a function of the cultural prescription in support patterns under the patriarchal family system in which the support of a parent relies upon the child with whom one shares the household. The survival of the patriarchal family system is evident. The daughters-in-law are still the most important family member for support of an aged parent. In accordance with cultural tradition and gender roles, daughters-in-law are strongly involved in providing instrumental support toward their parents-in-law. This is consistent with the finding that daughters are mainly involved in giving emotional support whereas sons and their wives are strongly involved in providing financial and instrumental support (Kim, 1982; Park, 1984). Thus, it appears that the current practice of parent support adheres strongly to cultural tradition. Change in these relationships is occurring at a very slow rate.

Socioeconomic factors have a profound impact upon familism, filial responsibility, and supporting behavior. The health status of the parent and the educational level of married women were found to indirectly influence supporting behavior through familism and filial responsibility. Consistent with these findings, the greater variance of educational level, co-residence, and supporting behavior toward parents-in-law than toward one's own parents seems to suggest that supporting behavior for a parent-in-law is based on obligation. Daughters-in-law have a stronger filial responsibility toward their parents-in-law than toward their own parents, as the culture prescribes. Although traditional family ways have shifted to emphasis on emotional relationships and affective bonds in Western culture, obligation exists as the foundation of family solidarity in Korea.

In conclusion, a widespread concern of older people and families in contemporary Korean society is the dependability of children, particularly married women, in the face of societal and legal changes. However, concern derived from the evidence of changes in the socioeconomic and cultural context has not been substantiated. The life of an aged parent is intricately tied to that of children, and the actual supporting behavior rendered by middle-aged women has remained intact. Although economic support for the aged has waned, support for the aged remains very much a family matter.

The findings of this research have serious implication for future social policy. The major finding that filial responsibility has a strong impact on supporting behavior provides the ideological basis for government leaders to foster family support in Korea. Since support of the aged parent has become an issue of public concern, the Korean government has emphasized the importance of family support and the undesirability of government intervention. Government strategy has been support to the family rather than directly to the aged. This strategy may be appropriate and may be continued.

References

Adams, B. N. (1970) "Isolation, Function and Beyond: American Kinship in the 1960's", *Journal of Marriage and the Family* 32: 375–397.

Bengtson, V. L.; Dowd, J. J.; Smith, D.H. & Inkeles, A. (1975) "Modernization, Modernity, and Perceptions of Aging: A Cross-cultural Study", *Journal of Gerontology* 30(6): 688–695.

Bengtson, V. L. & Cultler, N. E. (1976) "Generation and Intergenerational Relations: Perspectives on Age Groups and Social Change", in Binstock, R.M. & Shanas, E. (eds.), *Handbook of Aging and the Social Science*, pp. 135–155. New York: Van Nostrand Reinhold Co.

Bengtson, V.L. & Treas, J. (1987) "Family in Later Years", in M. Sussman & S. Steinmetz (eds.), *Handbook on Marriage and the Family*, pp. 614–618. New York: Plenum.

Choi, B.E. (1990) "Intergenerational Family Relationships and Life Satisfaction among Korean Aged Parents", *Journal of Korean Gerontology* 10.

Choi, J. S. (1970) "Comparative Study on the Traditional Families in Korea, Japan, and China", in R. Konig (eds.), *Families in East and West: Socialization Processes and Kinship Ties*, pp. 202–210. Paris: Mouton.

Choi, J. S. (1971). *Hanguk Kajok Yongu* (A Study of the Korean Family). Seoul: Minjung Sokwan.

Choi, S. N. (1980) "The Changing Family Patterns and Welfare of the Elderly", *Journal of Korean Gerontology* 2: 12–32.

Choi, S. N. (1985) *Welfare of the Aged in a Modern Society* (in Korean). Seoul: Hongikjae.

Circirelli, V. (1983) "Adult Children's Attachment and Helping Behavior to Elderly Parents: A Path Model", *Journal of Marriage and the Family* 45: 815–825.

Cowgill, D. (1980) *Aging around the World*. Belmont: Wadsworth.

Cowgill, D. & Holmes (1972) *Aging and Modernization*, Appleton Century-Crofts. New York: Meredith Corporation.

Kim, T. H. (1982) *Family Support for the Aged in Korean Society* (unpublished Ph.D. Dissertation). Seoul: Korea University.

Koh, Y. B. (1979) "Changing Status and Welfare of the Aged", *Journal of Korean Gerontology* 1: 25–30.

Korean Gallup (1990) *Life Style and Value of the Aged in Korea*. Korea Gallup.

Korean Ministry of Health and Social Affairs (1980) "Changing Family Patterns and Social Security Protection: The Case of Korea", in *Changing Family Patterns and Social Security Protection*. New Delhi: International Social Security Association Regional Office for Asia and Oceania, pp. 39–46.

Lang, A. H. & Crody, E. M. (1983) "Characteristics of Middle-Aged Daughter and Help to Their Elderly Mother", *Journal of Marriage and the Family* 45: 193–201.

Lee, G. R. (1980) "Kinship in the Seventies: A Decade Review of Research and Theory", *Journal of Marriage and the Family* 42: 923–934.

Lopata, H. Z. (1978) "Contributions of Extended Families to the Support Systems of Metropolitan Area Widows: Limitation of the Modified Kin Network", *Journal of Marriage and the Family* 40: 355–364.

Mancini, J. (1984) "Research on Family Life in Old Ages: Exploring the Frontiers", in W. Quinn & G. Hughston (eds.), *Independent Aging: Family and Social Systems Perspectives*. Rockville, MD: Aspen.

Park, J. G. (1979). *The Problem and Prospects of the Aged* (in Korean). Seoul: Ewoo.

Park, J. K. (1984) "A Study on the Support System for the Aged and the Function of Imformal Support Systems", *Journal of Korean Gerontology* 4: 103–126.

Palmore, E. B. & Manton, K. (1974) "Modernization and Status of the Aged: International Correlations", *Journal of Gerontology* 29: 205–210.

Seelbach, W. C. (1978) "Correlates of Aged Parents' Filial Responsibility, Expectations and Realizations", *The Family Coordinator* 27: 341–350.

Stoller, E. P. (1983) "Parental Caregiving by Adult Children", *Journal of Marriage and the Family* 45: 851–857.

Sung, K. T. (1991) "Family-Centered Informal Support Networks of Korean Elderly: The Resistance of Cultural Traditions", *Journal of Cross-Cultural Gerontology* 6: 431–447.

Sung, K.T. (1995) "Measures and Dimensions of Filial Piety in Korea", *The Gerontologist* 35: 240–247.

Sussman, M. B. (1985) "The Family Life of Old People", in R. Binstock & E. Shanas (eds.), *Handbook of Aging and the Social Sciences*. New York: Van Nostrand Rheinhold Co.

Yoon, J. (1985) *Social Psychology of Aging in Korea* (in Korean). Seoul: Choonang Chucksung.

Please remember that this is a library book,
and that it belongs only temporarily to each
person who uses it. Be considerate. Do
not write in this, or any, library book.

DATE DUE

DEMCO 38-296